Strategic Management and Business Analysis

Strategic Management and Business Analysis

David Williamson, Wyn Jenkins,
Peter Cooke and Keith Michael Moreton

ELSEVIER
BUTTERWORTH
HEINEMANN

AMSTERDAM   BOSTON   HEIDELBERG   LONDON   NEW YORK   OXFORD
PARIS   SAN DIEGO   SAN FRANCISCO   SINGAPORE   SYDNEY   TOKYO

Elsevier Butterworth-Heinemann
Linacre House, Jordan Hill, Oxford OX2 8DP
200 Wheeler Road, Burlington MA 01803

First published 2004

British Library Cataloguing-in-Publication Data
A catalogue record for this book is available from the British Library

Library of Congress Cataloguing-in-Publication Data
Strategic management and business analysis/David Williamson
      p.   cm.
   Accompanied by a CD-ROM, which provides a range of strategic analysis
tools, Powerpoint tutorials, and support files.
   System requirements: System requirements for accompanying
CD-ROM: operating System that runs Microsoft Office 97, or is capable of
running Excel (version 97) and Powerpoint (version 97).
   Includes bibliographical references and index.
1. Strategic planning.   2. Business planning.   3. Business enterprises–
Evaluation.   4. Business enterprises–Evaluation–Case studies.
I. Williamson, David, 1954–

HD.30.28.S729286 2003
658.4'012–dc22

ISBN 07506 42955

For information on all Butterworth-Heinemann publications
visit our website at www.bh.com

Typeset by Integra Software Services Pvt. Ltd, Pondicherry, India
www.integra-india.com
Printed and bound in Great Britain

Contents

CONTENTS

Introduction

Our experience has shown that students and managers benefit enormously when they apply systematic analytical frameworks to strategic problems and issues. Building on this, this book helps students and managers evaluate the strategic health and position of an organization by:

- Asking the reader to follow an easy-to-understand framework. The framework encourages the asking of important questions, and then supports the answering of these questions by directing the reader to support materials in the book and on the accompanying CD. It is important to emphasize that the framework complements, and cannot be a substitute for, managerial insight and creativity.
- Providing a range of strategic analysis tools to structure the strategic analysis task. The strategic analysis tools, PowerPoint tutorials and support files on the CD assist the asking of 'what-if' questions and the production of high quality presentations and reports.
- Supplying detailed advice on how to approach case studies, which is important because they are used extensively in the teaching of strategic management.

Because we believe that strategy is most successfully learnt when it is applied, the book invites the reader to be the practitioner and to apply the strategic questions in three main ways:

1. By encouraging the evaluation of the reader's own organization.
2. By encouraging students and managers to access publicly available company and market data and to take on the role of a potential investor.
3. By encouraging the use of case studies, with students and managers acting as consultants.

The book has three parts, with the second and third parts supporting the framework outlined in part one.

Part 1

This outlines our framework for strategic analysis and provides the basis for:

1 Analysing the strategic position of 'real-life' and 'case study' organizations;
2 Generating and evaluating strategic options;
3 Understanding and operationalizing strategic change processes.

Part 2

The chapters in this section support the answering of the questions asked in Part 1. By exploring the issues surrounding the questions they also introduce the student and manager to the wider academic literature.

Part 3

This section provides guidance on how to analyse case studies. This is followed by four case studies of companies positioned at different points along their supply chains.

In writing this book we have had to be highly selective on what should be included within the text. Indeed, our approach to strategic analysis means that this book can reinforce and support other strategic texts, and that these other texts can support and reinforce the material in this book. Our decisions on what should be included and excluded have benefited greatly from the views of the students and managers that we have taught, as has the structure and content of the book as a whole. We hope you find it interesting and that it results in the type of strategic analysis that your employer or professor would be proud of.

How to use the CD

The CD that accompanies the book contains a range of strategic analysis tools, PowerPoint tutorials and support files for strategically analysing organizations. When the CD is accessed a directory named 'strategic models' appears, and this contains the strategic analysis tools. Most of the strategic analysis tools have detailed instructions on how they are to be used, with many having help files and PowerPoint tutorials. System requirements, file access instructions and CD contents are outlined below.

System requirements

The files on the CD require an operating system that runs Microsoft Office 97 software or is capable of running Excel (version 97) and PowerPoint (version 97).

Accessing the files

When using the analysis tools you can copy individual files or all files to a directory of your choice located on your hard drive. You can also open individual files from the CD, but after entering data you will need to use the 'Save As' command from the 'File' menu in order to save changes made (it's not possible to save data to the CD).

The analysis tools are Excel files, with many having PowerPoint files embedded within them. Most of these files have macros within them and you will be prompted with a dialogue box, from which you should select 'Enable Macros'.

Analysis tools on the CD

Company Capability Profiling

File Name: Ccp.xls
Support Features: Help sheet within the file.

Strategic Positioning, ACtion and Evaluation analysis (SPACE)

File Name: Space.xls
Support Features: Help sheet within the file.

Strategic Positioning, ACtion and Evaluation analysis (SPACE) Teaching Aid

File Name: SPACE-Teaching aid.xls
Support Features: Instructions on screen.

Boston Consulting Group (BCG) Matrix

File Name: Bcgmatrix.xls
Support Features: Help sheet within the file and an embedded PowerPoint file that can be launched from the menu sheet.

General Electric's Industry Attractiveness/Business Strength Matrix

File Name: Gematrix.xls
Support Features: Help sheet within the file and an embedded PowerPoint file that can be launched from the menu sheet.

Life Cycle Portfolio Matrix

File Name: Lifecycle.xls
Support Features: Help sheet within the file and an embedded PowerPoint file that can be launched from the menu sheet.

Financial Analysis Model: Ratio Analyses

File Name: Ratio.xls
Support Features: Help sheet within the file. Test data appears when the file opens and this can be cleared using 'Clear Data' button.

Value Chain Analysis

File Name: Valchain.xls
Support Features: Help sheet within the file and an embedded PowerPoint file that can be launched from the menu sheet.

Team Self-Perception Model

File Name: TeamDiagnostics.xls
Support Features: Follow 'on screen' instructions.

Porter's Five Force Theory

File Name: Porter.xls
Support Features: Non-finctional model (for presentation purposes only).

Support files on the CD

How to construct a Strategic Plan

File Name: Strategic Plan.ppt
Support Features: Power Point presentation.

Developing a Business Plan

File Name: Business Plan.doc
Support Features: Contains detailed instructions on how to produce commercially acceptable business plans.

Directory of sources of information for strategic analysis

File Name: Directory of Information.doc
Support Features: Contains an extensive list of online sources of information that can be used in the strategic analysis of organizations.

Acknowledgements

As with most projects, this book benefited enormously from the support and help of many people. We are grateful to our MBA and Masters students, who commented upon and refined our ideas and approach. We must also thank the very patient and supportive team at Elsevier Butterworth-Heinemann, especially Maggie Smith, Jackie Holding and Iona Coppen. Other unsung heroes include Chris Franses at Staffordshire University for the hours spent pursuing references and permissions and Padma Narayanan at Integra Software Services for the care and professionalism shown at the proofs stage. Perhaps not unexpectedly, our greatest thanks go to Renia Williamson, Kathy Jenkins, Helen Cooke and Joyce Moreton for their enduring patience and surrogate proofreading duties.

PART ONE

The Four Big Questions You Need to Ask

A framework for strategic management

The big questions in strategic management

Strategic management is concerned with shaping the destiny of an organization. It is about:

- Putting an organization into a competitive position.
- Sustaining and improving that position by the deployment and acquisition of appropriate resources and by monitoring and responding to environmental changes.
- Monitoring and responding to the demands of key stakeholders.

For organizational strategists to achieve these aims they must be able to answer the following key questions:

1. Where is the organization now?
2. What options are open to the organization?
3. What is the best way forward for the organization?
4. How can this be achieved?

We have developed a framework around these questions so that managers and students can apply a structured approach when they try to answer them. The intention is to produce robust answers so that we can improve our chances of developing and implementing winning strategies. Yet the answering of these questions can be very difficult – which is why we have broken the questions down into their component parts to make the process more manageable.

Guidance Note 1.0

We are not suggesting that effective strategic management can be achieved by using frameworks and models blindly. Our argument is that they can be very useful if they are used appropriately, especially when managers and students understand the limitations of both the models they use and the data that goes into them. When this is understood, they can act as a lens that provides insight into strategic problems and processes. The overriding aim is to provide a framework and structure that encourages the acquisition of knowledge and skills so that managers and students can participate in the development of organizational strategy. The approach is pragmatic, and as such it recognizes that frameworks and models are imperfect representations of complex realities, and that they should be used to aid thinking rather than act as a substitute for it.

CHAPTER 1

The first big question: Where is the organization now?

It is logical to answer this question at two distinct organizational levels:

1   The corporate level or multi-strategic business unit (SBU) level.
2   The single business or SBU level.

Guidance Note 1.1

A strategic business unit (SBU) can be defined as a unit that produces products or services for which there is an identifiable group of customers. Organization divisions or units are frequently defined on this basis, with an adhesive company, for example, having an automotive division, a packaging division, and a DIY division. Units can also be defined geographically (e.g. Australian and European divisions). In some organizations divisions are defined both by product group and geographical location (e.g. Australian automotive division). The corporate centre normally allows the divisions to operate with varying degrees of operational and strategic autonomy within an overall centrally controlled framework. Organization structures and centre divisional relationships are discussed in Chapter 5.

Figure 1.1 outlines the basic corporate model. Individual businesses are seen as part of a corporate whole, with corporate strategy being concerned with decisions about the management and composition of that whole. Within

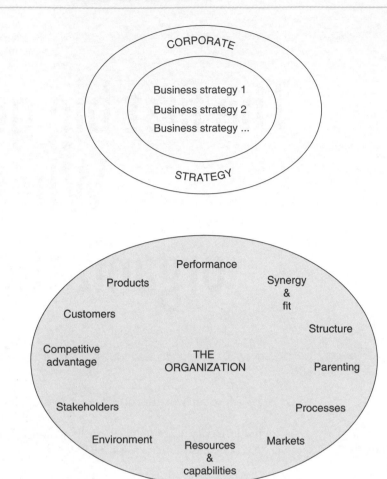

Figure 1.1
Corporate and business
strategy.

Figure 1.2
Understanding strategy
in organizations.

the corporate whole, individual businesses have to be managed and business strategies pursued. The overall corporate strategy and the strategies of sister businesses will influence the strategy of an individual business. Figure 1.2 provides an overview of the major variables that have to be considered when trying to understand the strategies of an individual organization.

1.1   The analytical process

To understand a complex corporate (multi-divisional) organization we have to have a process that is both holistic and reductionist. This is because corporate and business level analyses are interwoven – we cannot do one without considering the other. The framework or process that we use can be compared to an algorithm since it follows a procedure that helps the reader ask key questions about the organization being studied. When using the algorithm we would recommend that you:

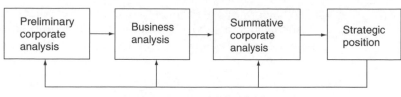

Figure 1.3
The iterative nature of strategic analysis.

Continuous revision until all evidence is considered

- ■ Move backwards and forwards within the procedure until the assessment of the data leads to a natural conclusion (see Figure 1.3).
- ■ Recognize that the data you are analyzing may be limited.
- ■ Arrive at your conclusions with care in light of the inherent limitations of the analysis.
- ■ Be prepared to argue for your conclusions from the available evidence, remembering that managers have to operate in situations of incomplete knowledge.

The analytical process is divided into three related parts:

1 Preliminary corporate analysis.
2 The analysis of business units.
3 Summative corporate analysis.

1.1.1 Preliminary corporate analysis algorithm

PC1 What products and markets does this organization supply/serve? What are its business units?

PC2 What is the formal structure of this organization?

PC3 What is the financial performance of each business? What is the contribution of each business to the overall financial performance of the whole?

PC4 Who are the major stakeholders in the organization? What are the issues that are important to these stakeholders?

Conduct an analysis of each business.

1.1.2 Individual business analysis algorithm

B1 Who are the consumers of the unit's goods and services?

B2 Why do its customers choose this business unit's products? What need is being met? What are the key success factors in this market?

B3 What are the trends in key performance indicators for this business?

B4 What are the resources (see Guidance Note 1.2) within and around the organization that allow the organization to provide products that customers will buy? To what extent can the business performance be explained by an understanding of an organization's resources?

B5   What are the characteristics of the markets that this business serves? What are the factors that exist outside the business unit that impact on its ability to provide goods and services? Can trends in performance indicators be explained by this analysis?

B6   What is the dominant logic/organization paradigm that guides this business's decision-making and contributes to the way strategy develops?

B7   Do the business's key players have a coherent vision of what they want the business to be in the medium and long term? Are this business's ambitions a coherent part of the vision for the corporate whole?

B8   What are the strengths and weaknesses of the business?

B9   What are the opportunities and threats that exist for this business?

B10 What is the strategic position of this business?

Feed this analysis into summative corporate analysis.

1.1.3   Summative corporate analysis algorithm

SC1 What is the relationship between the corporate centre and the individual businesses? What are the processes by which strategy develops in the business units and in the organization as a whole?

SC2 What are the relationships between the individual businesses? Are they supporting, neutral or disadvantageous?

SC3 What are the factors outside the organization that influence the organization's activities?

SC4 What are the strengths and weaknesses of the organization?

SC5 What are the opportunities and threats that exist for this organization?

What is the overall strategic position of the organization?

Guidance Note 1.2

In our view of strategic management the *resources* of an organization are its *assets* and *competences*. Assets are the resource endowments the business has accumulated over time and include investment in plant, location and brand equity. A competence encompasses the skill, ability and knowledge that organization members have individually or collectively which allows them to undertake an activity or activities to contribute to the transformation of inputs into outputs (see Chapter 9).

Guidance Note 1.3

Analysis is a process of data sorting and classifying followed by evaluation. The initial questions in the algorithm emphasize the

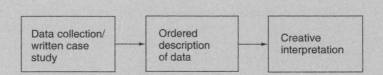

Figure 1.4
The analytical process.

importance of understanding the key influences on, and the activities of, the organization, while later questions lead into the evaluation of those activities. This allows analysts to be creative and to move from the 'what' questions outlined above to the development of their own 'why' and 'how' questions. This is depicted diagrammatically in Figure 1.4.

In many class-based exercises the data for a full analysis will not be available (indeed in most situations the data will be incomplete). Even when company accounts are available there is no requirement for divisional accounts to be published. Most analysis is therefore limited by a lack of data – but the good analyst recognizes these deficiencies and highlights them. Managers have to make decisions with limited data, and it is therefore important to acknowledge the limitations of the data and the caveats that this may place on conclusions drawn. Competent data sorting and ordering, followed by creative interpretation, allows managers to minimize their decision-making risks in situations of incomplete knowledge.

1.2 Preliminary corporate analysis

Q-PC1 What products and markets does this organization supply/serve? What are the business units and what products/markets does each unit supply/serve?

This can be difficult to answer because some organizations operate in more than one business area and they do not have neatly structured and easily identifiable product groups or SBUs. It is also possible for companies to have structures that reflect the views of their senior managers and owners on how they should operate, or that these structures are an outcome of history and previous conveniences. This means that we should look beyond organization structure when answering this question. It is possible, for example, to classify businesses according to the markets they serve or with the technology they employ. From a technological/supply side perspective an industry can be defined as a group of companies that find it easy to switch their production facilities to manufacture each other's products. Grant (1995) suggests that the automotive industry is usually defined to include the manufacturers of light vans and trucks because these can be relatively easily manufactured on the same plant as cars (the difficulty lies in deciding what is 'relatively easy'). From a market/demand side perspective, if customers consider the products of the two firms to be substitutes for each other, then the two firms can be considered to be competing in the same market as each other. Defining industries by supply-side criteria can lead to wider definitions than those obtained by using demand-side criteria. Deciding which definition to use therefore depends on the situation we wish to come to grips with. Ansoff (1987) has observed that many answers to the question 'what business are we in?' are too broad to be meaningfully understood. For example, are Morgan Cars in the same automotive industry as Ford?

The way that a single business or corporate portfolio is described is therefore important because it delineates the unit of analysis – the analysis of Morgan's environment is a very different task from the analysis of Ford's environment. Ansoff (1987) consequently defines mission in terms of customer needs, and the role of the firm is to meet customer needs through the deployment of resources. An SBU can therefore be conceived as an organizational unit that is focused on supplying the needs of specific customer groups through the deployment of specific resources.

Academic concepts:

- Market segmentation (Guidance Note 1.4 in this chapter).
- Industry analysis (Chapter 7).
- Portfolio analysis (Chapter 11).

Q-PC2 What is the formal organization structure?

In order to be strategically effective an organization needs to communicate its strategy internally and externally, and the structure of an organization can either help or hinder this communication. The way that an organization is configured can therefore impact on strategy implementation, how stakeholders are served, on strategy creation and development, what environmental signals are noticed, and what resources and skills are developed.

Organization structures are also useful to the analyst because they give clues to those roles and activities that the company considers important; organization structures are symbolic in that they indicate functions and activities that are considered important to the organization. Organization structures and unit size can also give clues to the balance of power between divisions and the corporate centre.

An important issue within and across units is the extent to which there is a *common thread* (Ansoff, 1987). Consequently, for a single business organization competitiveness is enhanced if there is a fit between activities (Porter, 1985), and for corporate organizations if there is a fit between units (Porter, 1987a; Prahalad and Hamel, 1990) and if there are any 'parenting' benefits derived from the centre (Campbell et al., 1995, 1998).

Academic concepts:

- Organization structures (Chapter 5).
- Value chain analysis (Chapter 9).

Q-PC3 What is the financial and business performance of each business? What is the contribution of each business to the overall financial performance of the whole?

This should be carried out at an early stage of the analysis. It is important to remember that comparisons over time and with other organizations are useful ways of gauging organization performance. Portfolio models can also be used to evaluate the performance of individual business within the corporate whole, although this should not be done until each individual business is analysed so that the data that is fed into the portfolio models is as robust as possible.

Guidance Note 1.4

Portfolio models have been criticized, and even abandoned by some writers of textbooks, because they say they are inappropriate and misleading analytical tools. We do not take this view, as we believe they can be a powerful conceptual device, especially when the earlier caveat – that models should encourage strategic thinking and not smother it – is adhered to.

Academic concepts:

- Financial and strategic performance analysis (Chapter 10).
- Portfolio analysis (Chapter 11).

Q-PC4 Who are the stakeholders in the organization?

It is important to identify those people and organizations that have an interest in the company being analysed. Since suppliers and customers of each business are organizational stakeholders, a broad discussion of stakeholders could include a myriad of people and organizations. The focus should therefore be on identifying stakeholders that have the power to influence corporate level activities. These can include large shareholders, governments and trade unions. The power and interests of these stakeholders affect the processes by which strategy develops at the corporate level and in each individual business.

Academic concepts:

- Stakeholders and strategic processes (Chapter 6).

1.3 Individual business analysis

Having developed a view on the organization's corporate strategy through the answering of the preliminary corporate analysis questions, our attention now shifts to the analysis of individual businesses within the corporate 'whole'. When each business has been analysed, the corporate analysis can be resumed and issues such as shared competences and resources, and the nature of the fit between businesses, can be examined.

To answer the big question 'where is the organization now?' for each individual business, it is best to ask smaller and related sub-questions. This ensures that important component questions are not overlooked and that all appropriate data and information is collected.

Q-B1   Who are the consumers of the business unit's goods and services?

It is a good idea to identify the people and/or organizations that purchase the business unit's products and wherever possible to classify them into groups or segments. By doing this we can produce data to estimate the proportion of the available market that the organization serves. The data can also be used to compare the performance of the company to that of its competitors, which can be an ongoing comparison if the data is collected regularly.

Guidance Note 1.5

A market segment has been defined as a group of consumers who can be classified on specific dimensions. Consumers may be individuals, in which case classification is along dimensions such as age, income, life style, and socio-economic group. Consumers can also be organizations, in which case classification is along dimensions such as volume usage, manufacturing or service process and inventory control process. The segment must be easily identifiable and distinguished from other segments (Hooley et al., 1998).

A description of an organization's products and the market segments that use them is a description of the organization's product market mission. In consumer markets the person who uses the product is often the person who pays for the product. In industrial markets purchases are made by organizations and the people in manufacturing and purchasing departments are key decision-makers. In public sector organizations the purchaser and the user can be different; for example, school pupils and their parents as distinct from local and national government. In any strategic analysis it is important to identify purchasers as well as users (see Chapters 4 and 10 for a discussion of stakeholders).

Q-B2   Why do its customers choose this business unit's products? What need is being met? What are the key success factors in this market?

Marketing and psychology texts will discuss in depth why people buy products or services. For our purposes we will simplify the answer to this question to: Customers buy a product because they perceive that its purchase will improve their ability to achieve desired objectives (meet needs). An issue for a purchaser is that this requirement is met at an acceptable cost. Different customers will also have different perceptions of their needs and these needs will be conceptualized within their utility potential. Put simply, some purchasers will be prepared to pay for a basic product and no more, whilst others will be prepared to pay a premium for a differentiated product; that is, they will be prepared to pay for benefits that derive from additional features. Models that are useful in discussing these topics are those concerned with identifying product and service competitive advantage. They are also useful when we try to develop explanations for organizational performance.

Academic concepts:

- Competitive advantage and success factors (Chapter 8).

Q-B3   What are the trends in key performance indicators for this business?

An organization's performance can be assessed by financial and non-financial measures. For organizations in the private sector financial success is the only long-term guarantee of survival, whereas for non-private sector organizations the criteria upon which success is judged can be more complex. But whatever the company, great care has to be taken to ensure that appropriate indicators are used.

Guidance Note 1.6

Examples of performance indicators

For-profit organizations	
Financial indicators	*Non-financial indicators*
Sales turnover	Market share
Earnings per share	Product quality
Return on sales	Brand recognition
Asset utilization ratio	
(sales/assets)	
Share prices	
Return on Capital	
employed	

Not-for-profit organizations (e.g. University)	
Financial indicators	*Non-financial indicators*
Unit cost of education	Student attendance
Revenue generated	Student retention
from fee paying	Student achievement
Students	Former students' employment
Revenue generated	Inspection grades
from funding	
agencies	

Academic concepts:

- Financial and strategic performance analysis (Chapter 10).
- Portfolio analysis (Chapter 11).

Q-B4 What are the resources within and around the organization that allow the organization to provide products that customers will buy? To what extent can the business performance be explained by an understanding of an organization's resources?

In order to supply services and products an organization requires resources. These can include skills and knowledge that are held tacitly within the organization. Strategic analysis should therefore seek to understand the relationship between market success (the sale of products and services) and the resources that are utilized to produce and deliver those products and services.

Academic concepts:

- Resources and competitive advantage (Chapters 8 and 9).
- Organization culture (Chapter 7).
- Strategic processes (Chapter 6).

Q-B5 What are the characteristics of the markets that this business serves? What are the factors that exist outside the business unit that impacts on its ability to provide goods and services? Can trends in performance indicators be explained by this analysis?

There are three areas that need to be considered when we answer this question:

1 The organizational environment.
2 The competitive environment and the characteristics of the markets the business serves.
3 The wider national, international, socio-economic, political and technological environments.

An analysis of a company's organizational environment provides a platform for understanding how a company's business strategy is related to the overall corporate strategy, and whether there is synergy or allergy between business units in the performance of their operational activities. It can also shed light on any explicit or implicit competition between business units for funds, which is why it is discussed more deeply within the corporate strategy part of the algorithm.

Academic concepts:

- Corporate parenting (Chapter 5).
- Environmental analysis (Chapter 7).
- Industry analysis (Chapter 7).
- Strategy development processes (Chapter 6).

Q-B6 What is the dominant logic/organization paradigm that guides this business's decision-making and contributes to the way strategy develops?

Prahalad and Bettis (1986) coined the phrase dominant logic to describe the logic that managers and others use to comprehend and justify the organization's purpose and environment. This is important because managers make decisions on the basis of this view. If their logic gives them a view of their environment that is consistent with the production of competitive products then the organization has a chance to thrive. If it does not the organization will decline until its management is able to implement a recovery strategy or the business is liquidated. In a multi-company organization, where managers from different businesses have to interact, the ability to operate with different dominant logics can be very important. This is especially true for corporate level managers because it is likely that they will have to operate within a number of dominant logics, which increases the level of complexity and difficulty that they will have to deal with. Johnson (1988) developed the concept of an organization paradigm supported by a cultural web, and this is important because it provides a framework through which the dominant logic concept can be operationalized.

Academic concepts:

- Organization paradigms, dominant logic and strategic processes (Chapter 6).

Q-B7   Do the business's key players have a coherent vision of what they want the business to be in the medium and long term? Are this business's ambitions a coherent part of the vision for the corporate whole?

Is there evidence that the future of the business can be founded on a resource base that is developable from the present resource base, through internal development, liaison between other units in the portfolio, or by acquisition? Does the organization's management have a clear vision of where they want this business to be?

Q-B8   What are the strengths and weaknesses of the business?

This question leads the analyst to assess the individual businesses from an internal perspective. A key issue is whether it's a strength or a weakness for the business to belong to the corporate whole? More generally, does the business have a balance of strengths and weaknesses, do strengths exceed weaknesses or do weaknesses exceed strengths? (Please see Q-B10 for a more detailed discussion of this issue.)

Q-B9   What are the opportunities and threats that exist for this business?

This question leads the analyst to assess the business from an external perspective. (Please see Q-B10 for a more detailed discussion of this issue.)

Guidance Note 1.7

In our analytical approach we have outlined how corporate and business strategies are interwoven. The purpose of the analysis is to determine the overall strategic strengths and weaknesses of each business and the corporate whole, so that we can assess the prospects for the organization based on the available information. From this assessment we can make judgements on the choices open to the organization and the strategic options it might pursue. This is discussed more fully in Chapters 3 and 4.

Q-B10 What is the strategic position of this business?

This involves an assessment of strengths and weaknesses, opportunities and threats (i.e. SWOT analysis), and is likely to include an analysis of the following issues:

- What are the organization's strengths and weaknesses?
- Does the organization have more strengths than weaknesses, a balance of strengths and weaknesses or more weaknesses than strengths?
- How dynamic is this organization's environment?
- How attractive are its markets?
- What are the key performance indicators for this business? What are the trends in these indicators?
- Is it financially strong?
- Should it be optimistic about its future or will it be fighting for survival?

The process of answering these questions will inevitably lead to a discussion of options and whether the company should pursue any of the identified options.

Academic concepts:

- SPACE (Strategic Position and Action Evaluation) (Chapter 11).

1.4 Summative corporate analysis

Q-SC1 What is the relationship between the corporate centre and the individual businesses? What are the processes by which strategy develops in the business units and in the organization as a whole?

Research by Campbell et al. (1995) indicates that successful organizations develop relationships between the parent and its subsidiary that vary from the distant to the close. They have developed a typology that classifies these relationships as:

- Strategic planning relationships.
- Financial control relationships.
- Strategic control relationships.

Strategic planning relationships are defined as relationships in which the centre actively participates in strategy development and implementation. This is an appropriate relationship when the portfolio is made up of related businesses and centre managers have a 'feel' for the businesses in the portfolio. It can encourage the development of long-term perspectives and lead to businesses sharing and developing capabilities that can confer strategic advantage to a number of product groups. In inappropriate circumstances it can lead to irrelevant procedures and unnecessary paper work, lack of ownership of tasks by those undertaking them, demoralization of divisional managers and strategy being developed by senior managers out of touch with the market place.

Financial control relationships are defined as relationships in which the centre's main concern is setting financial targets but delegates strategy development to the business unit. It is appropriate for corporations that are unrelatedly diversified, where the direction and control from the centre is targeted at motivating managers. This can motivate managers to focus on short-term performance and quickly identify short-term weaknesses in strategy. It does not, however, encourage co-operation across units or the development of long-term strategies.

Strategic control relationships are considered intermediate, lying somewhere between financial control relationships and strategic planning relationships. In these relationships strategies are developed by the business units and approved (or not) by the centre. The constraints found in the financial control style can also be found in strategic control relationships, yet the emphasis on short-term financial performance can be offset by the incorporation of strategic objectives into the agreed strategy. The organizational paradigm can also have an important influence on strategy development.

Academic concepts:

■ Corporate parenting (Chapter 5).
■ Strategy development processes (Chapter 6).

Q-SC2 What are the relationships between the individual businesses? Are they supporting, neutral or disadvantageous?

Is there a strategic fit between the businesses in the organization portfolio? Do they share value chain activities? Are there common and shared capabilities that allow synergies across the organization as a whole and confer competitive advantage on to specific units? Do the activities of some businesses reduce the effectiveness of others in the portfolio?

Academic concepts:

■ Resources and competitive advantage (Chapters 8 and 9).
■ Portfolio analysis and financial fit (Chapter 11).
■ Corporate parenting and strategic fit (Chapter 5).

Q-SC3 What are the factors outside the organization that influence the organization's activities?

It is important to recognize the factors outside the organization that influence its behaviour at both the corporate and business levels. The various factors that impact on the performance of individual businesses also have a cumulative effect on the organization as a whole. Indeed, the rationale for unrelated diversification has been the spread of risk. The nature of the business environments can also impact on the way the centre manages its relationships with the subsidiaries. Contemporary thinking in government, consultancies and business schools can also influence the way organizations behave. Examples of this include:

- The way that organizations in the 1950s and 1960s implemented strategies of corporate unrelated diversification.
- The way that many public sector organizations in the UK in the 1980s and 1990s were either privatized or required to operate in quasi markets using the management tools developed from the private sector.

Academic concepts:

- Environmental analysis (Chapter 7).

Q-SC4 What are the strengths and weaknesses of the organization?

The strengths and weaknesses of each business should be taken into account and the impact of these on the corporate entity should be considered. The strength and weakness assessment should revisit the questions covered above and should therefore relate to:

- the financial and business performance of each business.
- the contribution of each business to the overall financial performance of the whole.
- the strengths and weaknesses of each business.
- the fit between each business.
- the impact of stakeholder, including management and ownership, interests and actions, on the organization.
- the appropriateness of the organization structure.
- the relationship between the corporate centre and the individual businesses.

Q-SC5 What are the opportunities and threats that exist for this organization?

The opportunities and threats faced by each business should be taken into account and the impact of these on the corporate entity should be considered. The opportunities and threats assessment should consider:

1   External opportunities and threats:

- The impact of outside factors on each business.
- The net effect of outside factors on groups of individual business.
- The sum of the effect of outside factors on the corporate whole.

2   Internal opportunities:

- The possibility that some internal resource or strong capability may be the source of a market opportunity not yet obvious from external monitoring.

What is the overall strategic position of the organization?

A key question in answering this question relates to whether the corporate portfolio is balanced, and if it is self-funding and financially strong? Also, are the individual businesses more effective in the corporate portfolio than outside the portfolio? If so, why? The analysis of the question should also include an assessment of the following issues (which are very similar to those given for an individual business unit):

- What are its strengths, weaknesses?
- Does the organization have more strengths than weaknesses, a balance of strengths and weaknesses or more weaknesses than strengths?
- Does the organization's management have a clear vision of where they want this business to be?
- Should it be optimistic about its future or will it be fighting for survival?

The process of answering these questions will inevitably lead to a discussion of options and whether the company should pursue any of them (as it did for a single business unit).

Academic concepts:

- Portfolio analysis and strategic fit (Chapter 11).
- Corporate parenting (Chapter 5).

CHAPTER 2

The second big question: What options are open to the organization?

2.1   Strategic choices at the corporate level

Strategic choices at the corporate level can involve decisions about:

- Business closure.
- Business disposal.
- Business acquisition.
- Business re-organization.
- Business start up.
- The impact of doing nothing different.

Even in the case of a single business organization, a corporate level perspective might be important because an option may involve a diversification that can be best managed by creating a divisional form of organization.

A useful starting point is to compare the financial performance of these various options to the financial performance of the current business (i.e. the do-nothing-different option). This is important because a key strategic objective is to safeguard and improve shareholder value, and to do this the options must improve upon existing levels of performance. The analysis should also consider if the identified options have 'strategic fit' and whether they will have a positive or negative impact upon the financial balance within the corporate portfolio.

It is equally likely that the success of the corporate whole will depend upon the ability of senior management to fit together individual businesses, via appropriate 'parenting', so that their full potential is realized (Campbell et al., 1995). As a consequence, we emphasise an holistic approach that recognizes the need for both financial and strategic coherence.

Portfolio balance   Portfolio models, such as the Boston Consulting Group (BCG) matrix and the General Electric (GE) matrix, are useful devices for examining multi-business organizations. Understanding how the businesses 'fit' together is important because it may be necessary, for example, to use money from a cash-rich company to fund a growing and cash-hungry company. Shareholders must be happy that this is an effective use of their money, which is why the business being funded must benefit 'strategically' from being in the portfolio (Porter, 1987a).

Strategic fit and parenting   If organizations develop incrementally over time, then situations can arise where inter-business synergies are lost and the scope for corporate parenting is eroded. In these circumstances it may be necessary to divest non-core businesses if the assessment is that there are no synergies or opportunities for parenting. Owen and Harrison (1995) have discussed the de-merger of ICI in this context:

> ICI's problem wasn't an unusual one. Changes in markets and technologies had overtaken the logic that held the component businesses together and bound them to the corporate parent. The parenting skills on which ICI's earlier success had been based were no longer appropriate.
>
> (Owen and Harrison, 1995, p. 133)

Senior management teams are therefore required to fully understand their businesses so that they can maximize synergies between them. This means that we must understand and appreciate the role of 'parents' in assessing strategic fit and in the leveraging out of competitive advantage:

> Critical success factor analysis is an important base for assessing fit. It is useful in judging whether friction is likely to develop between the business and the parent. A parent that does not understand the critical success factors in a business is likely to destroy value. It is also useful for judging how similar the parenting needs of different business are.
>
> (Campbell et al., 1995, p. 123)

We suggest that options for each business are generated and then evaluated in the context of the whole organization. It is clearly important that the portfolio of businesses should be constructed in such a way that the organization can fund its ambitions.

2.2 Strategic choices at business unit level: Product–market matrices

The strategic analysis outlined in Chapter 1, which culminated in a SWOT analysis, provides a good platform for selecting and generating strategic options. SPACE analysis (Strategic Position and ACtion Evaluation – after Rowe et al., 1994) can also be used to identify options at the business unit and product level, and the technique is discussed in detail in Chapter 11.

An alternative approach is to use product–market matrices, as these focus on the products and markets that a business can serve. They can be especially powerful in terms of the options they generate, which can, in turn, be evaluated against the product–market mission being pursued. The process of referencing future and potential activities against current activities is therefore about current and potential market activities. And since these market opportunities cannot be sustained without an appropriate matching of resources, skills and value chain activities, the matrices in Figures 2.1 and 2.2 are outlined as a way of identifying options at the business unit and product level. Figure 2.1, based on his original model, was subsequently updated by Ansoff by adding a third dimension. The three dimensions are Market Geography (New–Present), Market Need (New–Present) and Product–Services Technologies (New–Present), and are concerned with an external perspective of markets and products, while Figure 2.2 makes a link between internal competences and the product–market mission.

Guidance Note 2.1

This is an appropriate time to remind readers that models are used to guide thinking and may not be direct replications of reality. The product market matrix model can appear confusing unless this is realized, as some potential strategic activities could be placed in different boxes depending on the *manager's judgement*. For example:

Figure 2.1
Product–market Matrix.
1. Market Geography;
2. New; 3. Present;
4. Market Need;
5. Product-services
Technologies.
Source: (after Ansoff,
(1988) *The New
Corporate Strategy*. New
York: John Wiley,
pp. 82–84. Copyright ©
The Estate of H. Igor
Ansoff).

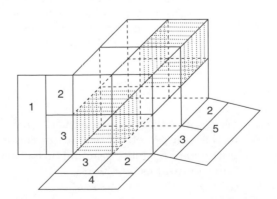

PRODUCT/MARKET

	Maintenance	Development
Maintenance	**Box E** Maintaining present resources to serve present market segments	**Box F** Moving into new products and markets with present resources
Development	**Box G** Delivering present products with new resources	**Box H** Delivering new products and/or entering new markets with new resources

RESOURCE PORTFOLIO

Figure 2.2
Product/market compe-tence portfolio matrix.

■ We characterize computer modifications such as 'memory' or 'chip speed enhancement' as fitting into Box A. So the product has been developed but the development is not likely to put the business in a new competitive position against competitors – but is likely to *maintain* the competitive position. However, if the change were such that a competitor was unable to match the change then a new competitive position would be *developed*. Thus firms that can maintain and incrementally improve their product features and/or sustain or enhance customers perceptions of benefits are likely, in the long run, to achieve an advantage over those that do not.

■ Again we characterize turnaround and recovery strategies as probably fitting into Box A. Turnaround strategies may involve some alterations to product and marketing but they are recovery rather than development strategies.

This implies that resources and market knowledge underpin decision-making and not the constraints of model itself. We urge readers to consider situations on their merits, recognizing both the advantages and disadvantages of the models they use.

The matrices in Figures 2.1 and 2.2 can be used to generate a number of possible options for a business unit.

2.2.1 Market maintenance, product maintenance strategies for growth (holding/increasing market share)

This could be the position in a highly competitive environment and may require a constant improvement of product and service features because customers' perceptions of quality (as fitness for purpose) are changed by rapidly advancing technology and the offerings of competitors. The main concern of firms is to maintain or enhance their sources of market advantage – be it cost or differentiation based – the personal computer market exemplifies this well. Typical strategic responses include a drive to improve quality, production processes, and customer service with, for example, marketing/product maintenance strategies supporting current or required competencies. In order to maintain its market position a manufacturing company might:

- have to change inventory control systems that require new competencies in the use of information technology (Box G).
- have to ensure skills are maintained by introducing a staff training programme and updating resources incrementally (Box E).

When an industry is in its early stages of development there can be competition between products and competitors, and between different technologies (operating systems in personal computers and video recording formats are good examples of competing technologies). In these situations rival technologies can be 'made' obsolete by effective strategy.

2.2.2 Market maintenance, product maintenance in situations of adjustment and turnaround

The analysis of the business may indicate that the organization is in a situation where some adjustments in strategy content and/or implementation are required as an antidote to decline. The decline may be in the early stages or may be so advanced as to require urgent action.

Figure 2.3 illustrates how organizations lose touch with their market and how their product is 'de-positioned' by the market changing faster than the firm's strategy. An organization can lose its brand image and reputation and slip from position 'C' to position 'D'. This is the case when a product market position is not maintained and customer expectations of the standard product increase.

A business may find that it is losing market share; it may have operating inefficiencies and have products or services that are not competitive. In these situations the competence portfolio is likely to need updating. It is also likely that the organization culture is no longer responding in an effective way to its environment. Slatter (1984) indicates the following factors cause a firm to decline:

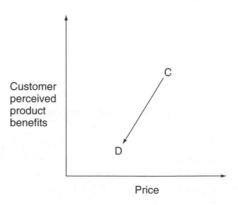

Figure 2.3
De-positioning of
product or service.

- Poor management.
- Inadequate financial control.
- High cost structure.
- Lack of marketing effort.
- Competitive weakness.
- Big project acquisitions.
- Financial policy.

Some firms will be in hopeless situations, others with good management can be revived. Turnaround techniques are discussed in Chapter 4.

2.2.3 Product maintenance, market development strategies for growth

This can occur when a company seeks opportunities in a different geographic area or wishes to reposition a product to appeal to a wider or different market segment. An example is the repositioning of Skoda by Volkswagen. The concept of repositioning is illustrated in Figure 2.4.

In Figure 2.4, the company launches or acquires a product in position 'A', which has basic tangible features (in the case of a motor car it might be an adequate engine, seats and bodywork). The company then improves the tangible and intangible features (intangible features include reputation and brand image) of the product. At the same time the product price is increased incrementally (perhaps via point 'B') so that ultimately position 'C' is achieved. Although there may be no advantage in leaving a high volume/low price market to move into a low volume/higher price market, it can be an appropriate strategy where the lower price segment is smaller than a higher priced segment (as in the automotive industry, see Chapter 8). So, even though the product is not new (although it might be modified) the organization makes strenuous efforts to change the customers' perception of its benefits.

Figure 2.4
Repositioning of
product or service.

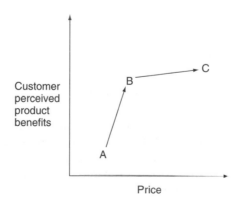

2.2.4   Market maintenance, product development strategies

This is an appropriate option when the strategic analysis suggests that there are opportunities for the business to develop new products for customers. These products may meet a present need that is served by other suppliers or may be a new need. In this situation there may be a requirement to develop new competencies as well as exploiting current ones (Boxes F and H).

2.2.5   Product development, market development strategies (related and unrelated diversification)

Diversification can be considered from two different strategic perspectives:

1   A 'market'-based perspective.
2   A 'resource'-based perspective.

From a market-based perspective a related diversification will involve moving into new products and markets that have similar dimensions to the ones currently being served. In this scenario products and markets are chosen that have similar features to the ones currently being served. For example, a perfume retailer whose historic market consist of females may move into the manufacture and sales of men's undergarments. In this case selling, branding and distribution would have similar features for both product market missions. A car producer who moves into manufacturing light vans may find some marketing commonalties e.g. brand name and distribution, as well as relatedness in production, etc.

If we wish to explain relatedness from a resource-based perspective we could argue that there is relatedness when the current competences and resources of the organization can be used as market entry facilitators and possibly sources of advantage in new markets. The greater the overlap of primary value chain activities the greater the relatedness. There may also be a requirement to develop new competences in primary activities (Boxes 'F' and 'H'). In unrelated diversification there is little overlap in primary value chain activities but the diversification is justified on the basis of secondary relatedness, especially in the area of general management.

2.3   Summary

In this chapter, we briefly discussed option generation at both corporate and business levels. The development of options for a multi-business firm is clearly a complex task and all options generated cannot be implemented. Indeed, whilst option generation implicitly involves a rough cut selection process, a much more detailed evaluation of possible ways forward is required before specific recommendations can be made. Ways of doing this are described in Chapter 3.

The procedure that has been outlined for option generation and evaluation has three stages:

- *Step 1* From the analysis produce a series of options for each business.
- *Step 2* Assess how the options selected for each business fit into the corporate vision.
- *Step 3* Make choices and recommendation based on the ideas developed in Chapters 3 and 4.

CHAPTER **3**

The third big question: What is the best way forward for the organization?

To answer this question we need to assess the options generated for each business in the context of the corporate whole. A framework for doing this has been developed and can be expressed as a series of questions.

3.1 The FIRM evaluation of options

1 Will the strategic option *Fit* with our present activities and lay down the foundations for the long-term prosperity of the organizations?
2 Will the strategic option have an *Impact* on the organization's performance within agreed time frames?
3 Can the *Resources* required to implement the option be obtained?
4 What are the features of the change option that is proposed and to what extent can the change be *Managed*?
5 In short, has the option a *FIRM* basis?

The four evaluation criteria are outlined and discussed more fully in the following sections.

3.1.1 The F in FIRM

Will the strategic option fit with our present activities and lay down the foundations for the long-term prosperity of the individual business and the corporate whole?

The new initiatives must seek to:

- Remove, reduce or compensate for any weaknesses identified in the corporate portfolio and in individual businesses. For an organization in a declining situation this may be the key emphasis. If an organization has a lot of weaknesses a turnaround strategy may be an urgent requirement before any other actions are appropriate.
- Build on resource strengths. For example, does the new initiative allow for the sharing of assets or the transferring of skills in such a way that competitive advantage is gained.
- Lead the organization into developing or acquiring skills that not only allow for the expected advantages but also lay down foundations for long-term strategic development.
- Build on opportunities that allow the organization to exploit its resources vis-à-vis its competitors.
- Does the proposed strategy give an opportunity to steal a march on competitors, or is the opportunity such that a disadvantage will occur if it is not taken? Is the opportunity also a potential threat?
- Seek to minimize threats that already exist in the organization's environment or reduce the organization's exposure to opportunity-taking by competitors.

3.1.2 The I in FIRM

Will the strategic option have an impact on the organization's performance within agreed time frames?

There is no point in pursuing strategies that make little difference to the performance of the organization in a time scale that is not acceptable to stakeholders. Because of this the returns from the proposed strategy must be estimated using appropriate techniques. In 'for-profit' organizations the impact of a strategy is usually measured in financial terms (although other measures like market domination via market share can be primary strategic objectives), and techniques for estimating and judging financial performance are discussed in Chapter 10.

3.1.3 The R in FIRM

Can the resources required to implement the option be obtained?

Since there is little point in developing strategies for which resources cannot be obtained, it is important that realistic judgements be made on the ability of the organization to acquire such resources. Resources can include capital to fund acquisition of buildings and equipment, raw materials, labour, skills, management expertise and sales outlets etc., and frameworks for assessing resources are discussed in Chapter 9.

3.1.4   The M in FIRM

What are the features of the change option that is proposed and to what extent can change be managed?

A number of writers and researchers on strategy have focused their attention on the cognitive nature of management. Organizations were said to have perspectives (Mintzberg, 1987), cultural webs and paradigms (Johnson, 1987), and dominant logics (Prahalad and Bettis, 1986). Consequently, if an organization is in a situation where the world-view of key managers and staff is at odds with its environment, the likelihood is that the organization will become dysfunctional. Examples of situations where there is the potential for a misalignment of world-view and environment are:

- When an organization diversifies into a new market and the common perspective of the organization is unable to understand the 'rules' of this market.
- When an organization's members lose touch with the needs of their customers because of complacency.
- When an organization is faced with a significant environmental change because of privatization or regulatory changes.

Managers who wish to make perspective-breaking changes should therefore expect resistance. Similarly, the change process may be much less complex to manage where world-views are consistent with the environment, as the implementation programme is likely to be a continuation of a strategy that has a shared and coherent corporate vision. This means that the most difficult kinds of changes to execute are those that require an organization to change its world-view or perspective, as they may require significant and complex organizational changes if they are to be successfully introduced.

This leads us to consider whether changes plotted on the product/market and product/market competence portfolio matrices (see Chapter 22) are within or outside the organization's dominant logic. Any proposed strategic change that requires new competences and capabilities may therefore require dominant logics that differ from those currently used in running the business. This means that corporate managers in multi-business and multi-national environments may have to operate with multi-dominant logics if they are to attend to the affairs of their different businesses.

Johnson's (1987) concept of the organization paradigm supported by a cultural web is a useful way to operationalize the concept of an organization's dominant logic. Figure 3.1 expresses these ideas within a matrix.

Box 1 and Box 3 situations are those where organization members in key strategic and/or operational positions have world-views/cultural webs that are not sympathetic to the proposed change. Such situations may involve the development of new competencies for expansion or may be situations where turnaround strategies are necessary for survival. These circumstances are encountered by organizations entering changed environments either through the incremental growth of competitive action (e.g. the situation encountered by Marks and Spencer in the late 1990s) or by

**RELATIONSHIP WITH
ORGANIZATION PARADIGM**

	Inconsistent Doing things differently	**Consistent** Doing things better
Incremental (Slow)	Box 1	Box 2
Step (Fast)	Box 3	Box 4

RATE OF CHANGE REQUIRED

Figure 3.1
Organization paradigm
and rate of change
required matrix
Source: (after Balogun
and Hailey (1999)
*Exploring Strategic
Change*, Prentice Hall,
Europe, reprinted with
permission from
Pearson Education
Limited).

a change in environment brought about by legislation. Clearly, the sooner an organization is able to 'sense' the need for change the sooner it can avoid situations of 'strategic drift' and the need for remedial actions, which are often painful, if it is to remain competitive. Yet this may be difficult because the dominant paradigm of the organization is likely to resist this 'sensing' of the need for change unless the situation becomes dramatically grave or a sense of urgency is deliberately precipitated (see Chapter 6). Although difficult, there is evidence that dominant logics can be influenced and changed through 'selective' recruitment, training and retirement programmes (see Slatter (1984) for a classic discussion of turnaround and recovery strategies).

Guidance Note 3.1

It is worth noting that managers perceive cost cutting to be a significant weapon in turnaround strategies. Indiscriminate cost cutting can, however, effect the long-term survival of the organization. The balance between long-term and short-term survival strategies can therefore cause managerial dilemmas – the turnaround strategy of a college that became debt bound focused on cost reductions through staff redundancies, and although this helped in the short term, it reduced the number of courses, which reduced the number of students, which reduced revenue even further.

Boxes 2 and 4 illustrate positions where the change to be undertaken does not require a change in dominant logic. Typically initiatives like the implementation of total quality management and business process re-engineering would fit into Box 4. In Box 2, changes are more adaptive and are allowed and encouraged to take place over time, and are exemplified by slowly improving the skills within the workforce, the development of computer-based inventory control systems, and the development of modified products to maintain markets, etc. Changes in Boxes 2 and 4 are necessary to improve the organization's performance and are less likely to meet resistance compared to the changes in Boxes 1 and 3.

If change is to be implemented it is important to estimate the attitudes of key stakeholders to that change and be prepared to respond to their views. In order to do this it is necessary to identify who the key stakeholders are and to estimate their interest in any given issue and their power to facilitate or block change. Estimations of power in organizations are an important step for change managers, and Burns (2000) suggests that power stems from:

- Control over information.
- Control over resources.
- Formal authority.

Examples include trade unions who have power over labour resources, experts who have control over information and knowledge, and shareholders who have the power to vote out managers (if they are organized).

The power–interest matrix shown in Figure 3.2 is a useful way of representing the interplay between different levels of interest and power.

Assessing the manageability of change of different options is important because it may be the basis upon which options are accepted or rejected. Also, changes that are considered vital for organizational survival can be prepared for, as the tasks should be easier to overcome if we have a better knowledge of the potential problems to be faced.

3.2 Summary

The FIRM framework for evaluating options has been outlined, and the options generated for each business that you look at should be critically evaluated using this framework. On the basis of this analysis, the optimal way forward for each business should be weighed against the long-term welfare of the corporate whole. In some circumstance this may mean that a business should be disposed of to create a more beneficial corporate environment, or sold to fund the aspirations of others.

The short- and long-term implications for shareholder value and funding should be considered – and this is likely to necessitate the production of short-, medium-

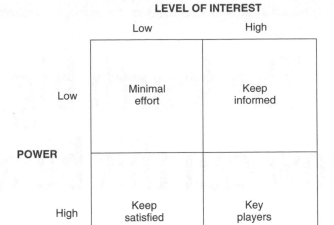

Figure 3.2
Power–interest matrix
Source: (after Mendelow,
1991, p. 216, Repro-
duced with permission
from Pearson Education
Limited).

and long-term financial predictions under different possible scenarios. The analysis
should include estimates of future company worth and how the new strategies will
impact on other stakeholders such as employees and customers.

A schematic overview of the key analysis stages for a multi-business organization is shown in Figure 3.3.

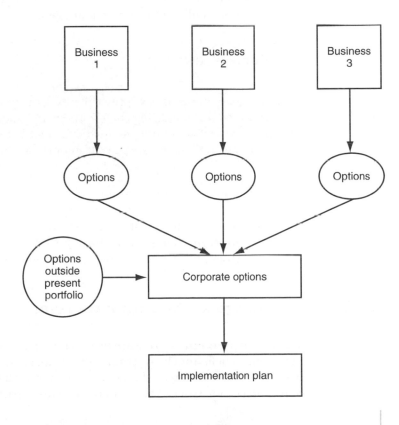

Figure 3.3
Options analysis
procedure.

CHAPTER 4

The fourth big question: How can this be achieved ?

By following the procedures in Chapter 3 we should have developed *FIRM* options for the organization being studied. These are options that:

- are appropriate for the organization's situation.
- are capable of making a worthwhile impact.
- can be resourced.
- in our judgement can be managed.

Guidance Note 4.1

In this chapter, we discuss prescriptions for managing change. It must be emphasized that managing change in real life situations requires sensitivity and judgement about unique situations. So the prescriptions given are not meant to be definitive – they are frameworks to inspire thinking.

This chapter is structured as follows:

1 Strategic change at the corporate level.
2 Strategic change at the business level.
3 Strategic change in different circumstances.

4.1 Strategic change at the corporate level

The role of the centre is to ensure that each unit in a corporate portfolio gains the maximum benefit from being part of the portfolio. Managers should also be aware of the way that units can be clustered within an overall framework to maximize the opportunities for synergy and parenting. This is particularly important in post-merger or post-acquisition periods when corporate centres endeavour to reconfigure their organizations. It may be appropriate to bring units together or separate them. Changes at the business level may have an impact on the whole organization, with some businesses possibly funding other businesses, while other businesses could be given preference for investment over others.

Questions for guiding thinking on these issues include:

Will the business portfolio of the organization change? Will there be less or more businesses in the group's portfolio?

These questions can prompt a discussion of the implications with respect to the disposal of companies, the acquisition of companies, company mergers and new business start-ups. Careful consideration will have to be given to the financing of corporate level change. For example, some businesses may be sold to fund expansion or improvements in other businesses. If additional investment is required, it is important to identify sources of funds and the impact that this will have on the financial structure of the organization. The long-term consequences of key financial ratios and the trends in these ratios need to be understood.

Will the proposed changes require that there is a change in the relationship between the corporate centre and the individual businesses? Will the proposed changes require changes in the relationships between individual businesses?

The strategic options chosen may require that the overall governance of the organization is changed and that the role of the centre and its relationship to individual business is modified. It may be appropriate for individual business to co-operate. A key issue is to identify the parenting relationship between the centre and the individual businesses and the opportunities for synergy across businesses.

4.2 Strategic change at the business level

Strategic change at the business level is the level where people become involved. The impact of corporate restructuring has to be managed within the individual businesses, and the ways that change is managed will be context-dependent. Expanding from a success is quite different from turning round an organization in crisis. The challenge is different when the proposed change requires a change in the way the organization's members understand their world.

Questions for guiding thinking on these issues include:

Will the proposed changes affect the consumers of the business's products, if so, how?

It is important to estimate the impact that change has on customers – because the nature of that impact should be anticipated. Some impacts are desired and are expected to have a positive impact on consumers, while other impacts may be trade-offs, which some consumers may not like (it is important to realize that there may be some unanticipated customer reactions). If products are to have different features that make them more competitive, then the mechanism for communicating these changes needs to be in place.

If new segments are targeted, perhaps in a different country, do the distribution and the promotion of the products parallel current practice or do they require new practices? Do the proposed changes require the organization's products to be sold into different markets in different international locations? What impact will this have on manufacturing, distribution and marketing?

Do the resources of this business require changes in order to implement the new strategy? If so, how?

Will the new strategy require resources to be changed, modified, or/and increased? Will resources have to be extended or developed?

Is the world-view or paradigm of the business unit compatible with the proposed strategic direction?

A strategy that is counter to the culture of the unit will be difficult to implement. If a change in strategic direction is necessary for long- or short-term organization survival this may be an appropriate route. Indeed, the very nature of the situation may be a driver for change and may be used by organization leaders as a catalyst for change. The effective communication of a crisis can be the lever, which facilitates change by challenging peoples' confidence in the existing certainties. Festinger's (1957) theory of cognitive dissonance indicates that people prefer their theories or beliefs to be consistent so if they can be convinced that their behaviour is inconsistent with their organization's survival, and hence their security, they will find alternative employment or change behaviour.

If we revisit the product/market resource portfolio matrix in Figure 4.1 and the organization paradigm and rate of change required matrix in Figure 4.2 we can consider the implications of managing change under the conditions suggested by the nature of the change in the organization's resource mix. Changes that are likely to be consistent with the development of the present organizational paradigm are more likely to occur when the organization is changing incrementally from a successful position. These changes can involve the maintenance of the current world-views held by all levels of organization member but are also likely to influence their evolution as initiatives become embedded in the organization.

PRODUCT/MARKET PORTFOLIO

		Maintenance	Development
RESOURCE PORTFOLIO	**Maintenance**	**Box E** Maintaining present resources to serve present market segments	**Box F** Moving into new products and/or markets with present resources
	Development	**Box G** Delivering present products with new resources	**Box H** Delivering new products and/or entering new markets with new resources

Figure 4.1
Product–market resource portfolio matrix.

**RELATIONSHIP WITH
ORGANIZATION PARADIGM**

	Inconsistent Doing things differently	Consistent Doing things better
Incremental (Slow)	Box 1	Box 2
Step (Fast)	Box 3	Box 4

RATE OF CHANGE REQUIRED

Figure 4.2
Organization paradigm
and rate of change
required matrix
Source: (adapted from
Balogun and Hailey,
1999, p. 21).

4.3   Strategic change in different circumstances

In the remainder of this chapter we discuss strategic change in four different circumstances:

1   Managing change when the change is consistent with the present culture.
2   Managing change to accommodate different organization contexts.
3   Managing change when the change requires a culture change to maintain a successful position.
4   Managing change in turnaround situations.

4.3.1   Managing change when the change is consistent with the present culture

For example, Box E and F type changes in Figure 4.1 involve maintaining and developing the organization's present market position and product portfolio by developing the present competence and asset base. In healthy organizations changes will be grounded in present resources, but over time the organization will learn and grow. It will acquire new assets and skills as current products are produced in more effective ways and new products and markets are developed (Box G and H type changes).

The organization needs to manage change incrementally whilst understanding the changes in its own situation and its environment. Examples of factors that affect the nature and structure of organizations are discussed in Chapter 6 and include:

■   its position in its cycle (Greiner, 1972).
■   the position of its products in their life cycle.

The way that environments affect organizations are outlined and discussed in Chapter 7. Examples of factors that effect organizations include:

- demographic changes, such as the increased spending power of elderly people.
- government policy and legislation on interest rates and trade, etc.
- technical innovation through Internet use and genetic engineering, etc.
- sociological changes such as the redefinition of pornography and the increasing dominance of one parent families.

Healthy organizations adopt a philosophy of continuous improvement (sometimes manifested through Total Quality Management systems). This can involve the updating of products and process so that they are aligned to evolving customer needs. The continuous development of a firm's skills and its ability to absorb technical advances in its area of expertise can allow it to lead and develop customer expectations of value in products and services, thereby minimizing risks of competitive action. Companies can also build relationships with their customers and suppliers so that they can be proactive in defining the way their industry develops. In this situation the organization culture is likely to be healthy but evolving, so that it can manage the status quo whilst innovating in other areas. It can incorporate both *step* and *incremental* change, such as the launching new products and the opening new markets, and the slow and continuous improvement of competences and resources.

In continuous improvement projects the main players are usually first line managers, maintained by middle managers acting as a key link to top managers. In a healthy culture there would be open communication throughout the organization. Indeed, the empowerment of individuals and teams within organizations is one of the cornerstones of a continuous improvement approach (Bowen and Lawler, 1992; Oakland and Porter, 1999). The concept of teamwork should involve teams within the organization and across organizations. Organizations can also build teams with customers and suppliers. Yet the practice of cross-organization teams only works if team members believe that customers and suppliers benefit through teamwork, and there is a shared belief in win–win outcomes.

The ability to create successful teams depends on a number of factors:

- Team members must want to be part of the team.
- There must be a balance of appropriate abilities in the team.
- They must want the team to succeed.

It is clearly essential that the team should be appropriate for the task and that the task being undertaken has the support of top management. In addition to having clear objectives, the objectives should be agreed at the start of the project and should be regularly restated. The team should have a leader who is concerned with the three key areas of teamwork (after Adair, 1988):

1. The needs of the task.
2. The needs of the team.
3. The needs of the individual within the team.

To do this the team leader should:

- Ensure that all members understand the task and the plan.
- Be responsible for leading the team in developing the project or task plan that accurately reflects the task.
- Allocate tasks within the team.
- Agree milestones and performance measures.
- Ensure that the team maintains an effective work rate and its task focus.
- Encourage and discipline the team and individuals.
- Encourage the building of team spirit.
- Minimize tension and reconcile disagreements.
- Receive information from the wider organization and its environment and disseminate to the team.
- Disseminate information from the team to the wider organization.
- Check project outcomes with initial objectives.
- Help the team evaluate its own performance against objectives.

Step and incremental changes in this environment are likely to be within the organization paradigm and are likely to be accepted by organization members as beneficial. This means that planning in a supportive environment facilitates the implementation process. For example, teams from sales, research and manufacturing would plan a new product development. To further improve customer service the team could include customers.

The philosophy embodied in the UK Government's Investors in People initiative is a way by which organizations can link a continuous improvement process to the development of their people. It is a framework for establishing and sustaining deeply embedded belief systems in organizations, and when fully implemented it should exhibit the characteristics shown in Figure 4.3.

4.3.2 Managing change to accommodate different organization contexts

There are situations when organizations have to come to terms with operating one way in one environment and another way in another environment.

- When healthy organizations expand their market areas to different countries the structure set-up for this must accommodate the impact that this will have on the organization.

Healthy organizations may also have to accommodate a step change when they introduce new products to new markets when this requires the acquisition of new resources. If there is a significant difference in the before and after resource endowments, it may be wise to allow separate developments and the formation of new units within the organization (Skinner, 1974).

Principles	Indicators
Commitment The organization is fully committed to developing people to achieve its aims and objectives	1. The organization is committed to supporting the development of its people 2. People are encouraged to improve their own and other people's performance 3. People believe their contribution is recognized 4. The organization is committed to ensuring equality of opportunity (meritocracy).
Planning The organization is clear about its aims and objectives and what people need to do to achieve them	5. The organization has a plan (strategy) that is understood by everyone 6. The development of people is in line with the organization's aims and objectives 7. People understand how they contribute to achieving the organization's aims and objectives
Action The organization develops its people effectively in order to improve its performance	8. Managers are effective in supporting the development of people 9. People learn and develop effectively
Evaluation The organization understands the impact of their investment in people on its performance	10. The development of people improves the performance of the organization, teams and individuals 11. People understand the impact of the development of people on the performance of the organization, teams and individuals 12. The organization gets better at developing its people

Figure 4.3
Investors in people
standard
Source: (adapted from
www.dti.gov.uk/quality/
people, November,
2002).

4.3.3 Managing change when the change requires a culture change to maintain a successful position (Realigning organizations: urgently required but not yet desperate change situations – medium-term Box G and H changes)

When an organization's culture is not consistent with its long-term success (and in the worst possible case the firm's short-term survival) the organization requires realigning. Remedial action can be carried out gradually if the organization is in the early stages of strategic misalignment. If the crisis is more immediate the changes must have a rapid impact on organization performance:

Example 1
The organization has an opportunity to change the way it delivers its present goods or services because of technological changes that allow these products to be delivered in more effective ways. If the opportunity is not taken the organization will find itself at a disadvantage against competitors who do

adopt these technologies. The firm has to reconfigure its value chain or business model. Having made the change the organization may find that it is then able to develop into different products and markets because of the new culture. This has been the situation facing financial service firms as they adopt IT.

Example 2
In the public sector, the introduction of government reforms has required change to meet new performance indicators and adopt different work practices. These changes have not always been smooth and straightforward and have involved disputes involving hospital consultants, nurses, college lecturers and the fire brigade. This suggests that cultures in organizations are not homogeneous in times of change. Particular groups of workers will have different world-views from their managers. For change to be successful, different world-views in different parts of the organization have to be compatible.

Kotter (1995) suggests that organization transformation be modelled using an eight-step framework:

1   Establishing a sense of urgency.
2   Forming a powerful guiding coalition.
3   Creating a vision.
4   Communicating the vision.
5   Empowering others to act on the vision.
6   Planning for and creating short-term wins.
7   Consolidating improvements and producing still more change.
8   Institutionalizing new approaches.

We have adopted this eight point transformation framework as a basis for the more detailed review outlined below.

4.3.3.1   Establishing a sense of urgency

The first step in initiating a process for change is to establish the need for change. Burns (2000) calls this the *trigger* for change while Kotter (1995) refers to the creation of *a sense of urgency*. The next step is to effectively communicate that need to those who have to implement it. In crises or potential crises this support must be obtained quickly.

The purpose of all this activity, in the words of one former CEO of a large European company, is to make the status quo more dangerous than launching into the unknown. In a few of the most successful cases a group has manufactured a crisis. One CEO deliberately engineered the largest accounting loss in the company's history, creating huge pressures from Wall Street in the process. One division president commissioned the first-ever customer-satisfaction surveys, knowing full well that the results would be terrible. He then made these findings public.

(Kotter, 1995, p. 60)

Developing strategies for overcoming resistance to change can be considered using force-field analysis. The technique looks at the change process and the forces driving and resisting change, as shown in Figure 4.4.

The actions of the chief executives described by Kotter represent attempts to overcome entrenched belief systems that say that all is well. In these situations company members will believe that customers are happy and that products are not outdated despite evidence to the contrary (Johnson, 1988). Change managers must therefore:

- find ways of establishing the need for change before it is too late.
- weaken resistance to change.
- strengthen forces driving change.

4.3.3.2 Forming a powerful guiding coalition

One of the first tasks within many change processes is the formation of a guiding coalition or project team. This team will initially review and re-examine the implications of the change proposals so that they become committed to the proposal and take it forward. Deciding on the composition of the project team is clearly an important task for senior management. The composition of the team should reflect the nature and context of the task and it is essential that the change team has status – the authority and obvious support of the organization's leadership. The project team should have the power to effect change and this should be symbolized by the make-up of the group. The group should also include representatives of those who are to implement the changes.

One of the most important changes in strategy making in large enterprises over the last two decades has been the shift in responsibility for strategy formulation from corporate planning departments to line managers. One of the benefits of this transition is that the strategic planning processes provide a highly effective mechanism for dialogue between corporate and divisional managers and between general managers and functional specialists.

(Grant, 1995, p. 22)

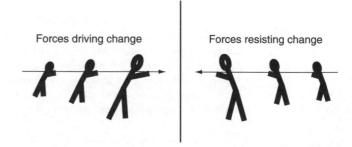

Figure 4.4
Force-field analysis.

4.3.3.3   Creating a vision

Having established the need for change, it is important to express that need in a form that can be understood by all. Measurable performance indicators are important but people need to quickly have 'a feel' for what is required. A clear statement of where the organization is going is essential.

4.3.3.4   Communicating the vision

Transformation is impossible unless employees can be convinced that it is achievable. Employees may have to make sacrifices and tolerate job losses amongst colleagues. Senior executives must show commitment to change by what they do and be aware of the symbolic nature of their actions. Writing newsletters about making sacrifices only becomes credible if the writer is seen to be making sacrifices. Senior managers must ensure that their behaviour backs the rhetoric or lower level employees will become cynical and not support change initiatives.

4.3.3.5   Empowering others to act on the vision

The systems and culture of the organization must be aligned to the vision outlined. The activities of the organization must be compatible with the vision of the future aspired to. One way to aid thinking about change is to draw *before* and *after* models as shown in Figure 4.5.

Modelling value chains and culture webs before and after the change initiative can allow people to focus on the requirements of the change process.

4.3.3.6   Planning for and creating short-term wins

Progress must be measured. This is why the organization needs to set objectives and performance indicators. Burns (2000) has identified two schools of change management theorists:

1   The advocates of planned change.
2   The advocates of emergent change.

The work of a number of writers, however, suggests that change can be managed in ways that involve both planned and emergent dimensions. Quinn (1978) captured the essence of this idea when he developed the concept of logical incrementalism. This process involves senior managers developing the

Primary activities now	⟶	Primary activities in the future
Secondary activities now	⟶	Secondary activities in the future
Controls and incentives now	⟶	Controls and incentives in the future
Resources now	⟶	Resources in the future
Organization structure now	⟶	Organization structure in the future
Dominant logic now	⟶	Dominant logic in the future

Figure 4.5
Before and after
activities.

overall direction of the organization but allowing lower level managers the room to develop and negotiate the methods by which that direction is followed. Kotter suggests that organizations should focus on achievable outcomes the achievement of which will be fed back into the system and psyche of employees. Winning will then become a habit. Short-term wins then become the foundation of long-term success.

The balanced scorecard provides a framework for translating a company's strategic objectives into a set of performance measures. This system seeks to align short-term performance indicators within a long-term perspective. This avoids organizations having incompatible long- and short-term objectives. Table 4.1 provides some insight into how these reward follies might manifest themselves in an organization.

Kaplan and Norton (1992, 1993, 1996) developed the balanced scorecard and it revolves around four separate but inter-linked management processes:

1 *Financial* Shareholder interests are best accommodated within a financial perspective (i.e. what are the financial expectations of corporate stakeholders and how should we measure these?).
2 *Customer* To succeed financially a company needs to create value for its customers (i.e. what do our customers value and what would they like to see improved – can we measure our progress on these issues?).
3 *Internal business process* Customer value can be enhanced by making internal processes more effective and efficient (i.e. can we improve customer service through more effective use of information technology – and can we measure how good we are at doing it?).
4 *Learning and Growth* Support for value-creating strategies requires ongoing support (i.e. improving customer service through superior IT integration is an ongoing process that requires the company to monitor how effective it is at innovation, learning and growth).

The scenario and the process for a company might be as follows:

■ A vision to be the first choice in their sector.
■ If successful, how will they look to their shareholders?
■ To achieve the vision, how must they look to their customers?

Table 4.1 Reward follies (Kerr, S., 1995, An Academy Classic: on the folly of rewarding A, while hoping for B, *Academy of Management Executive*, February)

We hope for	But we often reward ....
Long-term growth	Quarterly earnings
Teamwork and collaboration	The best team members
Commitment to total quality	Shipping on schedule, even with defects
Innovative thinking and risk taking	Proven methods and not making mistakes
Employee empowerment	Tight management control
etc.	etc.

■ To satisfy their customers what management processes must they excel at?

■ To achieve the vision, how must they learn and improve?

It is important that the four sets of performance indicators reflect and operationalize the organization's mission and strategy. An example of how a strategic vision can be translated into a balanced scorecard is shown in Figure 4.6.

Performance measures have to be cascaded down the organization so that managers can monitor their own implementation performance. This involves sub-units identifying their own set of actionable performance indicators in line with the overall strategic objectives of the company. The cascading process therefore communicates the strategic objectives to the managers and employees of the company, and acts as a motivational device because it involves them in the selection of appropriate performance measures. By converting strategic objectives into individual goals a 'personal scorecard'

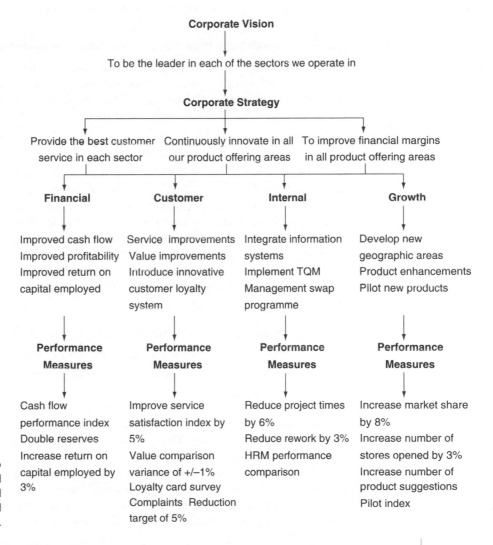

Figure 4.6
The strategic vision and the balanced scorecard (after Kaplan and Norton, 1993).

43

can be produced that can be carried around in a manager's pocket. These performance measures and targets can then be compared to the strategic objectives on an ongoing basis, providing feedback on how the strategic plan is being operationalized and how it might need to be amended in line with front line performance.

In summary, the benefits of integrating the balanced scorecard into the implementation process enable a company to:

- clarify its strategic objectives.
- structure its strategic objectives.
- measure its progress towards achieving its strategic objectives.
- communicate its strategy to its workforce.
- align its corporate and individual employee objectives.
- highlight the tensions and trade-offs required in meeting its strategic objectives.
- focus on its critical management issues.
- review performance to learn about and improve strategy.

4.3.3.7 Consolidating improvements and producing still more change

It is important that improved performance figures are used to inspire greater efforts, as individuals resisting change can take the early signs of improvement to claim that the job is already done. This is why there needs to be a continuous attack on the practices and structures that resist the corporate vision.

4.3.3.8 Institutionalizing new approaches

It is important that successful changes in systems, practices and attitudes are accompanied by the philosophy that catalyzed those changes. This will improve the probability of them becoming embedded in the organization culture itself. It is also important that organizations develop cultures that can adapt to change. Indeed, it is dangerous to consider change process complete and to over celebrate victories such that they then become the raison d'être for new rigid structures. Attitudes to continuous improvement must become embedded in the social norms of the organization.

4.3.4   Managing change in turnaround situations (Realigning organizations: urgently required and retrenchment and recovery – short-term Box G and H changes) (see Figure 4.1 on page 34)

Slatter (1984) suggested that antidotes for decline should be mapped to specific causes of decline. The potential causes of, and antidotes to decline are shown in Figure 4.7.

Slatter's research has indicated that firms in crisis can only be converted into firms that make above average profits if strong product market positions can be achieved. If this is not possible, because the products involved are in decline, it may be possible to sustain the firm in the short term and harvest

Cause of decline	Antidote
Poor management	New management and restructuring
Inadequate financial control	Improved financial control and localized costing and performance measures
High cost structure	Cost reduction, product market reassessment
Poor marketing	Improved marketing
Competitive weaknesses	Product market reassessment
	Cost reduction
	Improved marketing
	Asset reduction
	Growth by strategic acquisitions
Big projects	Asset reduction
Expensive acquisitions	
Financial strategy	Asset reduction
	New financial strategy

Figure 4.7
Causes of and antidotes to decline
Source: (adapted from Slatter, 1984).

cash before final liquidation. A lack of financial resources may also mean that short-term survival can be achieved by strong financial control and tight management, although the company will be finally defeated because of the lack of investment.

Guidance Note 4.2

We have discussed change in four different contexts:

1 Managing change when the change is consistent with the present culture.
2 Managing change to accommodate different organization contexts.
3 Managing change when the change requires a culture change to maintain a successful position.
4 Managing change in turnaround situations.

Real life organizations, however, rarely conform to textbox prescriptions, so we would urge you to take the ideas above and use them as a basis for reflecting on specific organizational situations.

PART TWO

Helping You Answer the Four Big Questions

Organization structure and strategy

An organization is a collection of resources that are linked together to transform inputs into outputs, and an organization structure is the framework that evolves (or is designed) to facilitate communication and co-ordination between organization members so that this transformation can take place. The way an organization arranges its resources, including its people, and the mechanisms that link these resources and make them cohesive, are dimensions of an organization's structure.

If organizations' environments were unchanging, an ideal organization structure would optimize the conversion of inputs to outputs and could be left to accomplish the task unendingly. It is difficult to imagine such a scenario because organizations operate in environments where consumers' choices can be fickle, where raw materials become scarce, where governments change laws and where shareholders expectations change. This suggests that organizational members invariably undertake routine and non-routine tasks.

Handy (1993) categorized four different types of organizational activities:

1 *Steady-state activities*   These activities are routines that account for most of the work of the organization, and are typical in routine manufacturing, sales and accounting.
2 *Innovation activities*   These activities are concerned with changing the things that the organization does or the ways that it does them. They are exemplified in such activities as marketing, product research and development, process development and innovative training.
3 *Crisis activities*   These are activities associated with dealing with the unexpected and are likely to be encountered by those departments and people who interface with the organization's environment.
4 *Policy making activities*   These activities are concerned with the overall guidance of the organization.

Handy suggests that if different parts of the organization are responsible for different sorts of activities then the culture (the norms, values and beliefs) and relationships in sub-units will differ. This means that the activities of an operations department in a high volume manufacturing plant are likely to have different internal and external relationships and controls from those of a design department. Although the organizational cultures are not homogenous, we would expect the sub-cultures to be compatible (otherwise we would probably see a mushroom cloud above it as it tears itself apart). So, whilst the control mechanisms and motivation may differ for senior managers, designers and assembly workers, the sub-cultures should be compatible in that they share a common sense of purpose (see Chapter 6). Different sub-units should be able to work separately but cohesively, so that they can be differentiated whilst remaining integrated within the corporate whole. In addition to this, the organization should be able to evolve so that its structure remains compatible with effective strategy creation and implementation.

These types of issues and the critical dimensions of organization structure that underpin them are explored through the work of the following key authors:

- Alfred Chandler.
- Larry Greiner.
- Henry Mintzberg.
- Michael Goold and Andrew Campbell.

5.1 The work of Alfred D. Chandler: Strategy and structure in large industrial enterprises

Chandler (1962, 1969) studied large American *industrial enterprises*. He defined an industrial enterprise as:

> ...a large private profit orientated business firm involved in the handling of goods in some or all of the successive processes from the procurement of raw materials to the sale to the ultimate customer.
>
> (Chandler, 1969, p. 8)

He observed that, as companies grew in turnover, employee numbers, geographical areas served, number of products sold or manufactured, etc., there was the possibility of an administration crisis before appropriate structures were developed.

Chandler concluded that new strategies created new administrative needs, but that executives could administer:

> Both old and new activities with the same personnel, using the same channels of communication and authority. Such administration must, however, become increasingly inefficient.
>
> (Chandler, 1969, p. 15)

Chandler's research indicated that the solution to complex growth on a number of dimensions – expansion by volume, geographical dispersion, vertical integration – was through a multi-divisional structure.

The generic multi-divisional structure as described by Chandler has the following features:

1 A general office.
2 Each division's central office.
3 Headquarters for the divisional departments.
4 The field units.

This is shown in Figure 5.1.

The general office or headquarters is responsible for planning, co-ordinating and appraising the activities of the quasi-autonomous divisions. The division's central office administers a number of functional departments. The managers of the functional departments are responsible for the administration of the field offices. Chandler distinguished between administrative and functional work. Administrative work is the domain of the company executives and is concerned with two kinds of tasks:

1 Those tasks that are concerned with the overall co-ordination and efficient operation of the enterprise.
2 Those tasks that are concerned with ensuring the long-term health of the organization.

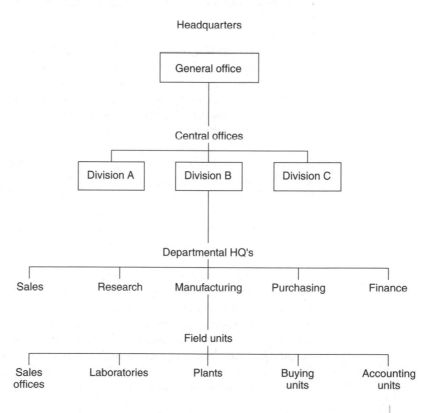

Figure 5.1
The multi-divisional structure
Source: (Chandler, A.D. (1962) *Strategy and Structure*, MIT, Boston, Massachusetts, p. 10).

51

Functional work involves the actual buying, selling, processing or transporting of goods.

In Chandler's model strategy development is largely the responsibility of the general office. Chandler noted that as strategy developed, successful organizations developed structures that supported its implementation. It was also recognized that strategy development could be hindered by the perceptions of managers, as their own history can constrain them in implementing structural changes. This was because either they were 'too involved with day to day tactical activities to appreciate longer range organizational needs or because they felt structural reorganization threatened their own personal position' (Chandler, 1962, p. 15). Chandler concluded that structural change not only served to make strategy implementation more efficient but also created an environment in which strategy would be made differently. The suggestion is that strategy influences structure, and that structure influences the way strategy is formed, which influences its content.

5.2 The work of Larry Greiner: Strategy, structure and organization growth

Greiner's (1972) ideas were developed in the early 1970s before information technology increased the possibilities for cross- and inter-organizational communication. Nonetheless, the propositions that are implicit in his work are an important contribution to the frameworks for understanding organization structures:

1 Organizations can and do fail if there is an inappropriate fit between structure, strategy and environment.
2 Strategy structure misalignments occur when organization structure is rooted in its history rather than its present situation.
3 Successful organizations overcome these problems by going through periods of evolution and revolution.

A period of evolution is when the organization experiences a long period of growth where *no major upheavals occur in organization practice*. A period of revolution occurs when there is substantial turmoil in organization life. The model says that organizations require different structures as they grow, and that organizations that survive are those that change their structures. This is best exemplified by profiling the life stages of a company.

Phase 1: Foundation and early growth
In the beginning the organization is staffed by its founders, who subsequently recruit employees as the company grows. It has a simple structure, with power resting with the founders, and where control and decision-making is achieved through informal communication. Handy (1993) has described the culture in embryonic organizations as a power culture in which the leader sees the organization as an extension of him or herself. As the organization grows the ability of the owners to maintain control is reduced until there is a crisis of

leadership. The informal manner in which the organization is managed is no longer adequate because it cannot:

- cope with higher production volumes;
- co-ordinate increased employee numbers;
- motivate employees who no longer identify with founding ideals;
- manage both support and primary activities.

The organization can survive this crisis by developing an organization structure that facilitates control and communication and allows specialist managers to run the company.

Phase 2: Direction

As a result of its growth the organization develops a functional structure (see Figure 5.2) that can support increased turnover in established and new product areas. The senior management team now becomes responsible for the direction of the company while those below it assume responsibility for the control of the functional tasks of production, distribution and marketing. As the organization continues to increase in complexity through the growth in the number of inputs, processes and outputs, there comes a stage when senior managers cannot cope with all the demands being made on them, and as a consequence junior managers are torn between following procedures or taking their own initiatives. The emerging crisis requires greater autonomy for junior managers, with failure occurring when senior managers remain reluctant to delegate, and when junior managers are unable to adjust to making non-routine decisions.

Phase 3: Delegation

At this stage the organization can survive by developing an organization structure that pushes some elements of strategic decision-making down the organization. This gives rise to a structure that retains functional elements whilst allowing the formation of autonomous units. As Figure 5.3 shows, responsibility for profit and cost control can be delegated down the organization by the formation of profit/cost centres.

In Figure 5.3, the Sales Manager of Product Group A could be responsible for the profit targets of Product Group A and have influence over manufacturing and R&D through the creation of an incentive bonus scheme. The

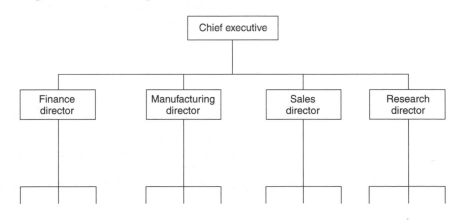

Figure 5.2
Functional organizational structure.

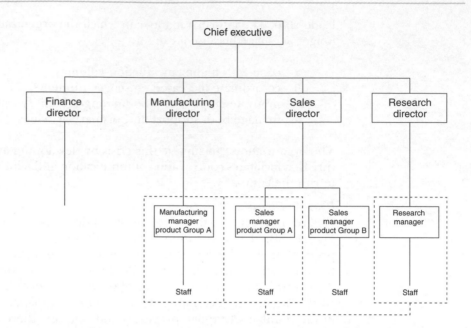

Figure 5.3
Autonomous profit –
cost centres.

structure would also allow R&D and Manufacturing to be profit centres, so that they could charge other Product Groups for work undertaken. Decentralized structures like these seek to give greater responsibility to local managers, with overall control being managed through output targets.

The decentralization of responsibility and power also encourages the development of relationships between middle managers, which can make senior executives uncomfortable if they feel that the growing influence of functional and line managers reduces their overall level of control within the diversified organizational structure. If managers do become parochial and run their own individual units as quasi independent businesses, then co-ordination and integration with the rest of the organization can be inhibited.

Phase 4: Co-ordination
The solution to these problems, according to Greiner, is to move to divisional structures that are co-ordinated by formal planning procedures within and across central, divisional and functional areas (see Figure 5.4). These structures can have activities that have both a functional role within divisions and be centrally co-ordinated: accounting and finance, for example, can have central and divisional arms. The danger with these structures is that they can become overbureaucratic and induce a crisis of red tape, and in these circumstances it is likely that organizations will have to progress to some form of collaborative structure.

Phase 5: Collaboration
In this phase the emphasis is on collaboration between divisional groups and between the centre and these groups, which can be made possible through a move to a more matrix style structure like the one shown in Figure 5.5. Greiner was optimistic that the use of matrix structures and the development of managers with appropriate behavioural skills would overcome 'red tape crises' in

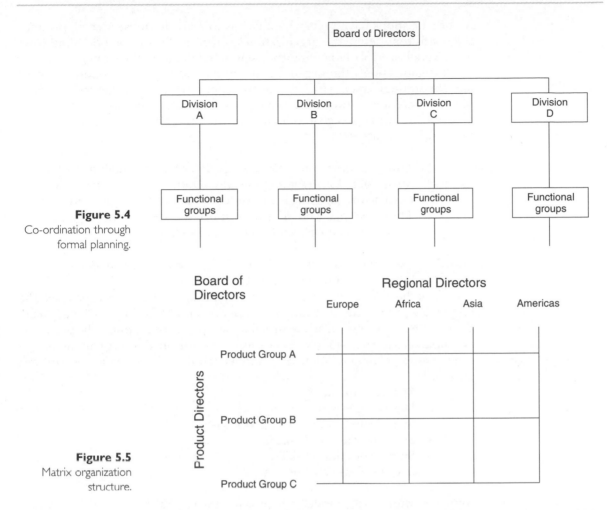

Figure 5.4
Co-ordination through formal planning.

Figure 5.5
Matrix organization structure.

larger organizations, even though it was not specified how these ideas would be put into practice.

In this matrix structure the divisional manager of Product Group A in Asia reports to both the Product Director and the Regional Director. It is designed to increase collaboration, although the multiple intersections within the matrix structure can be a source of potential conflict and confusion.

5.3 The work of Henry Mintzberg: Control and co-ordination in organizations

Mintzberg (2002) recognized that an organization's structure is not only dependent upon its age or size but is affected by other situational features, such as:

- the nature of the technology used in its transformation processes.
- the nature of the environment.
- the distribution of power inside and outside of the organization.

All organizations have units whose task is to provide the service or produce the goods that define the organization's purpose. This is the operating core. The overall control of the organization is in the hands of the strategic apex. In small organizations, the organization can consist of just the operating core and the strategic apex. However, as the operation grows a hierarchical middle line is created between the strategic apex and the operating core.

As the organization becomes more complex two additional groups of people may be required:

1   Those people who Mintzberg describes as analysts, who are responsible for designing the way others do work; this is the technostructure and it exists outside the hierarchy of line authority.
2   Those people who supply support services to the organization, such as legal advice and canteen facilities.

Mintzberg also suggests that every 'active' organization has an ideology (analogous to Johnson's cultural web (see Chapter 6)).

Each of these six components (i.e. the operating core, the strategic apex, the middle line, the technostructure, the support services and the ideology) plays a role in the production of an organization's outputs. For outputs to be produced organizations also have to have mechanisms of co-ordination. Organizational co-ordination, according to Mintzberg, is facilitated through six basic mechanisms:

1   Mutual adjustment.
2   Direct supervision.
3   Standardization of work processes.
4   Standardization of outputs.
5   Standardization of skills.
6   Standardization of norms.

By using Mintzberg's model it is possible to discuss the ways that communication and co-ordination can occur in different organization structures.

5.3.1   Communication and co-ordination in simple structures

In simple structures the prime co-ordinating mechanism is direct supervision by the strategic apex. The structure of a general store is shown in Figure 5.6, and in this structure co-ordination is through direct supervision, although mutual adjustment and formal/informal work standardization are also present. The process is informal, with the key driver being the owner manager.

5.3.2   Communication and co-ordination in machine organizations (e.g. traditional manufacturing firms)

The biggest part of the organization is likely to be the operating core. The prime co-ordinating mechanism in the operating core is work standardization, which means that the technostructure is important (although other mechanisms are also likely to be present).

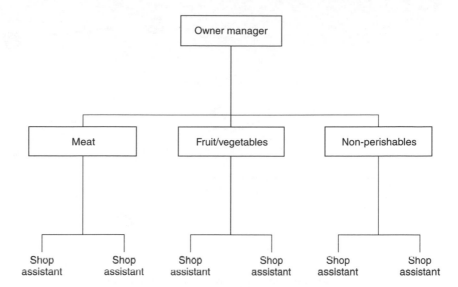

Figure 5.6
Communication and co-ordination in a general store.

Many traditional manufacturing firms have functional structures, which means that there is a requirement for control and co-ordination within and across functions. The co-ordination within functions will be significantly affected by the nature of the work done. Co-ordination in functions that are professionally staffed and involve the production of variable and complex outputs, such as research laboratories or design offices, will differ from co-ordination in functions that conduct routine repetitive tasks.

5.3.3 Communication and co-ordination in innovative organizations

In this kind of organization co-ordination will be characterized by mutual adjustment – but since many participants will have been through professional training there will also be skills standardization. This suggests that there will be some supervision, perhaps similar to that shown in Figure 5.7 which depicts the relationships of one person with four others (group size is 5).

In a group of 5 there will be 10 relationships. When the group size is 10 there are 45 relationships. This means that for a group size of n there are $(n - 1)n/2$ relationships. If a group of size n increases in size by 1 the number of relationships in the group increases by n. Groups will therefore require a different kind of co-ordination mechanism if they grow beyond a certain size because simple mutual adjustment will not be possible. Large-scale mutual adjustment could be possible, however, if groups have leaders or representatives who liaise with other groups. Mutual adjustment is then sustained by having a hierarchy of groups.

5.3.4 Communication and co-ordination in missionary organizations

Mintzberg describes an organization that is dominated by its ideology as a missionary one. The outputs of this type of organization and the activities of

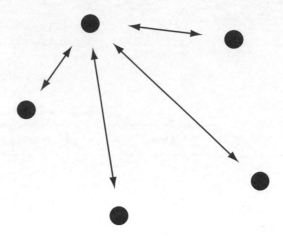

Figure 5.7
Communication and
co-ordination in innova-
tive organizations.

its members are largely controlled by the values that the organization member shares with his or her colleagues. Missionary organizations have strong cultures that are perpetuated by effective indoctrination of new members followed by reinforcement rituals, routines and symbols.

5.3.5   Communication and co-ordination in divisional structures

Mintzberg (1995) observed that the role of the centre in divisional structures is:

- to develop corporate strategy.
- to arrange the movement of funds between units.
- to devise and operate a performance control system.
- to appoint and replace divisional managers.

Divisional structures were designed to allow the centre to focus on decision-making in specific business areas. The objective is not to free the units from central control – it is to maximize the centre's ability to control units and to be able to communicate more effectively with them. Mintzberg (1995) writes:

> Alfred P. Sloan introduced the divisional structure to General Motors in the 1920s to reduce the power of its autonomous business units, to impose systems of financial controls on what had been a largely unmanaged agglomeration of different automobile businesses
>
> (Mintzberg, 1995, p. 648)

The nature of the relationship of the corporate centre to its divisions has also been investigated by Campbell and Goold (1988).

5.4 The work of Goold and Campbell and their associates: Management styles in divisional structures

Michael Porter (1987a) concluded that when companies acquired other companies, the result of the union did not always produce more shareholder value than when the companies operated independently. The suggestion is that the centre can either reduce or enhance the performance of a subsidiary business unit. A key issue is the relationship between each business in a corporate portfolio and the role that the centre has in creating value for each business. This value can be achieved either by directly injecting value-generating resources or competences into the business or by facilitating synergistic links between businesses where such synergistic value would not be created by the businesses acting alone. Simply injecting capital into a business is therefore unlikely to increase shareholder value, which means that if the corporate centre does not contribute to the business there is no rationale for the link to be maintained. Porter (1987a) suggested three ways in which the centre can add value:

1 By acting as a portfolio manager; in this scenario the centre acts as an informed banker and adds value by ensuring sound financial divisional control. The centre is expert in developing and implementing control systems.
2 By facilitating the transfer of skills between business units.
3 By facilitating the sharing of activities.

Campbell and Goold (1988) looked at how corporate centres add value to business units, and their findings suggest that corporate success depends on the style, the corporate centre adopts, how well it implements that style and the fit of that style with the organizational situation.

They suggest that there are three styles that can be successful:

1 Strategic planning style.
2 Financial control style.
3 Strategic control style.

5.4.1 The strategic planning style

The strategic planning style is characterized by:

- strong central leadership.
- an emphasis on co-ordination and co-operation (formalized mutual adjustment).
- mechanisms for thorough review and analysis.
- the setting of long-term strategic objectives.
- the willingness to change strategies to meet changing circumstances.

Organization structures in strategic planning companies are often of a matrix nature because it allows the centre to facilitate co-operation across a range of businesses. This approach seeks to create strategic options for business units that draw upon and utilize the expertise of the whole corporate entity. It would also provide an appropriate mechanism for the identification of synergies, through co-operation, across units.

5.4.1.1 Potential strengths of the strategic planning style

- The centre is able to challenge ideas and attitudes more competently than outside bankers and investors.
- By the process of interaction and leadership an effective central management can lead the business unit into developing more creative and ambitious strategies than would come out of single businesses.
- The centre can buffer the business unit from short-term financial pressures that stock markets and other investors may place on single businesses.
- The business unit can therefore adjust strategies in order to gain long-term benefits rather than be forced to concentrate on short-term financial targets.

5.4.1.2 Potential weaknesses of the strategic planning style

- Business managers have less clear-cut responsibilities and less autonomy, which can lead to de-motivation.
- The decision-making processes can be slowed down. In the worst cases the whole system can become unwieldy and bureaucratic.
- There is a risk that the centre can be seen to be autocratic and ill-informed, resulting in a perception, and sometimes a reality, that good opportunities are missed through a lack of fit with the overall corporate plan.
- An obsession with the long term can lead to the neglect of important operational issues and the need to generate profits in the short term.
- The business environment can be over-protected from harsh competitive realities, inducing complacency in business units.

5.4.2 The financial control style

The financial control style is characterized by:

- autonomy of divisions and local leadership.
- an emphasis on control through budgets (control by output standardization).
- strategy direction is set locally.
- the setting of financial objectives and allocation of resources based on the historical ability to deliver those objectives.
- tight financial control by the centre.

Organization structures in financial control companies stress independence, with divisions reporting directly to the centre with little cross-division liaison. There is no obvious added value from links between divisions.

5.4.2.1 Potential strengths of the financial control style

- Financial control organizations are more demanding of the business units than banks or stock markets. They impose tight controls which are tightly monitored, with under-achievement being quickly addressed. This can motivate divisional managers to think about their strategies so that they can deliver above average performance. The simplicity of accountability also provides managers with clear guidelines of the centre's expectations of them.
- The centre reinforces the focus on performance by allocating investment on the basis of performance. In a similar fashion, under-performing units will be divested. Financial control organizations search for acquisition candidates that are performing poorly with respect to return on assets, with the intention of turning them around through the application of financial control disciplines.

5.4.2.2 Potential weaknesses of the financial control style

- Some critics claim that the focus on short-term financial measures encourages revenue maximization at the expense of investment needs. Evidence suggests that financial control companies can miss out on long term and more speculative investments due to the desire to operate in financially predictable environments.

5.4.3 The strategic control style

Strategic control companies try to position themselves between financial control companies and strategic planning companies. Businesses are grouped into divisions but the centre maintains a closer interest on strategy than financial control companies. The intention of the intermediate position is to gain advantages that accrue to both financial control and strategic planning companies.

Strategic control companies:

- Try to ensure that subsidiaries do not get trapped into inappropriate mind-sets by allowing overlap of centre and subsidiary management functions, and by implementing strategic review processes (control by formalized mutual adjustment).
- Facilitate business unit collaboration without being over-active in the co-ordination of that collaboration.
- Provide access to resources so that subsidiaries can finance long-term or risky projects that would be difficult to finance through capital markets. The investments are supported because the centre has detailed and 'expert' knowledge of the subsidiary businesses. It also protects the business units from the short-term expectations of capital markets.

5.4.3.1 Potential strengths of the strategic control style

- It allows the individual businesses to take a long-term view on investment decisions and implementation performance.
- There is an awareness of the need to balance long-term goals and short-term performance.

5.4.3.2 Potential weaknesses of the strategic control style

- It can become bureaucratic and there is confusion between strategic control and financial control.
- The whole corporation may be unable to raise funds in situations where the individual businesses could.
- Business can be over-protected from the disciplines of the markets.

The ability of the centre to add value is therefore crucial to the success of these conglomerate companies. If the centre cannot add value then there is no justification for the link. The term 'corporate parenting' has been coined to describe the relationship between businesses in corporate portfolios. Good parents avoid the weaknesses of the strategic style and are able to add value to their 'children'. Campbell et al. (1995,1998) suggest that good parents positively intervene in situations where:

- The unit managers have a misguided conception of what the business should be – the market scope may be too wide or too narrow, or there is too much or too little vertical integration.
- The administration systems are too bureaucratic or are underdeveloped.
- Managers start to make inappropriate strategic decisions.
- There are opportunities for links with other businesses.
- Environmental change requires special expertise.
- This special expertise can be supplied to a number of businesses facing the same conditions.

Owen and Harrison (1995) recount that ICI split into ICI and Zeneca because one board was unable to give parenting advantages to what had become two distinct business groups.

5.5 Summary

The relationship between operating efficiency (strategy implementation), strategy creation and organization structure requires that strategic managers ask three important questions:

1 Is the present structure of the organization allowing the organization to operate as efficiently as alternative possibilities?

2   If we wish to make changes to the organization's outputs, are our choices constrained by our structure, and if we change strategy, can we change structure?

3   Does our structure constrain the way we develop strategy?

The underpinning economic logic is that organizations only grow to significant sizes when inputs are turned into outputs more efficiently by large organizations than small organizations (though other factors, such as monopolistic practices and innovation, are clearly important). Organizations that grow have to therefore 'find' structures that allow this growth. If structures do not accommodate growth economically, then growth will not occur – i.e. it must be more profitable to produce on a large scale rather than on a small scale. This means that there must be methods and structures to support increasing returns to scale if organizations are to grow. In other words, as organizations grow they must 'find' structures and processes that allow this growth to be profitable.

It is also worth noting that strategy has the potential to precede structure, as when production lines were introduced into car manufacturing, and that strategy can follow structure, if these production line methods are then applied to different industries. Organizations also take fewer risks when they accommodate new strategic directions within existing organizational configurations (structures, systems, resources). Peters and Waterman (1982) aptly said *they stick to the knitting*. The danger is that the new direction cannot be accommodated within existing configurations.

When organizations develop structures they develop systems of control, communication channels and cultural entities that subsequently affect how strategies develop. Miller (1986, 1987) has demonstrated how structure influences strategic decision-making and how particular kinds of strategies are associated with different kinds of strategic postures. Companies following cost leadership strategies will therefore manage their activities in different ways than those following differentiation strategies. Decisions about structural configuration will affect both operating efficiency and strategic decision-making. In other words, strategy implies structure and structure influences strategy creation.

CHAPTER 6

Strategy-making processes

In addition to recognizing the crucial role that managers play in shaping the destinies of organizations, it is important to acknowledge and to take into account other influences on strategy formation. Looking at strategy-making processes more generally, Mintzberg and Waters (1985) identified two dominant strategic patterns, which they subsequently termed 'deliberate strategy' and 'emergent strategy'. Deliberate strategy, as its name implies, advocates purposeful and planned actions using careful and logical analysis upon which impartial decision-making can be applied. Emergent strategy, on the other hand, incorporates the view that some (indeed many) organizations do not articulate and formulate strategy through formal processes, even though they have coherent business strategies. In this explanation of strategy formation, strategy is crafted rather than planned and is discernible as a pattern in a stream of actions. This is a useful definition for organization analysts as it allows strategy to be inferred from actions; the analyst is more likely to notice actions than to be present at the decision-making that provoked those actions. It also allows us to propose theories that account for these actions, and if the theories withstand scrutiny, they can be used to develop explanations that enable us to understand strategy formation processes. Yet it is also the case that theories of strategy making processes should be treated cautiously because they may be consistent with the facts but may not be true explanations. Mintzberg et al. (1996), for example, have shown how Pascale's analysis of Honda's entry into the US motor cycle market gave a completely different interpretation to events than did the Boston Consulting Group working from a rational planning/positioning perspective (Pascale, 1996).

6.1 Strategy-making dimensions

Numerous studies have emphasized the following dimensions as being particularly important in strategy formation:

- A rational dimension.
- An environmentally determined dimension.
- A political and cultural dimension.

6.1.1 The rational dimension of strategy

Strategy, in rational models, develops out of logical processes. The emphasis in early rational models was on strategy conception prior to strategy implementation, while later models (such as the logical incremental models of Quinn and the process and umbrella strategies of Mintzberg and Waters) recognized the limitations that managers have in realizing and understanding the totality of their environment. This would imply that managers formulate strategic directions in rational but imperfect ways.

6.1.1.1 Strategy creation preceding strategy implementation

Mintzberg (1994) describes two different strategy-making approaches under the headings 'design school' and 'planning school'. Both approaches work from the premise that strategy creation comes before strategy implementation. In the design school, strategy conceptualization resides in the hands (or the minds) of the organization's senior managers. The chief executive would normally be the key strategist, with implementation being carried out by subordinate managers – the underlying emphasis clearly being that strategy conceptualization should be kept simple and easily understandable. The design school originated in the 1950s and is seen by many as the foundation stone upon which modern strategic management is built.

The planning school, as the name implies, develops strategy out of careful analysis and planning. Early strategic planning models assumed that strategies could be developed in situations of complete knowledge, where the environment could be fully comprehended so that the strategic plan could be made with certainty. Experience and research have shown, however, that these expectations were frequently not realized. Lenz and Lyles (1985), for example, have criticized 'excessively rational' planning processes on the basis of studies carried out in financial and commercial organizations. They found that some strategic planning models treated the world of business and commerce as if it was easily reducible to predictable outcomes, disregarding managerial experience and ignored all data that could not be quantified. Wilson (1994) also describes the GE experience, one in which the planning process became an end in itself, and the planning staff, not the managers, took control of strategic planning. Grant (1995) reinforces this view when he outlines the feelings of Jack Welch, the Chief Executive of GE, who forcibly describes the strategic planning system of the 1970s *as slow, inefficient of management time, and stifling of innovation and opportunism.* More positively, Wilson (1994) describes how strategic planning became more effective when the planning process was *driven down into the organization.* In these circumstances strategic planning promoted *strategic thinking.*

Ansoff (1987) ascribes the failure of many strategic planning initiatives to the inability of organizations to sustain them once the initial enthusiasm had worn off. There are three main reasons, he argues, why strategic planning fails (after Ansoff, 1987, p. 196):

1 'Paralysis by analysis', which is induced when existing and previous strategic activity (i.e. their strategic plans) produced little by way of results in the market place.
2 Organizational resistance to the introduction of strategic planning into the business.
3 Withdrawal or relaxation of forceful support for strategic planning by top management.

Overcoming these potential hurdles was felt to be important, as Ansoff believed that formal strategic planning provided a framework for strategic thinking that was essential for improved organizational performance. It involved the integration of three management disciplines if strategic planning was to be effective:

> Strategic planning is only one of three processes which must be brought together to assure effective strategic adaptation. The other two processes are management capability planning and management of the overall process of strategic change.
>
> (Ansoff, 1987, p. 197)

This is especially important in turbulent environments since it can be linked to strategic control systems that enhance the management of change. It suggests that strategic planning can become strategic management if extra processes are integrated into it.

More negatively, the intensity of the criticism that has been levelled at strategic planning has been significant. Mintzberg (1994), for example, argues that strategic planning corrupts strategic thinking:

> Conventional planners may believe that managers are too involved in the details to reflect. But effective managers may know that only by being so involved can they reflect. To think strategically, in other words, they must be active, involved, connected, committed, alert, stimulated. It is the calculated chaos of their work that drives their thinking, enabling them to build reflection on action in an interactive process.
>
> (Mintzberg, 1994, p. 291)

Porter (1987b) attributes the failure of many strategic planning exercises to a lack of strategic thinking. He lays the blame for this in the separation of planning from action.

> Planning, must become the job of line managers, not of head office staff... Today every executive needs to understand how to think strategically.
>
> (Porter, 1987b, p. 28)

Grant (1995) expresses similar thoughts:

> One of the most important changes in strategy making in large enterprises over the last two decades has been the shift in responsibility for strategy formulation from

> Corporate planning departments to line managers. One of the benefits of this transition is that the strategic planning processes provide a highly effective mechanism for dialogue between corporate and divisional managers and between general managers and functional specialists.
>
> (Grant, 1995, p. 22)

6.1.1.2   The coalescence of strategy creation and strategy implementation

In a departure from previous thinking, Quinn (1978) observed that managers attempted to be rational, but because they were aware of the unpredictable nature of their environment, they relaxed some of the constraints usually associated with the design school. The strategic management process that he observed moved forward in what was described as a logically incremental manner. It involves senior managers developing an overall direction whilst simultaneously allowing lower level managers the room to develop and negotiate how that direction should be followed. This permitted senior managers to be more provisional in the sense that it allowed and accommodated sudden and unexpected changes in the business environment. The suggestion is that managers will be both rational and cautious as it is rational to be cautious in unstable environments! By constantly monitoring and interpreting the business environment a strategy can be consistent with its environment, and improve its chances of success.

The key features of logical incrementalism are outlined as follows (adapted from Quinn, 1978):

- In the initial phases of strategy development the top executives forecast the events that are likely to have the most impact on the company.
- They then try to develop a resource base and a corporate posture that can withstand all but the most devastating events.
- They select resources and market positions that they can competitively dominate, whilst simultaneously trying to maintain an ability to change.
- They then proceed incrementally, responding to unforeseen events as they occur, building on successes and cutting out losses from failed activities.
- They constantly reassess the future, finding new relationships and seeking to align the organization's resources to the environment, never quite achieving the perfect fit as events always keep changing.

Mintzberg and his co-workers investigated strategy formation over an extended time period using case studies (see Mintzberg and Waters, 1982; Mintzberg and McHugh, 1985) and they concluded that strategy had deliberate and emergent characteristics. They were seen to range from completely planned strategies, with managers in total control, through umbrella and process strategies where managers have some control, to imposed strategies with managers having no control. Their analysis also suggested that strategy development had the following eight features and development characteristics (adapted from Mintzberg and Waters, 1985):

1   Planned strategies assume that deliberate strategies *can* emerge from plans developed by the central leadership.
2   Entrepreneurial strategies occur when strategy is formed and led by an organization leader and can exhibit deliberate and emergent qualities.
3   Ideological strategies occur when all organizational members are dedicated to a common cause (strategies are largely deliberate).
4   Umbrella strategies occur when senior managers define strategic boundaries but allow lower levels to define specific market positions (control is through performance targets, exhibiting deliberate and emergent characteristics in what could be termed a deliberately emergent style).
5   Process strategies occur when organization leaders design the processes and systems upon which the organization's strategy creation and implementation is founded, leaving the details of strategy to emerge from these systems (again exhibiting deliberate and emergent characteristics in a deliberately emergent fashion).
6   Unconnected strategies occur when actors within organization follow their own desires. Coherent strategies emerge through the deliberate intentions of individuals and from the fact that these individuals have followed similar training schemes and have cognitively and organizationally equivalent standards.
7   Consensus strategies occur when actors mutually adjust through consistent trade-offs, with the strategies emerging from the consensus.
8   Imposed strategies originate outside the organization through the explicit imposition of the wishes of outside bodies, or implicitly by constraints on managerial choices.

These characteristics are similar to logical incrementalism in the partial acknowledgement of a strategic design and the concept of adaptive learning. They also differ from logical incrementalism in that strategies can form outside centrally devised frameworks, and because a number of mechanisms of strategy formation are possible.

6.1.2   The environmentally determined dimension of strategy formation

We can discuss environmentally determined strategy in two ways:

1   Past choice constrained strategy.
2   Externally imposed strategies.

Past choice constrained strategy   When we define strategic management as the management task that includes the activity of fitting an organization's resources to its environment, we are recognizing that an organization's strategy is constrained by its environment. As organizations commit more and more resources to particular market positions they become increasingly committed to those positions. Using an ecology metaphor, Hannan and Freeman (1977) suggest that as organizations adapt to a particular environment they become less flexible. Organization's choices are constrained not only by an explicit cultural dimension in the sense of 'What we believe around here' but also by what skills and resources are available, and in what context those skills and resources become valuable – the 'What we can do around here' question. In this sense strategies are constrained by path dependency (choices made in the past constrain choices that can be made now). If the environment changes substantially organizations that have been unable to adapt will fail.

Externally imposed strategies　Many organizations have to respond to the constraints imposed upon them by outside stakeholders. The actions of organizations, for example, can be constrained by the expected responses of competitors, suppliers or customers. Indeed, many public sector organizations, including those in the health and education sectors, are constrained by government regulation and funding.

6.1.3　The political and cultural dimensions of strategy formation

From a cultural point of view, understanding the beliefs and bureaucratic systems of organizations is essential if we are to explain the decisions that organizations make. Pettigrew (1973), for example, suggested that power was a dimension of decision-making, and that it should be taken into account when we try to explain the actions (and outputs) of organizations. He also suggested that in the pursuit of organizational goals it was rational for managers to be political if it produced what for them was the best strategy, and similarly, that the organizational politic should be rational if optimal solutions were to be produced. In a comparable fashion Allison (1971) noted that a decision that seems irrational from an organizational perspective may be rational from an individual or group perspective – suggesting that the political context of decisions is integral to any concept of organizational rationality. This is supported by the work of Guth and MacMillan (1986), who carried out a survey of middle managers and found that they were able to successfully intervene to selectively encourage or block important (strategic) decisions. There is also some evidence that managers use formal planning systems as vehicles to communicate their personal views and exert influence (Langley, 1988; Papadakis et al., 1998).

In line with the view that strategic decision-making is framed within a political and cultural context, Prahalad and Bettis (1986) argue that organizations have dominant logics, and that these logics are based on the mental maps developed in the organization's core business. For successful organizations the dominant logic underpins their success, although there is always the danger that management thinking can get stuck in a belief structure that is inappropriate because it fails to keep pace with changing situations. An explanation for such misalignments points to managers' perceptions changing more slowly than their environments, a finding corroborated in the work of Johnson (1987), Fletcher and Huff (1990), Narayanan and Fahey (1990), and Miller (1992). The work of Johnson, who developed the idea of the 'cultural web' shown in Figure 6.1, is particularly useful because it captures and distinguishes the factors that could constrain managers' world-views.

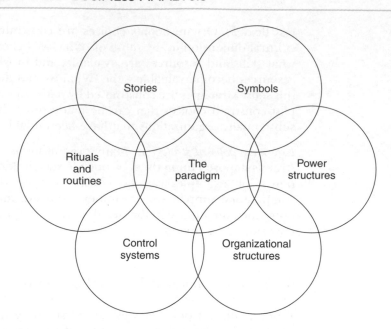

Figure 6.1
Cultural web
Source: (Johnson, G. and
Scholes, K., 1999, p. 59,
Reproduced with per-
mission from Pearson
Education Limited).

The central 'paradigm' represents the underlying beliefs that managers have about their organization. Johnson and Scholes describe the paradigm as 'the set of assumptions held relatively in common and taken for granted in an organization' (1999, p. 59). They distinguish between those assumptions that are implicit and unconsciously held and beliefs and values that are explicit, openly published, and discussed. Both sets of assumptions are said to be shaped and influenced by the other components of the cultural web:

Rituals and routines These activities establish relationships between organization members so that they know their places and roles in the organization. Members accept the rituals and routines because they are generally accepted to be the best way of doing things, and because their involvement reinforces their own membership rights. Rituals and routines can also have an important external effect, such as in the service sectors where they can be designed to inform and control customers. Johnson and Scholes, for example, highlight 'patient infantalising' in the National Health Service, where rituals and routines have the effect of making many patients feel they are being treated like children. More typical examples include degree ceremonies in universities, clocking in and out in factories, and stock taking in warehouses.

Stories The stories of the organization reflect those things that are important to the organization, such as tales of achievement and the doings of heroes and villains. They are signposts to what the organization considers important. Johnson and Scholes suggest that the stories of health service providers reflect an overriding passion for curing rather than for prevention and caring.

Symbols These are representations of power in terms of visible images of status (or lack of it) and examples include the allocation and specification of company cars, the size and decoration of offices, the wearing of uniforms, and in some organizations, the badges of rank. Symbolism can also be manifested in language and in the way people are described, as when customers are called clients and when passengers are referred to as customers. The content of language is also an important indicator of underlying assumptions, such as when universities talk of profit and loss more than they do standards and scholarship.

Power structures Power can be vested in ownership, by being a member of the elite professional group and by having control over valuable resources. Examples of power structures include consultants in hospitals, pension funds with large shareholdings, majority shareholders, trade unions, professional associations, professors in universities and technical experts in research led companies.

Control systems Organizations control their members through different types of reward and punishment systems. The principle is simple – organizational action can be driven by organizational rewards, and organization members respond to rewards more than they do to rhetoric (see Chapter 5). In periods of stability the rewards can be finely tuned so that they reinforce desired outcomes. Such tuning can be more difficult when strategic change is required because the reward system is likely to be embedded in the existing and established organizational paradigm. This can result in the company rewarding action 'A' when it wanted action 'B'. When strategic change is instigated it is therefore important to design the control system so that it can operate within the existing organizational paradigm, or that the organizational paradigm is changed, which can be very difficult, so that the control system can be made to work.

Organization structures Organization structures are frameworks that evolve (or are designed) to facilitate communication and co-ordination between organization members. Indeed, the way that its resources are arranged, including its people, and the mechanisms that link those resources and make them cohesive, are dimensions of an organization's structure. They also reflect the power structure in the organization as well as the level of importance that the organization puts on the control of certain key inputs and outputs.

The cultural web can also be a powerful tool in conceptualizing an organization's dominant logic on important strategic questions such as:

- Who are the organization's customers?
- What are their needs?
- What activities do we reward?
- Who are the most powerful stakeholder groups?
- How do we keep powerful stakeholder groups happy?
- What must we be good at to keep customer happy?

The health of an organization's dominant logic can be gauged by how consistent it is with the provision of outputs that satisfy customers. An organization can have an unhealthy dominant logic if it is so well established it prevents organization members responding adequately to environmental changes. If an organization cannot respond to environmental changes then its strategy cannot be consistent with success. For a commercial organization this might manifest itself as a tendency for its products to become less attractive to customers, with market share and profits declining. Johnson (1988) has described how the influence of an inappropriate organizational paradigm (i.e. an unhealthy dominant logic) means that incremental strategy development becomes illogical because it is based on an inappropriate perception of the environment. Organizations may also find that logics that are satisfactory for one industry or segment are not suitable for operating in other industries or segments. This can be linked to the idea of parenting, which is discussed in Chapter 5.

The influence and power of dominant logics on organizational behaviour is captured in the following scenario and story:

Start with a cage containing five monkeys. Inside the cage, hang a banana on a string and place a set of stairs under it. Before long, a monkey will go to the stairs and start to climb towards the banana. As soon as he touches the stairs, spray all of the other monkeys with cold water. After a while, another monkey makes an attempt with the same result that all the other monkeys are sprayed with cold water. Soon, when another monkey tries to climb the stairs, the other monkeys will try to prevent it. Now, put away the cold water. Remove one monkey from the cage and replace it with a new one. The new monkey sees the banana and wants to climb the stairs. To his surprise and horror, all of the other monkeys attack him. After another attempt and attack, he knows that if he tries to climb the stairs, he will be assaulted. Next, remove another of the original five monkeys and replace it with a new one. The newcomer goes to the stairs and is attacked. The previous newcomer takes part in the punishment with enthusiasm! Likewise, replace a third original monkey with a new one, then a fourth, and then the fifth. Every time the newest monkey takes to the stairs, he is attacked. Most of the monkeys that are beating him have no idea why they were not permitted to climb the stairs or why they are participating in the beating of the newest monkey. After replacing all the original monkeys, none of the remaining monkeys have ever been sprayed with cold water. Nevertheless, no monkey ever again approaches the stairs to try for the banana. Why not – because as far as they know that's the way it's always been done around here. And that, my friends, is how a company policy begins.
(Source: *Wake up to Wogan*, BBC Radio 2, 22 January 02, the programme producer Paul Walters who supplied a written copy of the quote, received it from a listener Mark Pils)

An important consideration when discussing strategy development is the nature of the power balance within organizations (Cohen et al., 1972; Mintzberg, 1979). When organizations have structures in which the strategic apex has considerable power strategy development is more likely to be centrally guided. Correspondingly, when power is dispersed evenly through organization strategy development is likely to emerge from various parts of the organization.

6.2 Integrative frameworks: Strategy-making as a complex amalgam of different processes

The work of Mintzberg and his colleagues initiated the concept that strategy was both deliberate and emergent and was formed by more than one mechanism. Indeed, the use of multi-model explanations is widely used to explain complex phenomena in other disciplines, such as surface adhesion in the natural sciences. The application of multi-model explanations are also important within the strategy making literature, with writers like Bailey and Johnson (1992, 1995, 1996) using more than one process model to explain strategic management processes. Explanations that developed out of the planning school tried to be overtly rational and were subsequently superseded and complemented by theories which recognized that 'realised strategy' arose out of situations where there was incomplete information and environmental unpredictability. This complexity can incorporate conflicting interpretations as well as multi-stakeholders with different and competing objectives (Johnson, 1987).

McLellan and Kelly (1980) point out that strategy formation in commercial organizations is characterized by mechanisms that have a number of top-down and bottom-up approaches. Chaffee (1985) states that strategy making processes incorporate linear, adaptive and interpretative processes. Linear processes are typified by the strategic planning model of Andrews (1971), while adaptive and interpretative processes progressively encompass the beliefs that are individually and collectively held about the nature of the organization and its environment. The three types of strategy making processes are progressive because organizations use increasingly more complex strategy forming processes as they evolve: from linear to adaptive to interpretative, there is organizational learning. Chaffee also suggested that different kinds of strategy making could co-exist in the same organization. This is supported by the cognitive mapping literature, which says that involvement in formal processes increases strategic sophistication, and that successful organizations are more strategically sophisticated than their less successful competitors (Narayanan and Fahey, 1990; Maznevski et al., 1993).

Work undertaken by Bailey and Johnson (1992, 1995, 1996), Hart (1992) and Hart and Banbury (1994) provided operationalized and integrative frameworks for describing strategic processes. Hart focuses on the roles that organization actors play in strategy-making and how senior managers use/ manage/tolerate different strategy-making modes. Bailey and Johnson take a different perspective and portray strategy as having different dimensions that help explain strategy-making within the context of those dimensions. In the Hart typology the emphasis is on managing process because he sees a link between strategy making modes and performance, which is subtly different than the Bailey and Johnson approach that recognizes that process can constrain managerial action and that strategic configurations can be a product of organizational context. The Hart typology proposed five strategy-making modes (Hart and Banbury, 1994):

1 *Command*   Where the chief executive and a few senior managers decide strategy.
2 *Symbolic*   Where strategy is driven by a mission and a vision for the future. The chief executive sets this vision and mission. The chief executive has a dream about where the organization will be in 20 years. This dream is communicated throughout the organization.
3 *Rational*   Where strategy is driven by formal structure and planning systems.
4 *Transactive*   Where strategy is made on an iterative basis involving managers and staff in an ongoing dialogue. The business planning in this organization is incremental involving everyone to some degree in the process. This organization continuously adapts its strategy based on feedback from the market.
5 *Generative*   Where most people in the organization are prepared to use their initiative. People are encouraged to experiment with innovative approaches. Organization members understand what the organization needs to achieve if it is to prosper.

Strategy modes that involve the whole organization are likely to produce more effective strategies than those that do not. Hart also points out that particular modes lead to particular performance outcomes. The rational mode, with its emphasis on decision control, can be associated with financial performance and profitability, whilst the transactive mode, which is more consultative and incremental, can be related to quality and social responsibility.

The idea that different strategic processes will emphasize particular performance measures is intuitively rational, though the idea that these can be separated out in the long run is less credible. For example, the separation of quality from profitability runs counter to other studies that specifically relate quality to profitability (Buzzel and Gale, 1987). Also, in a small organization a command mode of strategy-making could ensure high performance on a number of measures whilst in a large complex organization the interdependence of performance measures reduces the likelihood that each performance measure is not related to the sum of the strategy-making processes. In light of this it would seem more useful to consider strategy-making processes in context rather than relate individual modes to particular measures.

The underlying argument is that as organizations become more complex the strategy-making processes must match that complexity, with more people becoming involved in the process (Ansoff (1987) termed this the 'requisite variety hypothesis').

Bailey and Johnson (1996) propose six dimensions of strategy development. These are Planning, Political, Incrementalism, Command, Cultural and Enforced Choice. It is argued that one or more of these describe the strategy-making process of any given organization. The number of possible combinations on six dimensions is forty-nine, although it is argued that only a limited number of configurations exist. Their research indicated that there were six dominant configurations:

1 *Planning*   Organizations which are predominantly planners have clear objectives, a commonly held concept of vision and mission and use precise plans to articulate intended strategy and its implementation.

One dominant dimension: planning.

2 *Rational command*   In rational command organizations a senior member or group dominates the strategy creation process using a planning framework. This description is very similar to the Design School approach to strategic planning that is outlined by Mintzberg (1994).

Two dominant dimensions: planning and command.

3 *Logical incrementalism*   Logical incrementalism is a process that incorporates missions and objectives, and although the objectives are planned, organizations are cautious about setting them rigidly because the environment changes. The overall process is incremental since the objectives change over time due to the build-up of strategic and operational pressures, triggering reassessments and new objectives until future pressures trigger further reassessments.

Two dominant dimensions: planning and incremental.

4 *Muddling through*   Political, cultural and incremental dimensions dominate this configuration. Progress is made by players bargaining for their own particular objectives within a framework based on history and a clear understanding of what is, and what is not, allowed. Incrementalism results not only because of reactive adjustments to accommodate a changing environment but also because of political and cultural influences opposing significant change (Lindblom, 1959).

Three dominant dimensions: cultural, political and incremental.

5 *Externally dependent*   In this situation strategy is imposed by force outside the organization. Power to modify outside influences is likely to be in the hands of those who understand and can relate to powerful external players. This situation is typical of organizations being controlled by other organizations.

Two dominant dimensions: enforced choice and political.

6 *Embattled command*   As the name suggests, this typifies situations where a leader is charged with turning an organization in crisis around. It is frequently found in smaller organizations in turbulent environments, as well as in failing subsidiaries where a new leader is parachuted-in to address the situation. Embattled command has also become more prevalent in the public sector, with failing schools and hospitals attracting widespread media attention.

Two dominant dimensions: command and enforced choice.

The view that structure influences strategy is also well established within the strategic management literature. Miller (1986) argues that there are particular structural configurations associated with particular strategies. In competitive environments, for example, certain configurations of strategy and structure confer superior performance, and organizations which fail to move towards these configurations tend to ultimately perish. The idea of different strategy-making configurations offers the possibility that in different organizations different people will have different roles in strategy development, and that strategy can be developed within as well as at the top of organizations. There is also the possibility that different decisions will also be made by different processes.

CHAPTER 7

Organization environments

The Collins English Dictionary (1991) defines a plant's or animal's environment as:

> The external surroundings in which a plant or animal lives which tend to influence its development and behaviour.
>
> (Collins English Dictionary, 1991)

We can also define an organization's environment as the external surroundings in which the organization operates, and this can include its competitors (and non-competitors), suppliers, buyers and governments. Organizations act to both shape their environment and to respond to events that occur in it. In light of this, and since multi-divisional organizations operate in a number of industries and countries, we suggest that each business unit is investigated using the following procedure:

- Define the industry or industries in which the organization operates. This should include an estimate of industry size by some measure of turnover, the identification of industry segments and the geographic extent of the industry.
- Identify the organization's or unit's competitors.
- Conduct an analysis of the industry or industries using Porter's Five Forces Model (Porter, 1980, 1985).
- Identify the forces in the wider macroeconomic environment that are impacting on the unit and its competitors. Assess the significance of these forces and the potential for change that they could induce.
- Discuss the opportunities and threats to the organization that the environmental analysis raises.

7.1 Industry definition

Levitt (1960) attributes the decline of the US Railway industry to the inability of its management to define their industry environment (i.e. *the business they were in*) in such a way that the opportunities and threats could be recognized, understood and managed. The importance of industry definition, and how it impacts on organizations in different ways, is amply demonstrated by a DuPont Corporation example. The DuPont Corporation sold 80 per cent of all cellophane traded in the USA, but was able to claim in an antitrust case that they were in the flexible-wrap market rather than the cellophane market. The argument rested on the premise that consumers regarded close substitutes as competitive products, and their share of this wider defined market was below 25 per cent. This was accepted because the cross-elasticities of demand between cellophane and other flexible wrap products indicated their substitutability (Frank, 2000).

Examples of this kind demonstrate that the task of defining an organization's environment and the industries in which it competes can be difficult, and the way that it is defined depends on both economic and perceptual factors (Prahalad and Bettis, 1986; Johnson, 1988; Frank, 2000). This is why it is so important that we correctly define it within our strategic analysis, as it will significantly affect the outcome of the whole analysis and the actions based on that analysis.

Grant (1995) suggests that businesses can be usefully analysed by looking at the markets they serve and/or by the technology they employ. So, from a technological/supply side perspective, an industry can be defined as a group of companies that would find it easy to switch their production facilities to manufacture each other's products. Grant points out that the automotive industry normally includes light vans and trucks because it is assumed that they can be manufactured by car companies using the same technology. From a market/demand side perspective, if customers consider the products of the two firms to be substitutes for each other, then the two firms can be considered to be competing in the same market as each other. The more consumers see products as similar the more these products can be said to be substitutes for each other and competing with each other. And because individuals and corporations have limited spending power, every purchase is a trade-off against every other purchase. This has led to consumer choice being modelled as step process, as the following example of a car purchase demonstrates:

- The purchaser has to decide whether to buy a new or used car.
- He/she then has to decide what generic type of car to buy: big, small, four-wheel drive, etc.
- Then he/she has to decide which specific car to buy.

These choices will depend on disposable income and perception of needs. It is likely that different people will place different weights of importance on economy, comfort, status, etc., and that for the population as a whole there will be a number of segments based upon these preferences. The important point in this, or any other type of analysis, is that it provides a rich picture of the organization's competitive environment. Industry definitions should not restrict our analysis, and we should be prepared to explore different conceptualizations if this increases our understanding of an organization's context.

A technique that helps us to define industry membership, which is important if we want to assess an organization's competitive environment, is strategic group analysis (Porter, 1980).

7.2   Identifying the organization's competitors: Strategic groups

A group of firms who have similar strategic approaches and operate in similar ways are said to comprise a strategic group. If a market is homogeneous, such that all consumers have needs that are met by products and associated services (delivery method, after sales care, etc.) that have very similar features, then strategic groups will emerge on internal dimensions. If customers have differing needs, the market can be differentiated, and strategic groups can emerge on market and internal dimensions. As a general principle, organizations will seek to compete on dimensions that differ from those of their competitors so that they can minimize competition – and a strategic group map can sometimes identify areas where there is limited or no competition. They also provide a blueprint for adopting similar competitive positions to those of their rivals as knowledge disseminates across the industry and common recipes develop (Spender, 1989).

7.2.1   Constructing strategic group maps

The first stage is to identify dimensions or characteristics that distinguish firms from each other. Examples of such dimensions are product line breadth, brand image, number and type of distribution channels, product features, service features, cost position, price policy, geographic reach, degree of vertical integration and market segments served.

The second stage is to plot the firms on a graph with the axis represented by two minimally correlated dimensions. Repeat this procedure using a variety of axes until a pattern emerges that consistently groups companies together. If the grouping reveals that there are more than one company in at least one group, and more than one group emerge, competitive strategic groups have been identified. If this cannot be achieved then two conclusions can be drawn:

1   The industry is homogenous and the companies in the industry compete on the same basis.
2   The industry is completely heterogeneous and each firm forms its own strategic group.

There can be deviations to this, as when regionally based companies with similar strategies do not compete with each other (e.g. local breweries or village shops do not compete with each other but may compete on the same strategic dimensions). Companies with similar market dimensions can also differ on internal dimensions. Manufacturing processes, quality assurance, inventory control, people management and training are examples of dimensions for comparing resource endowments across organizations. It is possible that companies that compete on the same market dimensions have different resource endowments, or that companies with similar market positions have similar resource endowments. Companies that form the same strategic group on both resource endowments and market position are very similar organizations, and if they choose to compete they will be able to imitate or counter each other's moves. If a member of the strategic group instigates a price (or non-price based) strategy then every other member is capable of imitating it. In this situation the players may be forced into positions that minimize profits unless they can collaborate in some way. A strategic group is only likely to generate above average profits relative to the rest of the industry if:

- There are barriers of entry to the group from other industry groups or from new entrants to the industry.
- The group is an oligopoly that implicitly or explicitly behaves in such a way that above average profits are not traded away (see next section on industry rivalry).

Porter (1996) argues that if organizations follow similar market strategies they will inevitably end up with similar resource configurations because they all benefit from the dissemination of knowledge. Benchmarking, re-engineering and total quality management are cited as examples of technique diffusion. The net result of this is not competitive advantage for individual firms but convergence of market positions and resource configurations leading to hyper-competition.

7.3 Structural analysis of industries: Porter's five forces model

A key concept in Porter's five forces model is the view that some industries are attractive and others as less attractive. The ability to identify industry attractiveness is therefore important, and Porter argues that industries can be characterized and evaluated by looking at, and analysing, the following five forces:

1. The threat of substitute products.
2. The threat of new entrants.
3. The power of buyers.
4. The power of suppliers.
5. The rivalry amongst industry members.

7.3.1 The threat of substitute products

If the product of an industry can be substituted by that of another, the purchaser of that product has choices that extend beyond rival products. For example, margarine may be a substitute for butter, and going to the cinema can be a substitute for a meal at a restaurant. When analysing a specific segment it is advisable to identify the products that are direct competitors and those that are not considered direct competitors, especially when these alternatives could be first choice purchases if circumstances were to change slightly. For instance, branded food goods may be considered competitors of unbranded goods in broad definitions of markets but substitute products in more segment-focused definitions. The purchasers of medium range cars would not consider smaller cars as possible purchases under normal circumstances, but might consider them if there was a rapid increase in petrol prices or if they began to feel societal pressures for greener motoring.

Substitute products are a strong threat when:

- they offer a similar level of benefits at proximate prices.
- the consumer will not incur switching costs in moving between alternatives.
- the consumer is price sensitive.

7.3.2 The threat of new entrants

When new entrants enter an industry they bring extra capacity to the industry. If demand is increasing the new entrants can use this capacity to meet the increased demand. This is frequently the case during the growth stages of an industry, but as the industry matures demand growth slows and new entrants will have to start competing with existing companies for a share of existing demand. In this situation the new entrants will have to gain market share by offering similar products at competitive prices or by redefining the market to increase product demand. If the new entrants have similar product features and benefits to that of existing providers, then the new entry threat is by imitation. When this type of imitation produces a similar competitive position and a similarity of resources, the entrants will face the following entry barriers:

- economies of scale.
- access to secret technology (patented and not patented).
- brand recognition.
- capital costs of entry.
- access to distribution channels.
- lack of experience in carrying out operational activities leading to learning gaps, producing cost disadvantages.
- high customer switching costs.
- access to low cost inputs (e.g. labour).
- legislative barriers to entry.

Porter's framework has been criticized because of its implicit assumption that industry structure is the major determinant of company profitability. The critics of this view contend that business processes are sources of advantage and that competitors with different strategies can overcome established structures by doing things differently (Barney, 1991; Baden-Fuller and Stopford, 1992). New entrants can also enter an industry by acquiring the assets of existing companies, so that the mix of companies remains the same but new resources are introduced to the company by the new ownership – and this could lead to changes in ideas and the introduction of new strategies.

When industry entrance and exit is relatively easy, industries are described as contestable. These situations occur when entry is associated with relatively low sunk costs. If the assets required for entry can be used for other purposes then exit is easier than when the assets are unique. The profits of companies within contestable industries are also moderated by this threat. By way of contrast, the larger the sunk costs of entry the greater the profits available to existing firms without attracting new entrants. This position, according to Schumpeter (in Lipsey and Crystal, 1999), is not sustainable since even in monopoly situations the possibility of obtaining high profits will, in the long run, lead new entrants to circumvent barriers to entry by inventing new 'leapfrogging' products or new production techniques. Schumpeter called this process *creative destruction*. Creative destruction precludes the very long run persistence of barriers to entry to industries that earn large profits.

7.3.3 The power of buyers

Buyers (customers) are powerful when the following conditions exist:

- There are few buyers who purchase in large quantities.
- Buyers have low switching costs.
- Buyers have choices because there is a large volume of sellers.
- The product or service supplied is not an important one.
- The buyer has the ability to produce the product supplied (backwards integration).
- The buyers have information about the costs of production and other buyers' prices.

The impact of powerful buyers can be significant because they can negotiate prices down and reduce industry profitability.

7.3.4 The power of suppliers

The factors that influence buyer power are similar to those that influence supplier power, they just act in the opposite direction.

Supplier power is high when:

- there are few alternative sources of supply and there are many buyers.
- a particular buyer is not an important customer to the supplier.
- the product or service supplied is an important input for the buyer.
- the buyer cannot make the product cheaper than the supplier can.
- there are no substitutes for the supplied product.
- the supplied product has a good brand reputation, especially when this branding is important to the final product.

7.3.5 The rivalry amongst industry members

Two extreme possibilities form reference points for this part of the analysis:

1 Competition between industry members is low. Each industry member is content with its market share and gets involved only minimally with competitive activity. The main concern is to maintain industry profitability by tacit co-operation.
2 Competitive rivalry is high and is manifested in direct and indirect price cutting, promotional activities and discounted products.

Rivalry tends to be high when:

■ Demand is growing slowly or declining. This causes greater rivalry when it is difficult to leave the industry (i.e. when sunk costs are not recoverable and fixed assets cannot be sold or turned to other uses).
■ Customers can switch products easily (products are undifferentiated).
■ New entrants, especially if they are cross-subsidized by rich parents, are seeking to gain market share by price cutting.
■ Industry members are of similar size and have similar market power.
■ There is excess capacity, especially where this results in high fixed costs. In this situation some industry members may be prepared to sell at prices that exceed variable costs but do not necessarily cover total costs. This is likely when companies can differentially price products to different customers so that total revenue exceeds total costs for a complete product mix, with some customers or segments paying lower than average prices.
■ Industry members believe that gaining increased market share will lead to long-term profits through economies of scale and experience effects, and believe that these can be achieved by driving out weaker competitors before an industry matures.

7.3.6 Using Porter's five forces model in organization analysis

The Porter framework can be used at a variety of levels: the evaluation of an industry based on a wide definition and then breaking this wider definition into smaller chunks to clarify specific issues. In evaluating the environment of Toyota, for instance, the following conceptions of industry may be appropriate (depending on the nature of the analysis):

■ The world automotive industry.
■ The world car market.
■ The North American car market.
■ The European car market.
■ The Asian car market.
■ Various national markets.

- The small car market.
- The luxury car market.

The analyst has to define the industry in light of the required task, which is why the analysis of Morgan Cars requires a different approach to an analysis of Toyota. The point of the analysis is to gain an understanding of why organizations are thriving or are not thriving, and to develop ideas for future strategies. It is important that we understand how changes in industry structures are being shaped, or could be shaped, by:

- the actions of industry members.
- the driving forces present in the wider macroeconomic environment.

7.4   The impact of the wider environment on firms and industries

The impact that the wider environment has on firms and industries can be significant, which is why it is important that we understand and recognize the forces that impact on the organization and the industry it operates in. If governments produce increasingly restrictive legislation on polluting cars, for example, each member of the car industry will have to develop or licence 'greener' engines.

Two of the most important environmental forces impacting on organizations are the globalization of markets and organizations and the development of the Internet. Although difficult, a cause and effect approach has to be adopted when assessing the drivers of such environmental change. The Internet arose out of political and technological forces acting on governments, becoming a transnational communications tool that then impacted on manufacturing logistics and the globalization of markets, etc. It can be argued that it was governments seeking trade agreements, with the development of physical and electronic communications, and the convergence of cultures through increased communications, that underpinned the globalization of markets. The global activities of some organizations then made it necessary for competitors to follow suit in order to gain economies of scale, and/or to identify low cost manufacturing nations.

7.4.1   Auditing of environmental driving forces

This can be difficult task because it involves:

- the recognition and identification of environmental factors as early as possible.
- the assessment of the impact of their driving forces.
- the assessment of the rate of change that will, or is, taking place.

A procedure for carrying out the task would first identify the forces acting on the organization. This is likely to include the analysis of industry reports and will involve speaking to managers and experts to see what is in the 'pipeline'. A commonly used and comprehensive framework for identifying key environmental pressures is PEST analysis. It identifies environmental forces under four headings, these being Political, Economic, Sociological and Technological.

7.4.1.1 Political factors

Organizations are influenced by the responses of governments to activities in the wider business environment. Pressure groups, for instance, will purposely target governments in the hope that it will influence or change policy. This is also true of business, with trade and management associations applying political pressure to support perceived needs. More broadly, events such as terrorist attacks in the USA can significantly and adversely affect airlines and related industries. Wars have historically reduced the availability of raw materials, which has adversely affected some businesses, while others, such as armaments producers, have benefited. Governments can also create conditions that encourage or discourage the growth of strong businesses in their countries. Porter (1990) has described how government action can create conditions which, though intended to protect home business, leave them vulnerable (in the long run) to firms that have had to survive unprotected and competitively tougher market places.

Examples of the types of events that governments react to include:

- Wars.
- Terrorist attacks.
- Government stability.
- Economic stability.
- Legislation (e.g. employment conditions, environmental impacts, transportation, foreign trade).
- Membership of trading blocks and alliances.

7.4.1.2 Economic factors

The economic factors that influence organizations fall into two main categories; those that impact on their costs and those that affect their ability to sell. Examples of those that impact on cost are:

- Interest rates.
- The cost of inputs – some inputs impact across a range of industries (e.g. energy and fuel costs).
- Inflation rates.
- Exchange rates.

While examples that impact on their ability to sell include:

- The amount of disposable income in the economy.
- The growth rate of the economy.

- Inflation rates.
- Interest rates.
- Exchange rates.

7.4.1.3 Sociological factors

An organization's outputs are only valuable if people or organizations find them sufficiently useful that they will purchase them. Societal factors that affect the demand for goods and services are clearly important, and examples include:

- a concern for the ecological environment.
- attitudes to eating.
- the importance of status and fashion in clothes and other personal items.
- attitudes to the use of drugs and alcohol.
- beliefs about public and private control/ownership of utilities, education and health services.
- attitudes to trading with unpopular political regimes.

7.4.1.4 Technological factors

Technological changes cover the whole range of inventions and technological innovations that impact along the length of firms' value chains and on the lifestyles of producers and consumers. Significant technological developments over the last 50 years include:

- The development of computers and information technology leading to changes in product design through computer-aided design, the control of inventory, links between suppliers and buyers and the development of robotics and automated manufacturing.
- The development of non-computer-based ideas in manufacturing including just-in-time concepts.
- The development of drugs and pharmaceuticals leading to eradication of disease.
- Development of fertilizers and farming methods.
- Development of improved land and air transportation.

7.4.2 The impact of environmental factors on organizations and industries

Having conducted an environmental audit the next task is to identify the forces that are driving industry change and what impact these are having on firms and industries. It is especially useful to identify the rate at which change is taking place and whether the impact of a particular factor is the same across industries or varies for different groups of firms or specific organizations. Table 7.1 provides an example of how the process might be carried out.

Table 7.1 Assessing the impact of environmental factors

PEST factor	Industry	Impact on industry	Impact on organization	Threat aspects	Opportunity aspects
Terrorist attacks	Airline passenger	Reduction in passengers	Increase in competition	Weaker firms may go out of business	Stronger firms may achieve bigger market share and dominant position
Terrorist attacks	Security and surveillance	Increase in demand for services. Possible introduction of government and international standards	Decrease in competition, more demand for services	New entrants may be encouraged/Weaker organizations may not be able to match an increase in standards	Chance to expand quickly and improve product. Opportunity for specialized services
Increase in exchange rates, pound becomes stronger	UK manufacturing	Possibly more imports from abroad. Reduction of profit for home producers. Increase in rivalry	More difficulty in exporting but cheaper imports of raw materials	Loss of business to imports. Loss of market share. Weaker organizations may go out of business	Driver to increase internal efficiencies by designing lower cost products and processes

CHAPTER 8

Competitive advantage

Firms compete for sales revenue with other suppliers of goods and services. If a firm has a competitive advantage its products are both profitable and attractive to significant numbers of buyers. A theory that can explain how sustainable competitive advantage is achieved would be the philosopher's stone of strategic management. The theories of Michael Porter (1980, 1985) were thought to offer the answer, though subsequent research has exposed their limitations. Yet his ideas rightly remain influential, and they are outlined and critically reviewed in this chapter.

Porter (1985) suggested that a firm is able to achieve advantage through product differentiation or cost leadership. These two sources of competitive advantage coupled with the scope of activities for which the firm seeks to achieve them lead to three generic strategic positions:

1 A low-cost strategy over a broad target.
2 A differentiation strategy over a broad target.
3 A focus strategy involving either a low-cost strategy over a narrow target or a differentiation strategy over a narrow target.

Porter represents these strategies as shown in Figure 8.1.

A crucial point in the concept of generic strategies is the need for a firm, which wishes to achieve a competitive advantage, to make a choice about the type of competitive advantage it wishes to achieve. This is at the heart of Porter's argument and in order to pursue his ideas it is useful to examine his descriptions of each generic strategy.

8.1 Features of a broad cost leadership strategy

■ The firm sets out to be the lowest cost producer (of the industry standard product):

The strategic logic of cost leadership usually requires that a firm be the cost leader, not one of several firms vying for this position

(Porter, 1985, p. 13)

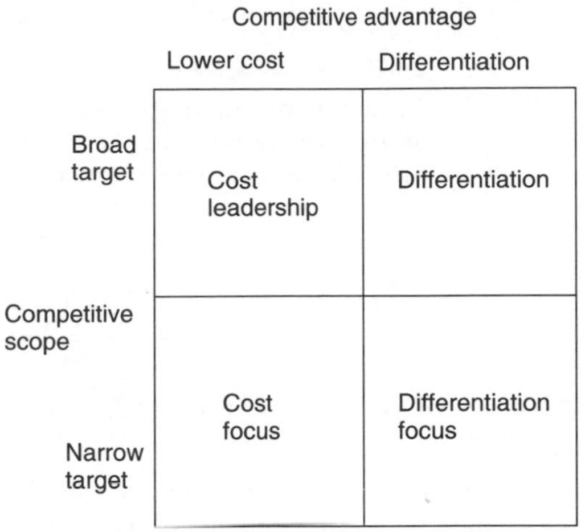

Figure 8.1
Generic strategic postures
Source: (Reprinted with the permission of The Free Press, an imprint of Simon & Schuster Adult Publishing Group, from *Competitive Advantage: Creating and Sustaining Superior Performance* by Michael E. Porter. Copyright © 1985, 1998 by Michael E. Porter).

- The firm has a broad scope and serves many segments.
- Above average profitability is achieved by the cost leader commanding prices at or near the industry average.
- Proximity in differentiation:

> A cost leader must achieve parity or proximity in the bases of differentiation relative to its competitors to be an above average performer, even though it relies on cost leadership for its competitive advantage. Parity in the bases of differentiation allows a cost leader to translate its cost advantages directly into higher profits than competitors'. Proximity in differentiation means that the price discount necessary to achieve an acceptable market share does not offset a cost leader's cost advantage and hence the cost leader earns above average returns
>
> (Porter, 1985, p. 13)

Porter also argues that in commodity industries it is not only the cost leader who gains above average returns but also those firms who are in the lower quartile of costs. If firms are price takers, any firm that can produce below average costs will make above average profits.

8.2 Features of a broad differentiation strategy

- The provision of product or service attributes that are valued by buyers:

> The firm seeks to be unique in its industry along some dimensions that are widely valued by buyers
>
> (Porter, 1985, p. 14)

■ Differentiation can be achieved in the product, its supply chain, and its marketing:

> Above average profitability is achieved by achieving ways of differentiation that lead to a price premium greater than the cost of differentiating. A differentiator cannot ignore its cost position because its premium prices will be nullified by a markedly inferior cost position
>
> (Porter, 1985, p. 14)

8.3 Features of a focus strategy

This strategy requires the firm to focus on a narrow segment. It is appropriate when those firms following broad strategies do not cater for the needs of significant segments either on the basis of cost or differentiation. For example, the specific segment may require a product that is more differentiated than the broad differentiator's (the product has a higher number of beneficial features or attributes). In some industries a segment may be prepared to forego some features on a broad cost leader's products in exchange for a lower price.

8.4 The consequences for strategic choice of Porter's generic strategies

Porter claims that organizations need to make choices that avoid having strategies which are based neither on differentiation nor on cost leadership. The need for distinct generic strategy and the dangers of being 'stuck in the middle' are emphasized. A point of confusion is whether a firm is a cost leader or a differentiator or whether the products or services it offers are sold on the basis of price or differentiation. Porter indicates that both criteria are required for success:

> Sometimes a firm may be able to create two largely separate business units within the same corporate entity, each with a different generic strategy. A good example is the British hotel firm Trusthouse Forte, which operates five separate hotel chains each targeted at different segments. However, unless a firm strictly separates the units pursing different generic strategies, it may compromise the ability of any of them to achieve its competitive advantage
>
> (Porter, 1985, p. 18)

A firm must commit its business units to one generic strategy and a unit with multi-product offering should position each product similarly. It is the relationship between resources and their deployment, and market positioning that underlines the premise of incompatibility between cost-based and differentiation-based strategies. Thus a firm that pursues a market position that is based on price can only make above average profits if its resources are also committed to low cost. Equally a differentiator is seemingly also committed to higher than average production costs to achieve differentiation but is in turn rewarded for that differentiation by being able to command a higher price. Porter implicitly associates low cost strategies with either average or near average prices for broad cost leaders, or below average prices for focused cost leaders:

> If a firm can achieve and sustain overall cost leadership, then it will be an above-average performer in its industry provided it can command prices at or near the industry average
>
> (Porter, 1985, p. 13)

> A classic example is Laker Airways, which began with a clear cost-focus strategy based on no-frills operation in the North Atlantic market, aimed at a particular segment of the travelling public that was extremely price sensitive
>
> (Porter, 1985, p. 17)

Differentiators are similarly predicted to incur the higher costs of differentiation but are rewarded by higher prices.

8.5   Commentary on Porter's generic strategies

Whilst Porter's framework has been widely adopted in the teaching of strategic management and inspired many research frameworks it is the subject of critical debate (e.g. Miller, 1986; Hill, 1988; Miller and Dess, 1993; Bowman, 1997; Walters and Lancaster, 1999; Campbell-Hunt, 2000). In a study of competitive strategy research Campbell-Hunt (2000) concluded that:

- Researchers use cost and differentiation as ways of classifying strategy and have investigated the merits of both in delivering competitive advantage.
- Presence or absence of specialization in competitive strategies cannot explain performance in many cases. Mixed designs may be appropriate under some conditions.
- 'Stuck in the middle' designs, those strategies that seek to produce lower than average product costs with differentiation, are possible in some circumstances. Some resources facilitate the production of both differentiation and reduced costs.

Campbell-Hunt also suggests that differentiation can take on a number of forms and can be based on marketing variables, sales variables, quality reputation variables and product innovation variables.

The advocates of resource-based explanations of competitive advantage have criticized the static nature of Porter's framework with its emphasis on market positioning (e.g. Barney, 1991; McWilliams and Smart, 1993; Peteraf, 1993). They argue that superior performance can be better explained by recognizing that differences in firm resource endowments can explain differences in the nature and costs of outputs. However, as Srivastava et al. (2001, p. 783) have noted: 'the demand side of market conditions requires the transformation of any firm's resources into an offering that customers can view and experience and determine whether or not they wish to purchase it.'

8.6 Cost, price and differentiation relationships

In order to discuss the relationship between cost, price and differentiation, the following framework is proposed – that we describe products or services by three variables:

1. Degree of differentiation.
2. Relative cost to the producer.
3. Relative price to the customer.

For the sake of simplicity a number of assumptions are made: The degree of differentiation is measured by the number of attributes of the product that give perceived customer benefits; the more perceived benefits the product has, the greater is its perceived value to the customer; the standard product or average product will have a standard range of benefits; the differentiated product will have more benefits.

In order to consider some possible product positions we initially consider nine combinations of price, cost and differentiation (as beneficial attributes) in the matrix shown in Figure 8.2. In order to simplify our discussion we have considered eight cases where each of the three variables takes two values high and low, and have represented the standard product as one with average price, average cost and an average level of benefits.

8.6.1 Low cost, low price, low benefits strategies: Positions proximate to position E

A number of authors have indicated that cost leadership strategies are usually associated with price-based competition (Bowman, 1997). Firms which charge average prices for an average product can only make above average profits if its costs are lower than average. Bowman (1997) argues that if average prices are charged then it is unlikely that more than average market share will be achieved. If a firm wishes to achieve a relatively high market share using a price-based strategy it will have to charge lower than average prices. Firms who charge lower than average prices for standard products will only make above average profits if their costs are lower than average. If price reductions against the average are made then market share gains will be made that make both experience and scale advantages possible, but since lower prices are being charged, above average profitability may not accrue, especially in

Relative level of perceived benefits	Relative cost	Relative price	Identity letter	Features of strategies proximate to position
High	High	High	A	Differentiation strategies (fits Porter's description)
High	High	Low	B	Untenable, internal costs too high
High	Low	High	C	Market differentiation with cost advantage, unlikely in Porter taxonomy
Low	High	High	D	Untenable, consumer unlikely to choose over standard product
Low	Low	Low	E	Possible tenable position for focus cost leader. A broad cost leader would approach this position
High	Low	Low	F	Market differentiation with cost and price advantages, unlikely in Porter taxonomy
Low	High	Low	G	Untenable, consumer may choose under some circumstances too costly for producer to sustain
Low	Low	High	H	Untenable
Average	Average	Average	I	The standard product

Figure 8.2
Possible strategic
postures matrix.

the short run. However, if a firm can reduce costs via innovative product and/or process designs that cannot be copied then lower costs for products can be achieved without relying on scale effects. In order to be above average performers, firms following low price market strategies for proximate standard products need to have lower than average costs. If firms have average costs and decide to try to achieve lower costs through scale and experience effects, they will, in the short run, achieve lower than average profits until these scale effects have an impact. This is a risky strategy because they are vulnerable to attack from firms who have lower costs based on non-scale effects. There is also the possibility that others may follow the same strategy and the resulting competition benefits no one but the customer.

We conclude that in order to follow a price strategy based upon low cost a firm must have:

- Lower than average costs.
- Lower than average price.
- An average level of benefits.

Firms striving to be cost competitors in non-commodity industries have to make sophisticated decisions about product definition. If they fail to do this they may become price-setters that fail simultaneously to set prices which are attractive to those who wish to buy standard products at the lowest possible price and to deliver products with sufficient features to attract buyers who wish some differentiation. The other possibility is that a firm markets a product with more features than the 'standard' customer is prepared to pay for but less than the 'differentiator' customer wants. It ends up selling a partially differentiated product at a standard price and making lower profits because of the costs of unwanted differentiation – it becomes 'stuck in the middle'.

Porter has observed that when firms seek to become cost leaders (i.e. the lowest cost supplier in the industry) with very similar products they can find themselves in an unattractive industry where all technological gains are competed away. This presupposes that all gains are imitable and transferable. Inimitability can be sought through economies of scale (initially risky until achieved, see above), exclusive control over important inputs, patents and government licenses or franchises (Frank, 2000).

A sustained leadership position may be achievable if the external market is static and the firm has access to unique advantage conferring resources. A focused cost-/price-based strategy requires the 'average' product to be modified to meet the needs of a segment which does not require or is prepared to forgo some benefits in return for a lower price. This position will be nearer the position E than that of the broad cost/price competitor. Successful focused cost/price competitors will have lower costs and prices than the broad cost/price competitors. A danger for the focused competitor is that their target segment may develop increased expectations and become subsumed into a segment served by a broad cost leader.

8.6.2 Porter's differentiation strategies: Positions proximate to position A

Porter argues that in order to achieve differentiation, differentiators will incur costs and thus their costs will be higher than average. Thus both focused and broad differentiators will approximate to position A. The danger for differentiators is that they may get left behind if cost-based competitors increase product features as consumer expectations rise (consumer expectations are not static – cars now have radios and central locking as standard features, and computer chip speed and memory are constantly changing as suppliers both respond to and shape consumer demand) and differentiated parts of the market risk becoming subsumed into larger segments that are more price competitive. Another danger is that in trying to maintain a differentiated position in a changing market, features that are not attractive to the segment may be mistakenly incorporated into the product so as to add cost without any perceived benefits.

8.6.3 · Positions that indicate both cost and differentiation dimensions: Positions proximate to position C and F

Position C is market differentiation with relative low costs and a relative high price. Position F is market differentiation with relative low costs and a relative low price. These appear to be very attractive positions if they can be achieved profitably. Porter suggests that this is unlikely because of the additional costs of differentiation.

> Achieving cost leadership and differentiation is also usually inconsistent, because differentiation is usually costly
>
> (Porter, 1985, p. 18)

Trying to achieve differentiation at low cost can lead to a 'stuck in the middle position' by mistakenly marketing a product that exceeds the requirements of a cost leadership position but fails to meet the needs of the customer with high benefit requirements.

However, an alternative perspective is also possible – if a product with a high level of benefits is produced at a low cost because the firm has developed some skill and resource that has hitherto been unavailable, then two possibilities exist:

1   The case where the skills and resources are imitable and transferable in some finite time. In this case the innovator of the particular resource or skill could elect to try to achieve market share by using cost advantages to reduce prices and seek to change customer perceptions of the standard product. In this way they attempt to establish a broad position based on the redefinition of both the standard product and the nature of the market. Then by the time competitors have been able to acquire the resources and skills required the originator will have gained a position of advantage through the development of economies of scale. If economies of scale are not possible the differentiator with a low cost position could seek to distance itself from competitors by using the superior profits to maintain advantages. This could be achieved by redeveloping the product to raise customer expectations through increased research and development and marketing.

2   The case when the skills and resources are not imitable. In this situation the firm with this position can sustain profits unless demand for its product subsides. The firm also has the options outlined in the first scenario.

8.6.4 Untenable positions: Positions proximate to position B, D, G and H

Position B   High benefits, high cost, low price. This is clearly not an internally sustainable position though it may gain market share in the short term.

Position D   Low benefits, high cost, high price. This position is unlikely to gain any market share and is externally unsustainable.

Position G   Low benefits, high cost, low price. This position is unlikely to be internally sustainable or gain sustainable market share.

Position H   Low benefits, low cost, high price. This position is unlikely to gain market share but may be able to move to a position proximate to E and adopt a focus cost leadership position by lowering price.

8.7   Explaining competitive advantage: A market perspective

People and organizations with finite amounts of money to spend have to make choices between alternatives. Those with relatively high levels of disposable capital can elect to purchase high price products with lower opportunity costs than those with lower levels (Frank, 2000). Segments appear in some markets and these segments are to some extent defined by the spending ability of the market's population. The ideal position for a firm is to be the only supplier into a specific market or segment. Firms who seek above average profits would presumably wish to operate in an attractive segment where there is little competition but which is big enough to generate profitable sales.

A market may be a commodity market like agricultural markets where few segments have appeared or like the car market where a number of segments have appeared. In markets where segments exist, market positioning by segment is possible. However, if more than one competitor enters a segment price-based competition can be fierce even amongst would-be differentiators. For example, the car industry is divided into a number of segments and competition exists in each segment.

In many markets there are a number of products each having features that are designed to appeal to particular segments. These features are perceived by users to give them benefits. In the UK car market products differ on a number of dimensions, such as engine size, comfort, body size, perception of brand. Each product has a price, and as Figure 8.3 shows, they can differ considerably.

The cars sold in the UK range from relatively high price luxury cars to relatively low price small cars. The bulk of sales, however, are generated by cars that are priced between £8,000 and £20,000 (see Figure 8.4).

The number of cars sold in the UK in 2001 was 2,458,769; the top ten best selling cars accounted for about 40 per cent of sales. More expensive cars and lower cost cars appeal to smaller segments.

Car make and type	List price (£)
Perodua Nippa	4624
Daewoo Matiz SE 5 door	6595
Vauxhall Vectra 1.6 club 4 door	13,235
Ford Mondeo 1.8 LX 4 door	14,645
BMW 520 4 door	23,540
Lexus GS 3.0 door auto	28,450
Mercedes SL500 2 door Auto	68,940
Ferrari 360M Coupe Modena 2 door	103,248

Figure 8.3
Selected car prices
Source: (© Parker's Car
Price Guide, Emap
Automotive Ltd).

Car	Price range (£)	Units sold in 2001	Market share (%)
Ford Focus	10,495–16,845	137,074	5.6
Vauxhall Astra	11,180–17,440	98,999	4.0
Ford Fiesta	8760–10,150	98,221	4.0
Peugeot 206	7995–16,195	97,887	4.0
Vauxhall Corsa	6995–13,495	93,729	3.8
Ford Mondeo	14,645–21,445	86,559	3.5
Renault Clio	7495–10995	79,843	3.2
Renault Megane	10,325–14,470	73,577	3.0
Volkswagen Golf	10,715–21,620	67,099	2.7

Figure 8.4
Top ten best selling cars
in the UK in 2001
Source: (© Parker's Car
Price Guide, Emap
Automotive Ltd).

When trying to understand competition in a segment, it is useful to identify the product/service dimensions that form the basis of competition. Price may be critical in one segment, benefits in another. In some segments consumers are seeking a balance of price and benefits. Consider Figure 8.5.

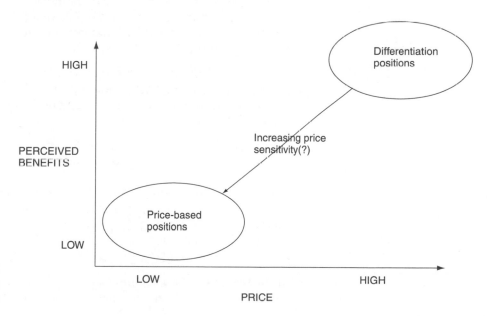

Figure 8.5
The impact of increasing
price sensitivity.

We can hypothesize that customers in segments at the top right of Figure 8.5 are likely to be more benefits sensitive and customers in segments at the bottom left more price sensitive. Products that are in the middle of these positions are likely to sell on some balance between benefits and price. However, all pricing decisions are best made with a knowledge of price elasticity. Middle positioned products may, however, differ in the nature of benefits they are offering so a number of viable positions may be available as long as there are segments which have needs that match these benefits. Some positions may not match a segment and be 'stuck in the middle'. Porter (1996) suggests that it is important for firms to select market positions that are compatible with delivering a bundle of benefits that the consumer values. If suppliers compete in the segment offering the same benefits they are reduced to competing on price. Working on the assumption that resource endowments are mobile, he argues that improvements in production techniques, e.g. using Total Quality Management, Just in Time inventory control and management, only deliver gains to consumers as competitors compete on price. So a better strategy is to choose market positions that are based on offering a unique service or product. However, in order to do this trade-offs are required; suppliers who try to offer a range of products giving a range of benefits at a range of prices are often doomed to failure as they try to meet the often conflicting demands of different segments.

In order to avoid hyper-competition in segments where a number of competitors are pursuing similar generic strategies, Porter indicates three distinct strategic positions:

1 *Variety-based positioning* This occurs when a competitor offers a sub-set of services that are used by a broad range of segments. He gives the examples of Jiffy Lube, who specialized in low price fast oil changes and Vanguard Group which specialized in low commission investment vehicles based on comparatively secure steadily performing stocks and bonds that incur low trading costs. All vehicle users need oil changes and many investors include Vanguard funds in a wider portfolio.

2 *Needs-based positioning* This involves focusing on all the needs of a particular segment. The example Porter gives is IKEA, who meet all the needs of their identified segment for home furnishings at a reasonable price.

3 *Access-based positioning* This is focusing on specific customer segments that are accessible in different ways; Porter gives the example of Carmike Cinemas who focused on running cinemas in small US communities (population <200,000). They adopted a low cost approach using standard cinema designs with fewer screens and less expensive projection technology than that used in big-city cinemas.

A key point in Porter's (1996) argument is that a position is only valuable if the activities required to deliver the customer needs of that position are also different. Porter's thesis is that in order to have a competitive advantage two criteria must be met:

1   A market position must identify customers with specific needs. The customers can belong to a particular segment (focus strategy) or can straddle a number of segments (broad strategy) meeting the common needs of a variety of customers leaving specific needs to other suppliers.
2   The market position chosen can be best delivered by a specific set of activities and those activities are unique to that position. If an organization attempts to straddle positions it finds itself unable to maximize its efforts in any position.

Sustainable competitive advantage depends on companies being able to develop and protect resource advantages by focusing on particular market positions. Implicit in this argument is that firms have the ability to not only identify and locate unique market opportunities but also to be able to develop market positions and resource configurations that are inimitable. In the sense of our model they must be able to set costs and prices that make the position attractive.

8.8   Explaining competitive advantage: A resource perspective

A resource-based perspective takes a slightly different view. In this competitive advantage accrues to firms whose internal resources are able to produce goods and services that consumers find valuable. Unlike Porter's unique position backed by unique activities, the resource-based perspective allows similar market positions to be the focus of competition whilst attributing superior performance to the superior resources of successful competitors. Thus market positions may be imitable but the most efficient organizations will have lower costs for all market positions. Definitions of resources and capabilities are discussed later in this book but can be regarded as the assets and skills available to the firm.

Peteraf (1993) argues that the resource-based perspective requires that four criteria be met if competitive advantage is to occur. These are that:

1   There is heterogeneity of resources across firms.
2   The acquisition price of assets must allow for future profits.
3   It has to be difficult/impossible for competitors to imitate or substitute profit-yielding resources.
4   Resources should be specific to the firm such that they cannot be traded.

8.8.1   Heterogeneity of resources across firms

This means that unless there are differences between the resources of firms there cannot be differences in their profitability (Barney, 1991).

8.8.2 The acquisition price of assets must allow for future profits

Resources have to be acquired at a price below their discounted net present value in order to yield profits, otherwise future profits will be fully absorbed in the price paid for the resource. Economists call this *ex ante* (before) *limits to competition*.

8.8.3 Difficult/impossible for competitors to imitate or substitute profit-yielding resources

The third concept of *ex post* (after) *limits to competition* says that some resources such as loyalty, tacit knowledge and relationships are developed over time and are built progressively. Trying to compress these activities into shorter periods under different conditions can prove to be unfruitful. Dierickx and Cool (1989) have suggested that there are five mechanisms at work that make it difficult for competitors to copy sources of competitive advantage. These are:

1   Time compression diseconomies, as when a firm tries to learn quickly something that took a rival much longer to learn; or tries to build trust and loyalty with sceptical dealers, employees or customers.
2   Asset mass efficiencies (the marginal cost of an asset falls as its level increases): these are the basis of 'virtuous circles', as when learning is easier in firms where the stock of knowledge is already high. This is also seen as an evolutionary process subject to trial and error, uncertainty, and learning by mistakes (see Nelson, 1991).
3   Interconnectedness among stocks of complementary assets (marginal cost falls as levels of complementary assets increase): as when the creativity of employees depends on how a firm is organized and on its management style. Hamel and Prahalad (1994) define a core competence as an integrated bundle of skills and technologies that are unlikely to reside in one person or team. Building a core competence, they argue, involves cumulative organizational learning that is difficult to time-compress (see above). It may also require generalists who are sympathetic to other disciplines because a core competence frequently requires integration across several of the firm's activities.
4   Slow erosion of existing stocks of assets.
5   Causal ambiguity (uncertain knowledge of how to imitate an asset): as with corporate cultures that facilitate productivity growth or organizational change. Since it is possible for resources to be accumulated over time it may well be impossible for competitors to specify which factors, and the role those factors play, in the accumulation process. Indeed, Nelson and Winter (1982) have argued that firms might not know themselves how their stocks of resources accumulated.

8.8.4 Resources should be specific to the firm such that they cannot be traded

Since they remain bound to the firm and are available for use over the long run, they become a source of sustained competitive advantage.

The practical value of a resource-based perspective, according to Peteraf, is that it enables managers to understand, preserve or extend their competitive advantage (with the strategic implications being dependent on the firm's specific resource endowment).

If, however, managers do not understand the resource basis of their competitive advantage there is a danger that they are unable to effectively develop strategy. When trying to understand how resources support advantage it is therefore useful to first identify the competences that the organization possesses in order to provide its products and services. It is also useful to ascertain whether this organization's competences are distinctly different from its competitors, and how this difference allows it to achieve advantage in the market place. There must be at least an advantage in price at the same benefits level or an advantage in benefits at the same price. It must be remembered that the internal competences of a firm are only sources of advantage when they deliver that advantage in the market place.

An analysis of competitive advantage requires the understanding of both a firm's market position (external capability) and its resources (internal capability). It is important that strategy makers understand both aspects of strategy. A danger is that a misunderstanding of either perspective can lead to the formulation and implementation of inappropriate strategies.

The internal problem is the potential inability to understand what the sources of advantage are. In this situation there is a danger that managers may undertake actions that destroy advantage delivering competences (Bowman and Ambrosini, 2000). The external problem is that managers will respond to external events without a deep understanding of the historic reasons for success and hence a lack of understanding of the current requirements of success (Johnson, 1988).

8.9 Bringing it together: Key success factors

An organization's ability to succeed in a business arena depends on its ability to develop a market position that is supported by appropriate assets and capabilities. In an industry all successful firms must be able to do some things well:

- They must have competences and resources that allow them to meet the needs of their customers.
- They must be able to identify and occupy an attractive market position – meet the needs of a significant segment.

Campbell et al. (1995) emphasize that different markets have different critical (key) success factors and that a potential problem for corporate managers is that an understanding of critical success factors in one industry may lead them to wrongly believe that the same success factors apply elsewhere:

> The concept of critical success factors is familiar to most managers. In every business, certain activities or issues are critical to performance and to the creation of competitive advantage. However, success factors differ among and even within industries. For example, those in bulk chemicals are not the same as those in speciality chemicals
>
> (Campbell et al., 1995, p. 123)

A competence in consumer marketing is therefore important for food suppliers who sell under their own brand, but a competence in business to business marketing is important for manufacturers who make own label brands for supermarkets. However, firms may sometimes change the rules of the game and key success factors may change – consider the revolution in cheap air travel instigated by companies like EasyJet. Nevertheless, some factors remain important, airlines always needed to fill aircraft, but they can change aircraft size.

8.10   Summary

We have outlined the work of Michael Porter on competitive advantage. This has led us to discuss how market position and the internal ability to sustain it, is important in gaining competitive advantage. Firms that have distinctive competences to provide product/service features, through either lower costs or unique benefits, which competitors cannot match, are more likely to be superior performers. Factors that lead to differences in firms and how those differences can lead to competitive advantage have been outlined.

CHAPTER 9

Auditing resources

In our view of strategic management the *resources* of an organization are its *assets* and *competences*. This avoids confusion as different authors have defined resources, assets and competences in different ways (e.g. Wernerfelt, 1984; Prahalad and Hamel, 1990; Barney, 1991; Kogut and Zander, 1992; Amit Schoemaker, 1993; Grant, 1995). For the purposes of our approach the key terms can be defined as follows:

1 Assets are the resource endowments the business has accumulated over time and include investments in plant, location and brand equity (Day, 1994).
   - A unique asset is one that a firm has that has not been imitated by other firms and allows the firm to carry out some activity or activities better than other firms.
2 A competence encompasses the skill, ability and knowledge that organization members have individually or collectively which allows them to undertake an activity or activities to contribute to the transformation of inputs into outputs directly or indirectly.
   - A threshold competence is one that all producers must have in order to make and deliver a particular product.
   - A distinctive competence is one that allows a firm to carry out an activity or activities better than competitors.
3 An organization exhibits capability in carrying out a range of activities. Thus a capability in marketing will include a range of competences in selling, promotion, etc.

In multi-business organizations competences and assets may be shared across business units. Indeed, this sharing is the rationale for these corporations to exist, and it is the reason why the analysis of resources must be focused at both the corporate and the business levels.

9.1 Auditing resources at a business level

The value chain is the main analytical tool for analysing resources at the business level. It is described and discussed in the following algorithmic procedure:

- Mapping a unit's activities.
- Auditing a unit's resources (identifying a unit's competences and assets).
- Identifying a unit's strengths and weaknesses.

9.1.1 Mapping a unit's activities using the value chain model

An organization can be modelled as a system that is concerned with the conversion of inputs into outputs. Since organizations operate in dynamic environments, their managers will be concerned with the continuing usefulness of these outputs, and how they can provide the greatest possible utility through the continuing development of business and/or corporate strategy.

The value chain concept depicts an organization as a transformation system made up of different sub-systems, each of which performs a series of activities that contribute to the organization's outputs. Michael Porter (1985) was a key proponent of the value chain concept, and his model clearly distinguishes primary and support type activities. Primary activities are those that are directly concerned with the production of the product or service and include inbound logistics, operations, outbound logistics, marketing, sales and service functions. Support activities are those that back-up the primary activities, and can include such things as human resource management, technological development, procurement and firm infrastructure. Primary and support activities are important because different firms or units can conduct their activities in different ways (i.e. have different business models), which means that different firms can have different value chains. A framework for analysing activities using the value chain model is outlined in Figure 9.1. The analysis seeks to identify how different parts of the value chain contribute to and affect the competitiveness of the organization. Careful analysis is likely to identify areas of competitive strength that will need protecting, and areas of weakness that will need strengthening.

Although the value chain model described by Porter had a strong manufacturing bias it can be applied to both public and private service organizations. For example, the primary activities of a university are to recruit, educate and assess students, so that they can produce graduates. Associated with these primary activities are support activities. However, universities also carry out research work, and the activities directly concerned with this endeavour could be regarded as the primary activities of a different value chain. A university can be regarded as a series of units that educate and a series of units that do research – or it can be regarded as a series of units that do both.

The analyst has to initially decide on their unit of analysis, conduct the analysis, and make links between not only support and primary activities but also between value chains. In the university example, human resources management will support the different teaching departments and the different research groups. In many organizations functional units match specific parts of the value chain but this may not always be the case.

Cost and value are added to the product as it passes along the value chain, and the final margin is the difference between the cumulative added costs and the cumulative added values. Adding value and/or accruing less cost in support and primary activities can increase margins. Support activities can

	Primary Activities					
	Pre Sales	Design	In bound logistics	Transformation	Out bound logistics	After Sales
Support activities						
Technology development						
Human Resources						
Marketing						
Procurement						
Finance						
General Management						
Activity assessment criteria						
Distinctive Competences						
Threshold competences						
Value added						
Cost added						
Margin						

Figure 9.1
A value chain model for analysing an organization's activities.

indirectly add value, for example by designing products that command higher market prices or lower production costs compared to competitors.

9.1.2 Auditing a unit's resources

Resource analysis at the business level has the following steps:

- The use of the value chain model to identify the activities carried out by the unit under consideration.
- The identification of the costs associated with each activity. (The estimation of costs when analysing cases can be particularly difficult for students because the data can be subsumed within consolidated corporate accounts and/or is not provided. An alternative approach is to compare costs by looking at the published accounts of competitors to see if they are higher or lower, and to see if it is possible to identify the activities that are responsible for the differences. It is also worth remembering the difference between economic costs and accounting profit: accounting profit ignores the opportunity costs of assets whereas economic profit includes the opportunity costs associated with alternative uses of assets.)

■ The identification of those activities that add value to the product and/or service compared to those of their competitors. If some activities add less cost than the equivalent activities of competitors then they may provide a source of competitive advantage. For example, inventory control is a cost within most value chains, although some methods of inventory control are more efficient than other methods. Alternatively, some activities add cost but result in other activities being more effective and efficient (e.g. quality assurance). Other activities may add benefits to the products and services and incur above average costs, but deliver above average prices. More generally, the analysis should identify activities that the organization does as well as its competitors and those activities that the organization does better or worse than its competitors.

■ That we use this acquired information to identify distinctive competences (competences in specific activities that give the firm competitive advantage) and general, shared and threshold competencies (those that provide parity with competitors). It also helps identify weaknesses in activities, areas where the organization requires more skill and/or assets to match the performance of competitors.

■ That we also identify assets that the organization uses in carrying out its activities. A useful classification, and one that can be used to identify assets within organizations, has been devised by Hooley et al. (1997), and a simplified version of the classification is shown in Figure 9.2.

Identifying assets and relating their utilization to particular activities highlights their importance. Computer systems, for example, can be important across a number of value activities, and the way that people use this asset to make links across value chains can be a source of competitive advantage. A particularly useful way of classifying assets requires the analyst to identify those assets that are unique to one organization (unique assets) and those assets that are available to all organizations. Unique assets can be the source of 'difficult to copy' competitive advantage.

9.1.3 Strength and weakness assessment

Examine the gathered information inductively to assess if:

■ There are any patterns of good/bad practice in activities?
■ Some activities are done well/badly?

Figure 9.2
Types of assets
Source: (Hooley, G., Möller, K. and Broderick, A. (1997) Competitive Positioning and the Resource Based View of the Firm, reprinted with permission of Pearson Education Limited).

Asset type	Example of tangible asset	Example of intangible asset
Physical (general)	Land, buildings	'Solidity' to investors
Financial	Cash in hand	Creditworthiness
Operational (specific)	Plants and machinery	Procedures and systems
Human	The people	Their abilities
Marketing	Customer database	Brand and reputation
Legal	Copyrights and patents	Reputation in litigation
Systems	Databases and MIS	Knowledge

- There are resources that are used in a number of activities?
- Links between activities can be recognized?
- There are unique assets and distinctive competences?
- We can say what the strengths and weaknesses inherent in the resources and activities are?

The most significant sources of advantages are those that are inimitable in the long run. A firm that has an advantage has, by definition, some short-term inimitability, and the key issue is how this position can be maintained.

9.2 Auditing resources at a corporate level

Portfolio models, such as the BCG Matrix and the GE Matrix, are useful devices for examining multi-business organizations. Understanding how the businesses 'fit' together is important because it may be necessary, for example, to use money from a cash-rich company to fund a growing and cash-hungry company. Shareholders must be happy that this is an effective use of their money.

In addition to analysing each unit, the corporate level audit needs to analyse the activities carried out by the centre. Ideally a senior management team must itself be assessed as a resource. This requires three principal types of assessments:

1 *Links between units* Are there linkages that exist across the units in a corporate portfolio? Do these links suggest that there is synergy between units? Does the centre effectively manage the whole organization so the benefits available from links are maximized? Is there evidence that capability is used across units as well as within individual value chains?

2 *The overall role of the centre* Is there evidence that central general management is a significant strength to all units, some units, or no units? This then leads to a discussion/assessment of the effectiveness of the parenting, synergy creating, role of the centre (Campbell et al., 1995). If the centre adds nothing to the unit then the unit is better off without the centre (Corporate parenting was discussed in Chapter 5).

3 *The strengths and weaknesses of the corporation* Consider issues such as:
- Is this a good/bad parent for each business, why/why not?
- Are there businesses that fit well/badly with the organization as a whole?
- Are there businesses that would be better off with other parents or by being independent?

9.2.1 Organizational profiles

A useful way of summarizing resource endowments at the corporate level is to build up a profile based upon the corporation's current activities. If this is done against six general headings (i.e. physical features, management features, financial resources, market position, product situation and environmental characteristics) a broad picture can be built-up that provides a summary of current knowledge and a basis for identifying missing data. Figure 9.3 shows how such an organizational profile looked for the PepsiCo Corporation in the early 1990s.

Area	Profile
Physical	*Founded*: In 1893 Brad's drink was concocted; in 1902 Pepsi Cola was registered. *Sales*: 1992: $21,970.9 million dollars. *Assets*: 1992: $4,842.3 million dollars. *Employees*: 1992: 338,000. *Structure*: 3 SBUs – Beverages, Snack Foods, Fast Foods. *Market share (1992): Beverages* – 31.3% of $35 billion (US); *Snack foods* – 11% of $35 billion; *Fast Foods* – KFC 8729 (48.6% of £7 billion (US) market), Taco Bell 4153 (69.6% of $4.6 billion (US) market), Pizza Hut 9454 (26.2% of $16.4 billion (US) market).
Management	*Organizational structure*: SBUs operate independently; Fast Food outlets operate separately with rivalry amongst them. *Organizational culture*: When acquisitions occur PepsiCo install their management to assert the PepsiCo culture (previous management are removed or placed into another SBU). Fast track approach to management development, hiring top graduates and promoting them on performance. Management of change is ingrained into their culture. *Degree of autonomy*: Operating divisions have autonomy but follow core central values and goals. Judged on results. CEO has hands off approach but is again performance driven. *Delegation*: High, within the agreed strategic planning objectives. *Motivation*: Employees are seen as main strength (it makes the difference in service sector). However, the drive to continually reduce cost base can lead to discontent. Franchisee problems within certain areas of Fast food SBU.
Financial	*Net Profit*: $1,193.3 million dollars (1992) *Liquidity*: Current ratio $= 1.12$; Quick ratio $= 0.94$. *Long-term solvency*: Debt to assets ratio in $92 = 38\%$, $91 = 41.6\%$, $90 = 32.7\%$, $89 = 40.9\%$. *ROCE*: 15.9% (1992) *Times interest earned*: 4.5 *Return on assets*: 12.8% *Margin*: 11.4% *Return on equity*: 23.2% *Debt to equity*: 1:1.62 *Cash flow*: Good
Market	*Beverages*: Second largest (world leader is Coca-Cola). *Snack foods*: Largest world player. *Fast foods*: Largest world player in fast food sector.

(continued)

Market share: Leader or close second in each sector. Looking to increase market share worldwide.
Future market demand: Very good globally but maturing in the US.
Buyer behaviour: Looking to develop strong brands to reduce threat of switching to substitutes due to price sensitivity.

Product

Portfolio analysis: High volume, low cost consumer industry. Good strategic fit between product groups
Product life cycle: Mature in US but at differing PLC stages worldwide. Significant global growth potential.
Technology employed: Beverages – are updating production. Fast food industry – are employing ways to make the kitchens more effective, to use less space, to require fewer people and to reduce costs by using central catering facilities. Snack foods – automatic ordering via hand held computers. Using information technology to capture information on market demand supports micro marketing profiling.
R&D for new product development: Seeking to develop new and innovative product experiences and standards of service (important in service sector and particularly in Fast food SBU).
Quality of product: For the market segments they serve the product quality is good.

Environmental

Competitors positioning: Beverages – Coca-Cola is industry leader, followers are own brands competing on cost; *Snack foods*: local competitors in national markets, while PepsiCo has more than half of US market; *Fast food* – leaders in their market segments but there are bigger market segments to operate in, e.g. McDonald's market leader in burgers. Ethnic food has high growth potential.
Social responsibility: Clean industry, environmental concerns about excessive packaging and litter in all their businesses. Changing demographics and lifestyles mean that all three divisions are in potentially growth industries, e.g. single people, married couples both working, less time for cooking. Health concerns.
Government legislation: Franchisee protection legislation, reduction in trade barriers, food legislation.
Political influence: Green lobby.

Figure 9.3
Organizational profile of PepsiCo.

9.3 Additional auditing techniques

This section discusses techniques that can be used to further explore and understand organization capabilities and resources, whether the unit of analysis is a single business unit or a corporation consisting of a number of units.

9.3.1 Bottom-up and top-down approaches

An alternative way to identify the competences of an organization is to systematically analyse a company from either a bottom-up or top-down direction.

In a bottom-up approach the raw material and process inputs are followed through to completed products or services, while for a top-down approach the finished products and services are broken down into their constituent parts. The two approaches are outlined in Figures 9.4 and 9.5.

Although there appears to be little difference between the two methods, the bottom-up approach may overlook or under-represent the customer, whereas for the top-down approach it is the starting point. The top-down approach looks at the overall picture and then seeks to identify the main revenue streams associated with the products or services that it provides for its markets. It then moves on to consider the technology, processes, knowledge and strategic assets associated with these products and services. Critically, can any of these be considered distinctive or unique? How are these then related to their underpinning subsystems, and again, what technology, processes and knowledge do they use? Also, are the subsystems related and is it the way that they combine that provides unique capabilities? The answers to these questions can then be tested against the three criteria set out by Prahalad and Hamel in Stage 5 of Figure 9.4.

9.3.2 The Hall and Andriani approach

A more detailed methodology for identifying the resources that underpin competitive advantage has been put forward by Hall and Andriani (1999). This is also a top-down approach because it focuses on the identification and assessment of competitive advantage from the customers' point of view. The first stage involves identifying what customers value. Checklists for ascertaining this in the product and delivery areas are shown in Figure 9.6.

These attributes are then weighted by importance in Figure 9.7 and it is then possible to identify the strength of the advantage by comparing the 'quality' of the attribute with the company's main competitor. It may also be possible to estimate the sustainability of the advantage in terms of the ease, or difficulty, of maintaining the attribute position relative to the competition.

Figure 9.4
A bottom-up approach: composition of products/services
Source: (Tampoe, M. (1998) Getting to know your organisation's core competences, in *Exploring Techniques of Analysis and Evaluation in Strategic Management* (ed. Ambrosini, V.), Hamel Hempstead: Prentice Hall Europe, reprinted with permission of Pearson Education Limited).

Stage 3 How do stage 2/3 resources influence customer-buying decisions?	Are there distribution competences, brand competences, selling competences?		
Stage 2 How does stage 1 feed into higher stage activities?	Are there competences, in product design	Are there process knowledge competences?	Is there institutional knowledge, key individuals, a commitment to service?
Stage 1 What are the key input resources?	What is/are the technology used, knowledge base, the ability to learn, the culture, the assets, the processes, the sources of raw materials?		

	Technical subsystems		Administrative/ institutional subsystems		Strategic assets	
Stage 1 Why does the customer buy?	Products or services bought by customer					
Stage 2 What are the main subsystems that make-up the product or service?	Technical subsystems		Administrative/ institutional subsystems		Strategic assets	
Stage 3 What are the core talents/processes feeding into level 3?	Identify core products and made components	Identify knowledge embedded in procedures or rules	Identify knowledge in individuals and groups	Process within: Distribution Marketing Warehoues Sales Finance	Patents Trademarks Copyright Licences	Raw materials and unique supply
Stage 4 What are the key input resources?	Technology, knowledge base, ability to learn, culture, assets, processes, raw materials and bought-in components (see using the supply chain to get competitive advantage).					
Stage 5	Resources Which of the resources, identified at stages 1, 2, 3 and 4 s satisfy the three tests of Prahalad and Hamel (1990): a) Can they be used to gain access to a wide variety of markets? b) Do they make a significant contribution to the perceived customer benefits of the end product? c) Can competitors copy them (i.e. Are there distinctive competences and/or unique assets?)					

Figure 9.5

A top-down approach: unravelling sources of competitive advantage

Source: (Tampoe, M. (1998) Getting to know your organisation's core competences, in *Exploring Techniques of Analysis and Evaluation in Strategic Management* (ed. Ambrosini, V.), Hamel Hempstead: Prentice Hall Europe, reprinted with permission of Pearson Education Limited).

Figure 9.6
Checklist for identifying
product and delivery
attributes that produce
sales advantage
Source: (Reprinted from
Hall, R. and Andriani, P.
(1999) Developing
and Managing Strategic
Partnerships, *European
Journal of Purchasing
and Supply Management*,
Vol. 5, with permission
from Elsevier Science).

Image: What is the image of your product? Is it important?
User statement: Does your product make the appropriate 'statement' about the user?
Price: Is a low price a key buying criterion?
Value for money: Is the achievement of a certain ratio of specification/price crucial?
User friendliness: Is it important for the product to be user friendly?
Availability: Is product range availability crucial?
Rapid response to enquiry: Is it important to produce designs, quotations very quickly? etc.

Figure 9.7
Weighting of sales
advantage
Source: (Reprinted from
Hall, R. and Andriani, P.
(1999) Developing
and Managing Strategic
Partnerships, *European
Journal of Purchasing and
Supply Management*,
Vol. 5, with permission
from Elsevier Science).

Key attributes weighting	Importance %
1 Price	35
2 Availability	30
3 Value for money	20
4 Rapid Response to enquiry	10
5 Image	5
Total	100

The second stage involves identifying the intangible resources that produce the weighted sales advantage attributes. Hall and Andriani suggest that you select the intangible resources from the 'four capabilities framework' shown in Figure 9.8 because it ensures that a full range of resources are considered. The attribute and its linked resource type are then entered into Figure 9.9.

Regulatory assets: *legal entities, often with property rights*	Positional assets: *assets which are legal entities*
Patents, Trademarks, Copyright Registered designs, Trade secrets, Contracts, Licences, Proprietary operating systems.	Reputation of company and products, Value chain configuration, Distribution network, Unique access to raw materials, Organizational networks, Installed operating systems e.g. ERP, EPOS, etc., Databases.
Functional resources: *individual or team skills*	**Cultural resources:** *the characteristics of the organization*
Employee know-how, Distributor know-how, Supplier know-how, and groupings of the above.	Perception of high quality standards, The organization's ability to: Manage change, innovate work as teams, Respond to challenge Tradition of Customer Service, etc.

Figure 9.8
The four capabilities
framework
Source: (Reprinted from
Hall, R. and Andriani, P.
(1999) Developing
and Managing Strategic
Partnerships, *European
Journal of Purchasing and
Supply Management*,
Vol. 5, with permission
from Elsevier Science).

Figure 9.9
Intangible resources
related to weighted sales
advantage attributes
Source: (Reprinted from
Hall, R. and Andriani, P.
(1999) Developing and
Managing Strategic
Partnerships, *European
Journal of Purchasing and
Supply Management*,
Vol. 5, with permission
from Elsevier Science).

Weighted key product attributes	Regulatory capability	Positional capability	Functional capability	Cultural capability
1 Price		Value chain configuration	Employee know-how	
2 Availability			Distributor know-how	
3 Value for money	Licences			
4 Rapid response		Operating system		Ability to manage change
5 Image	Trademarks	Reputation of products		Perception of quality

The strategic issue of how these intangible resources can be developed for competitive and market advantage can now be addressed. This involves consideration of how intangible resources can be protected, sustained, enhanced and exploited. For example, does management recognize and value the intangible resources of the organization and do they appreciate the length of time it took to acquire them? How safe are these resources and can they be protected in law? From a competitive advantage perspective, are the resources increasing or decreasing, and what can we do to ensure that they continue to increase? An example of the types of actions that can be undertaken to protect and develop the key intangible resources are shown in Figure 9.10.

By progressively narrowing down and ranking these capabilities we can more clearly identify a company's strengths, and this is pivotal for a strategy that seeks

Figure 9.10
Development scenarios
for key intangible
resources
Source: (Reprinted from
Hall, R. and Andriani, P.
(1999) Developing and
Managing Strategic
Partnerships, *European
Journal of Purchasing and
Supply Management*,
Vol. 5, with permission
from Elsevier Science).

The key intangibles	Protecting	Sustaining	Enhancing	Leveraging
1 Employee know-how		Reward in salary and bonus structure	Widen training opportunities	
2 Distribution know-how				Include in strategic alliance decisions
3 Licences	Protect sole licence agreements in courts			
4 Operating System				Integrate with distributors
5 Quality		Do not tamper with organization culture		

to maintain or expand the market share of a company. It is also crucial that management understand the potential consequences of a strategic move that undermines or abandons the capabilities that sustain existing competitive advantage, as this can result in a loss of market share and company failure.

From a strategic perspective, capabilities can be inputted into investment decisions, portfolio analysis, value chain analysis and decisions regarding strategic acquisitions, alliances and disposals. This information can also be used to more effectively gauge the competitive position of a company and the actions it might reasonably undertake.

9.4 Summary

We have defined resources as consisting of assets and competences. This led to an outlining of techniques for analysing the activities and resources of an organization at a business level. It also involved a discussion of the relationship between inimitable resources as distinctive competences and unique assets, and competitive advantage. The role of management as a resource in making links between units in corporate portfolios was discussed. In multidivisional firms, the role of the centre in recognizing opportunities for synergy between business units and its role in contributing to effectiveness of unit value chains was outlined.

Bottom-up and top-down techniques for auditing resources have also been discussed. Top-down techniques are important because they emphasize the primacy of the customer. The Hall and Andriani approach for making links between resources, product features, product benefits and competitive advantage was outlined to show how organizations might go about the task.

CHAPTER 10

Financial performance and investment appraisal

10.1 Evaluating financial performance

The ability to financially analyse a company is central to any strategic investigation, and a better understanding of financial performance can be achieved if we apply certain analytical tools. Indeed, the use of financial performance indicators are a key analytical tool for many investors and management consultants, especially when the emphasis is on evaluating past and current performance, and where projections on future performance are being made.

Access to financial information is obviously necessary if you are to financially evaluate a company, and this information is most likely to be contained within profit and loss and balance sheet statements. These statements provide a 'snapshot' on the financial health and standing of a company at a specific point in time. They are particularly important within strategic analysis because they provide the information for the calculation of financial ratios, which enable comparisons to be made with other companies in the same industry or sector. The ratios can be used to measure profitability, liquidity, corporate activity, the efficiency with which the company uses the assets that it has at its disposal, and how the stock market values the company. It is important that the data collected from the financial statements spans a time frame that enables a meaningful comparison to be made between companies and for financial projections to be made (e.g. 5 years). The collection of this financial data can be time consuming, especially so when it involves the dissection of the financial statements of competitors – although this is time well spent if it provides insight into the strategic decision-making processes of the key players within the industry or sector.

10.1.1　Using financial statements for strategic analysis

It is important to remember that financial statements contain data that is normally 12 months out of date. This is likely to be the most up-to-date information because companies have to produce, by law, annual operating statements of their preceding 12 months activities. The information that these statements contain is particularly useful because all companies have to provide equivalent types of information, which means that we can make quite robust comparisons between companies.

Financial statements can be used for the following:

- To support and underpin the data and information that is inputted into strategic models (e.g. SPACE, Life Cycle Matrix SWOT analysis).
- To analyse competitors who may pose a strategic threat by identifying their financial strengths and weaknesses, and how these might influence their strategic intent.
- To support strategic acquisitions and mergers through a detailed financial analysis of potential candidates.
- To analyse key customers and suppliers in order to anticipate demand and potential strategic activity.
- To compare internal cost centres with comparable cost centres within competitors, to identify significant variances, and to incorporate remedial action into the strategic planning process.
- To identify the growth potential and borrowing power of the organization.
- To assess if the company is vulnerable to decreases in revenue and possible corporate failure.

10.1.2　Written statements

Corporate reports also contain a written statement by the Chairman or Chief Executive Officer, and these provide a valuable resume of the company's activity and accomplishments over the previous 12 months, together with an insight into current business strategies and their expected impact on future corporate financial performance. These reports can also be 'economical' with the truth when performance is poor. If results are worse than expected and the interpretation of the Chairman or Chief Executive Officer looks overly optimistic, care needs to be exercised. In these circumstances additional research may be required to see if the projections and expectations are justified.

Written statements provide a useful context for considering the following questions:

- Has senior management identified any specific challenges or underlying trends facing the organization, and has corrective action been incorporated into their overall strategy?

- Does the report provide any insight into managements ability (and track record) to identify and implement strategic change?
- Are the strategic objectives within the report being achieved, and if not, is the current management capable of achieving them?
- Does the report contain a clear view of the business and does it state where the business is headed?

10.1.3 Analysing financial statements using ratio analysis

A financial ratio is a relationship, at a given point in time, between items on a financial statement. If the ratio is to have any meaning then the items must be synergistic (i.e. when put together they say something about the performance of the company). It is important to resist the temptation of calculating all possible ratios, because like strategic analysis in general, it should be a selective process where the emphasis is on the selection of ratios to identify and illustrate specific strategic issues and trends. It is also important that we do not generalize too broadly from ratios, as it does not automatically follow that weak ratios are a precursor to corporate failure. Although powerful, many other factors need to be dovetailed into ratio analysis if we are to arrive at a meaningful insight into present and future performance.

When ratios are used to compare industries or sectors then it is important that the companies should be of a similar size and sell similar products or services to similar markets. Although it is always difficult to project into the future, ratios can be calculated over several years and then plotted graphically in a time series to highlight changes over that period, and by extending the trend, potential future performance.

10.1.4 Ensuring validity of data comparison

Comparisons between trading years and other companies in the industry or sector can be made difficult in the following situations:

- Changes in accounting standards and methods – such changes can result in material changes to ratios calculated. These changes should be quantified if possible and their impact on the analysis explained.
- Accounting for exceptional items can create anomalies, and an assessment needs to be made as to whether they are a 'one off'. Companies frequently use this technique to cover a multitude of sins (including poor performance).
- Restructuring costs – like exceptional items these reduce margins and profits. Explanations for such costs very often lack detail and care needs to be exercised when assessing their strategic implications.
- The sale or acquisition of subsidiaries can make a material difference when assessing group structures.

These factors and situations need to be taken into account, and possibly compensated for, when comparing companies using ratios. If these types of situations are taken into account then they can only improve and enhance the insight that financial ratios provide.

Ratio analysis can be divided into five key areas: profitability, liquidity, leverage or gearing, activity analysis, and stock market valuations.

10.2　Types of ratios

10.2.1　Profitability ratios

These ratios indicate the degree of competence with which the company allocates the resources available to the resulting income generated. The main item used in profitability analysis is the profit and loss account, and this can give rise to confusion because two profit figures are given; one after interest and tax and the other before interest and tax.

In general, using profit before interest and tax is useful because it enables us to compare the trading performance of similar companies irrespective of borrowings that may have been used to finance those activities. Taking profit after interest and tax charges provides a more thorough analysis of a company's competitive strength, as there is a direct relationship to gearing (leverage), and this can be important in assessing whether the company is financially over-stretched. Profit after interest will fluctuate in line with variations in interest rates assuming profits before interest remain constant. The seven most commonly used profitability ratios are shown in Figure 10.1.

10.2.2　Liquidity ratios

Liquidity ratios can show whether a company can meet its short-term liabilities, which usually revolve around the ability of a company to manage its stocks and inventories, and the flow of cash coming into the company. This can be critically important because a company that fails to pay its bills (for its stock) is likely to cease to function. If a company is unable to generate sufficient cash itself, then it should have set up and put in place the financial facilities to cover its position. Poor liquidity and the inability to manage cash flow can lead to a loss in confidence from both creditors and financial providers, and if such problems are not addressed quickly, exposure to take-over or company failure may be a reality. Conversely, too much liquidity can reduce profitability as short-term assets usually infer that the company is failing to fully utilize its cash to produce higher levels of return. Indeed, the maintenance of the fine balance of keeping liquidity low whilst meeting all short-term obligations can be a key success factor. When the ratios are shown as trends over time they can be used as a comparative barometer of overall performance.

In general, low liquidity ratios are associated with a stable and predictable industry and sector environment, whilst high ratios can relate to unpredictable,

Ratio	Method of calculation	Analytical value
1 Gross profit	$\dfrac{\text{Sales} - \text{Cost of goods sold}}{\text{Sales}}$	The total margin available to cover operating costs and give a profit
2 Operating profit margin (return on sales)	$\dfrac{\text{Profit before interest and tax}}{\text{Sales}}$	A measure of the firm's profitability irrespective of interest and tax charges
3 Net profit margin (net return on sales)	$\dfrac{\text{Profit after tax and interest}}{\text{Sales}}$	Indicates the percentage of profit available for distribution and reinvestment
4 Return on total assets	$\dfrac{\text{Profit after tax} + \text{Interest}}{\text{Total assets}}$	Measures the return on total assets
5 Return on shareholders equity (net on net worth)	$\dfrac{\text{Profit after tax}}{\text{Shareholders equity}}$	Measures the rate of return on the shareholders investment
6 Return on common equity	$\dfrac{\text{Profit after tax} - \text{Dividends on preference shares}}{\text{Total stockholders equity} - \text{Partial value of preference shares}}$	Measures the return to common or ordinary shares
7 Earnings per share	$\dfrac{\text{Profit after tax} - \text{Dividends on preference shares}}{\text{Number of common or ordinary shares issued}}$	Gives the value of earnings for each ordinary or common share

Figure 10.1 Profitability ratios.

Ratio	Method of calculation	Analytical value
1 Current ratio	$$\frac{\text{Current assets}}{\text{Current liabilities}}$$	Shows the level by which short-term creditors are covered by assets that will convert to cash before payment becomes due on the liability
2 Quick ratio	$$\frac{\text{Current assets} - \text{Stock (inventory)}}{\text{Current liabilities}}$$	Measures the firms ability to pay off short-term creditors without the sale of stock or inventory
3 Stock to net working capital	$$\frac{\text{Stock (inventory)}}{\text{Current assets} - \text{Current liabilities}}$$	Shows the amount of working capital that is tied up in stock

Figure 10.2
Liquidity ratios.

volatile and cyclical environments. Likewise, companies having high levels of stock may be subject to increased risks, whilst a downward trend of stock values in relation to sales may indicate improved management practices (e.g. JIT stock management systems). There are three key liquidity ratios, and these are shown in Figure 10.2.

10.2.3   Gearing or leverage ratios

Gearing ratios provide insights into how much of a company's assets are financed by external sources of funding. The higher the ratios the greater the risk to the company, as large borrowings will be prone to interest rate changes that are beyond the control of management. Funds that are provided by ordinary shareholders can have a reduced dividend payment when times are difficult, whereas borrowed funds attract a market rate of interest that cannot be deferred or defaulted upon. Figure 10.3 shows the five most used gearing ratios.

10.2.4   Activity ratios

These ratios are useful for comparing individual companies to industry or sector standards. Figure 10.4 shows five activity ratios, and when used sensible they can indicate how efficient a company is in managing and generating a return from its assets.

10.2.5   Stock market ratios

Stock markets use a myriad of techniques to assess the value of companies, and the four ratios outlined in Figure 10.5 are used extensively within such evaluations.

Ratio	Method of calculation	Analytical value
1 Debt to asset ratio	$\dfrac{\text{Total debt}}{\text{Total assets}}$	A measure of the amount of borrowed funds put in place to finance the asset base
2 Debt to equity ratio	$\dfrac{\text{Total debt}}{\text{Total shareholder equity}}$	A measure of the amount of debt to the amount invested by the shareholders
3 Long-term debt to equity	$\dfrac{\text{Long-term debt}}{\text{Total interest charges}}$	An indication of the balance between shareholders equity and long-term finance
4 Times interest earned (interest coverage ratio)	$\dfrac{\text{Profits before interest and tax}}{\text{Total interest charges}}$	Shows the level of cover available before the company is unable to meet its interest commitments
5 Fixed charge coverage	$\dfrac{\text{Profits before interest and tax} + \text{Lease charges}}{\text{Interest and leasing charges}}$	Shows the company's ability to meet all finance charges

Figure 10.3
Gearing or leverage ratios.

Ratio	Method of calculation	Analytical value
1 Inventory or stock turnover	$\dfrac{\text{Sales}}{\text{Stock of finished goods}}$	An indicator of whether stock turnover is inadequate excessive
2 Fixed asset turnover	$\dfrac{\text{Sales}}{\text{Fixed assets}}$	A measure of asset utilization and sales productivity
3 Total asset turnover	$\dfrac{\text{Sales}}{\text{Total assets}}$	A measure of total asset utilization, useful when compared to the industry average
4 Accounts receivable	$\dfrac{\text{Annual credit sales}}{\text{Accounts receivable}}$	Shows the time period a firm takes to collect debtors (sales made on credit)
5 Average collection period	$\dfrac{\text{Accounts receivable}}{\text{Total sales} \div 365}$	Indicates the average time taken for debts to be received and turned to cash

Figure 10.4
Activity ratios.

Ratio	Method of calculation	Analytical value
1 Price earnings ratio	$$\dfrac{\text{Current share price}}{\text{After tax earnings per share}}$$	High ratios indicate low risk and high growth companies: low ratios indicate high risk and slow growth companies
2 Dividend yield on ordinary shares	$$\dfrac{\text{Annual dividends per share}}{\text{Current share price}}$$	Measures the yield to holders of common stocks
3 Dividend payout ratio	$$\dfrac{\text{Annual dividends per share}}{\text{After tax earnings per share}}$$	Indicates the proportion of profits paid as dividends
4 Cash flow per share	$$\dfrac{\text{After tax profits} + \text{Depreciation}}{\text{Number of ordinary shares issued}}$$	A measure of the funds available to the company after the payment of expenses

Figure 10.5
Stock market ratios.

10.3 Using ratio analysis with other strategic models

Ratio analysis can be integrated into, and be a valuable part of, the following strategic models:

S.W.O.T. analysis Ratios can be used to identify strengths and weaknesses. This can be integrated into future scenarios by trending the ratios forward.

S.P.A.C.E. analysis The 'industry strength' axis can be measured using ratios that gauge profit potential, financial stability and capital intensity. Likewise, the axis 'financial strength' can be measured using return on investment, gearing (leverage), liquidity, capital required, cash flow, and inventory turnover ratios. The 'competitive advantage' axis can also be inferred from the position of the company's products within the overall life cycle (see product life cycle below).

Industry attractiveness/business strength matrix Ratios can be used to weight and rate market size and potential growth, capital requirements, and industry profitability so that a composite measure can be arrived at for 'industry attractiveness'. The areas for measurement within 'business strength' are market share, relative profit margins and cost differences.

Life cycle matrix A company's competitive position can be gauged using the five types of ratios outlined above (i.e. profitability, liquidity, gearing [leverage], activity and stock market), whilst the industry stage in the evolutionary life cycle can be estimated by incorporating estimates of product life cycles (see product life cycle below).

B.C.G. matrix The industry growth rate and relative market share can be inferred from profitability, liquidity, gearing (leverage) and stock market ratios, as each of the four 'ideal' positions within the matrix can be compared to each other using these ratios.

10.3.1   Using ratio analysis in product life cycle analysis

As products progress through their respective life cycles distinct links can be made with financial performance. Product revenue will continue to increase until the product reaches maturity, sales will then decrease until the product is obsolete. Profitability will also decrease at this point as margins are under pressure from both competitor products and the need to invest in R&D to create new products. The stages of a product's life cycle and the types of strategies associated with each stage are shown in Figure 10.6. Ratio analysis can provide insight on the relative position of a product, and through forward trend projections of the ratios strategic positions can be anticipated and catered for.

10.4   Ratio calculation using the CD ROM

All of the ratios outlined in Chapter 10 can be calculated automatically on the CD. By selecting 'Ratio' from the menu, ratios can be calculated and graphed for a 5-year period, and then trended forward for a further 2 years. Analysis is supported through help menus and on-screen buttons, with detailed information being provided on how to use and interpret the ratios. We would encourage you to use the ratio analysis package, as it is a powerful investigative tool that can enhance and extend your strategic analysis of a company.

10.5   Investment appraisal

Investment appraisal or capital budgeting can be defined as 'the analysis of a proposed investment that is a long-term asset used by the business to yield a return over a period of time that is greater than one year.' Examples include the purchase of a warehouse or a fleet of delivery vehicles.

Market share	Introduction	Growth	Maturity	Decline
High (leader)	Sacrifice current profits to increase market investment	Reduce prices as costs reduce, putting pressure on competitors	Improve quality and increase advertising to fully utilize capacity	Maximize cash flow, reducing investment and advertising
Low (follower)	Increase market share by investment	Concentrate on market segment	Withdraw or reduce costs and prices	Exit from market

Figure 10.6
Product life cycle stages and associated strategies.

Capital budgeting assumes that funds are limited and that a decision has to be made between several investment alternatives. To simplify the analysis we make the following assumptions:

- The project's cash flows are known with certainty.
- The cost of capital is given and is the same for all projects.
- The expected net cash flows for the project will be realized at the end of the time periods in which they are expected to occur.

With these assumptions in place we can divide the capital budgeting process into five stages:

1 Search and identification.
2 Estimating cash flows (including discount rate selection).
3 Evaluating projects.
4 Selecting projects.
5 Post acceptance analysis.

10.6 Appraisal methods

The five most used techniques for evaluating investment projects are outlined in the following list (tutorial and exercises for each of the appraisal methods can be accessed on the CD):

1 Payback.
2 Discounted payback.
3 Average rate of return.
4 Net present value.
5 Internal rate of return and modified internal rate of return.

The process of calculation has been eased significantly as most spreadsheet software packages have in-built functions that can be used in each of the five areas. Choosing the most appropriate appraisal method depends on a number of factors, and these, together with a brief outline of the appraisal method, are outlined in the following sections.

10.6.1 Payback

This is the simplest method of calculation, and it involves selecting projects on the basis of repaying the investment amount in the shortest possible (or company stated) time period. In addition to its simplicity, the main advantage of payback appraisal method is the built-in safeguard against risk, because it always looks for projects that will repay capital in the shortest (or stated) time period. The main disadvantage is that it makes no allowance for taxation or capital allowances, and this is important because different allowances and tax benefits can be attributable to different types of projects. It also disregards the profit streams from projects once the payback period is over. This means that payback-based funding decisions could lead to under investment, which could have a very negative impact on long-term competitive advantage.

10.6.2 Discounted payback

Discounted payback uses a discount rate to discount down the net inflows to the project, with the cumulative value of these being used to determine the point at which payback occurs. This is considered to be more realistic because the value of monetary inflows decreases over time (due to inflation), and it is only by 'discounting' these can the original investment be properly recouped. The choice of the discounting rate is clearly important, for too high a rate will increase the payback period and make the project look unviable.

10.6.3 Average rate of return

The average rate of return calculates the profitability of an investment by relating the initial investment to the future annual average net cash flows. The method takes account of profits over the whole of the project's life, and its average profit is expressed as the rate of return on the initial investment. This calculation should be done after tax and capital allowances so that a more accurate profit figure is used.

Payback, discounted payback and average rate of return are the most traditional discounting methods, yet they all suffer from a lack of sensitivity with respect to reinvestment issues, differing project lengths and varying profit flows and patterns. They also suffer from the previously mentioned time value of money problem – money today is of more value than money tomorrow, so we should not treat the value of money in year one as the same as that accrued in future years. Issues like these can be more effectively accommodated in the net present value and internal rate of return appraisal methods.

10.6.4 Net present value

Net present value calculates the benefit of an investment project in terms of current money assuming that a rate of return must be earned. To calculate the NPV of an investment a discount rate is used on future payments and income.

10.6.5 Internal rate of return

The internal rate of return of an investment project is the break-even return level that equates to the project's present value of net cash flows against the projects initial investment.

10.6.6 Modified internal rate of return

This is a more sophisticated form of IRR and the calculation takes into account the re-investment of net flows. Two rates are required for this calculation, a finance rate and a re-investment rate.

10.6.7 Comparison of IRR and NPV

Although there is little difference between the two techniques, the IRR method has the advantage that it provides a better estimate of project risk. It is also preferred by many businesses because it focuses on the rate of return rather and not NPV values.

The IRR and NPV appraisal methods are both robust, yet neither should be used as a panacea within investment appraisal, as many other factors and analysis tools can be used alongside them to make the strategic decision-making more effective.

10.7 Summary

Financial analysis is an essential ingredient within strategic analysis. Importantly, the ease with which the tools and techniques that have been outlined can be used in strategic analysis is significantly enhanced if the CD is used. Indeed, the ability to carry out sophisticated financial analysis is only likely to be hampered by the availability of relevant financial data within consolidated corporate accounts and the unpredictability that inherently exists when extrapolating into the future.

CHAPTER 11

Models for aiding strategic selection

11.1   The analysis of diversified companies

A diversified company can have several businesses within its corporate portfolio, which increases complexity and necessitates that we look at:

- How attractive the portfolio is from different stakeholder positions (shareholders, bankers, etc.).
- The projected performance of the present portfolio.
- The enhancements that could be made to the portfolio to improve synergy and strategic fit (e.g. divest units to provide finance to improve overall performance and/or to finance acquisitions that would improve specific value chains).

The analysis of a portfolio uses all the analysis techniques for a single business company, and then builds on these by mapping and assessing the interaction and performance contribution of each portfolio member to the group as a whole. A procedure for carrying out these tasks is likely to include:

- The identification of existing portfolio strategies.
- The use of the strategic models described in this chapter to map and analyse the current position of the companies within the corporate portfolio.
- The analysis of the industries within which portfolio companies operate in so that future performance and potential can be evaluated.
- The benchmarking of individual company performance against the rest of the industry.

- The assessment of the interrelationships of portfolio members in respect of synergy and strategic fit.
- The assessment of whether individual portfolio companies fit with current and future corporate strategy.
- The analysis of the capital requirements of the portfolio (this should be quantified to give a ranking to strategic options and their investment strategies).
- The crafting of new strategies to improve portfolio performance (this may include acquisitions, divestments, investments in existing businesses, and the creation of synergy between businesses in the portfolio, such as shared distribution channels and other services to provide overall cost reductions and benefits).

11.2 Matrix techniques

A business portfolio matrix is a two dimensional array that graphically displays the strategic positions of the various businesses within a diversified company. The types of factors that influence and shape the strategic position of a company include:

- the industry growth rate.
- the amount of market share achieved by the company.
- the long-term projections for the industry.
- the competitive strength of the business.
- the stage in the product life cycle.
- the stage in the industry life cycle.

The three most widely used strategic models for analysing a diversified portfolio of companies are the BCG (or Growth Share) matrix, the Industry Attractiveness – Business Strength (or GE) matrix and the Industry Life Cycle (or Hoffer, A.D. Little) matrix (Hofer and Schendel, 1978).

11.2.1 Boston Consulting Group (BCG) matrix

The BCG matrix shown in Figure 11.1 compares the industry growth rate on the X-axis and the relative market share of the company on the Y-axis, with each business being plotted as a circle that is positioned according to its $X Y$ location. The circle size equates to the revenue contribution made by the business to the total revenue of the portfolio. Figure 11.1 shows the data that was inputted to determine the position and size of the circles so that we can compare the companies within the portfolio against the industry growth rate and their relative market share.

The position of each company on the BCG matrix in Figure 11.2 is deemed to have implications with respect to how the corporate group invests in each of the portfolio companies, and the types of strategies that they will then develop and execute.

Portfolio company	Market share	Largest rival % share	Relative market share	Economic growth (%)	Industry growth	Growth % differential	Revenue contrib. (%)
A	15	12	1.3	2	3	1	20
B	60	70	0.9	2	5	3	15
C	40	30	1.3	2	6	4	30
D	10	50	0.2	2	1	-1	10
E	15	10	1.5	2	-1	3	11
F	35	60	0.6	2	2	0	14

Figure 11.1 BCG data table.

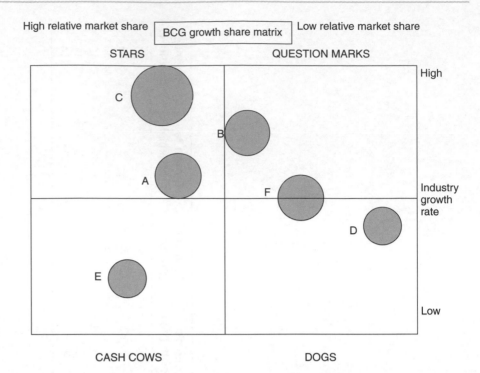

Figure 11.2
BCG growth
share matrix
Source: (after Hedley,
1977, p. 12).

The *growth rate* in Figure 11.2 is arrived at by taking the difference between the industry growth rate and the economic growth rate, with the resultant rate being either higher or lower than the economy as a whole. *Relative market share* (R.M.S.) is calculated by dividing the businesses percentage share of the total industry volume by the percentage share of its largest rival. For example, if a business has 30 per cent of the market by volume and its nearest rival has a 60 per cent share, its R.M.S. is 0.5. It therefore follows that only market leaders have an R.M.S. greater than 1. Many portfolio analysts feel that the axis for relative market share should be divided at 0.75 or 0.8 rather than 1 so that businesses with strong market shares that are not market leaders can be positioned in the two left-hand quadrants of the matrix.

There are four generic categories within the BCG matrix, and the characteristics of each generic type are outlined below:

1   Question mark characteristics:

- The business is in an industry growing faster than the economy.
- The business has a low relative market share.
- There is a low experience curve effect and the firm cannot exploit economies of scale.
- The business may not have the ability to compete against a larger rival.
- Investing large amounts of cash is needed to increase relative market share.
- Investment may not overcome the experience curve effect that rivals with a large relative market share possess.

- The parent company may invest in order to capture the rapid growth in the industry.
- The parent may divest if there are more attactive alternative investments.

2   Star characteristics:

- The industry growth rate is high and superior to that of the economy as a whole.
- High profitability and cash flow generation potential.
- High investment needed to maximize the benefit from the high industry growth rate.
- The business can take advantage of its experience curve and economies of scale.
- Such businesses can significantly boost the overall financial performance of the portfolio.

3   Cash cow characteristics:

- They have high relative market share in an industry with a low growth rate.
- They have the ability to generate large cash surpluses.
- As the industry is mature the investment needs are lower for sustaining market share.
- The business is likely to be an industry leader with high relative market share and experience curve benefits.
- The business will need to fortify and defend strategy to maintain its position.
- If a 'Cash Cow' becomes weak they can be divested so that cash can be invested in other portfolio companies.

4   Dog characteristics:

- Low growth rate and relative market share.
- Low profit margins through poor economies of scale and experience curve benefits.
- Poor generation of cash may prevent action to redress the situation.
- Divesting or liquidating the company may be the only feasible option.

11.2.2   BCG and corporate strategy

The BCG Matrix can be a useful strategic tool for highlighting businesses that provide strong cash flows and/or require an investment strategy. It raises awareness of the need to allocate financial resources correctly in order to optimize the performance of the overall portfolio. Perhaps more importantly, it sheds light on the sources of potential funding and where such funding should be spent, and provides a basis for strategies that effect movements within the matrix for the overall benefit of the portfolio. Investment and divestment strategies can be assessed, even though the matrix does not measure profitability directly.

Looking at the BCG matrix positively, it can:

■ Assist strategic decision-making, especially on investment expansion and divestment.
■ Help identify cash providing companies and companies that need cash injections.
■ Facilitate a better understanding of financial relationships between portfolio companies.
■ Be a useful tool when used in conjunction with investment appraisal techniques such as NPV and IRR.

Looking at the BCG matrix negatively, it can:

■ Artificially categorize businesses in high and low categories for relative market shares and growth rates when the reality is that many businesses have average classifications.
■ Be too simplistic to place a business in one of four cells (e.g. a market leader may be less profitable than a smaller rival). It may be more meaningful to analyse the movement of a portfolio company over a period of time to assess its general direction within the matrix.
■ Fail to determine which portfolio company provides the best return on an investment assuming finite resources are available.
■ Provide a blinkered perspective because relative market share and industry growth rates are too limiting in terms of their ability to capture the dynamics of strategic positions (e.g. a high relative market share does not guarantee high profitability because it assumes that there will be experience curve benefits and economies of scale).

11.2.3 Industry attractiveness matrix

The industry attractiveness matrix is a nine cell model that quantifies long-term industry attractiveness on the vertical axis and competitive strength on the horizontal axis. As Figure 11.3 shows, long-term industry attractiveness is divided into high, medium and low attractiveness while competitive strength is divided into strong, average and weak strength. The two axes are derived from several factors that are individually weighted and rated, and once the factors have been given values and weighted a circle is placed on the matrix where the co-ordinates intersect, with the size of the circle being directly proportionate to the individual company's revenue contribution to the whole portfolio.

11.2.4 Evaluating industry attractiveness

Industry attractiveness is an important factor within strategic analysis because attractive industries are seen to provide long-term growth opportunities and profit streams within the portfolio. The types of factors that impinge on industry attractiveness are:

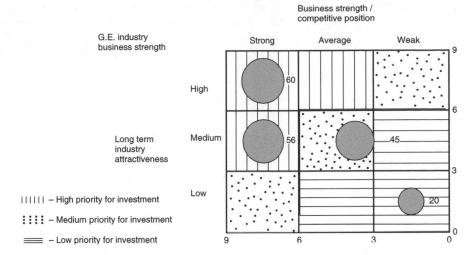

Figure 11.3
Industry attractiveness matrix (G.E. business/industry strength matrix) *Source*: (From *Strategy Formulation, Analytical Concepts*, 1st Edition by Hofer. © 1978. Reprinted with permission of South-Western, a division of Thomson Learning: www.thomsonrights.com. Fax 800 730 2215).

- *Market size and predicted growth rates*   High rates of growth and large market shares are highly positive factors.
- *The intensity of competition*   A lack of competition will result in higher profit margins.
- *Emerging opportunities and threats*   Low threat levels and promising opportunities provide competitive advantages.
- *Capital requirements*   Can the company finance high-level capital programmes and will the return on capital be acceptable to shareholders?
- *Strategic fit*   Synergy with other members in the portfolio can provide combinatory competitive advantages.
- *Profitability*   Margins and return on investment are directly affected by profits.
- *Social, political, environmental and regulatory factors*   Industries are affected by some or all of these factors and they can increase pressure on margins and profitability.
- *Risk and uncertainty*   High risk and uncertainty can result in business failure.
- *Cyclical and seasonal factors*   These factors can affect stability and cash flow.

These types of industry attractiveness factors will then require weighting with the total weights being equal to 1. They are then rated with each factor having a value between 1 and 10.

11.2.5   Evaluating competitive strength

Competitive strength factors are important because they influence a company's ability to gain competitive advantage. By assessing the competitive strength of a company we can compare it to other companies in the same industry. The types of factors that affect competitive strength are:

- *Relative Market Share* This is the ratio of a company's market share by volume to its nearest rival (e.g. if a company has a 25 per cent share and its nearest rival has 50 per cent the R.M.S. is 0.5), and the higher the R.M.S. the greater its competitive strength compared to its rivals.
- *Ability to compete on cost* This provides a strong competitive advantage over rivals. If competitors can achieve cost parity, then the time involved in achieving cost parity must be allowed for.
- *Ability to match rivals on key product and/or service attributes* Quality, technology, reputation, etc., can affect customer demand and competitive advantage.
- *Influence and bargaining power over buyers and suppliers* This can lower competition in the market place and provide competitive advantage.
- *Technology and innovation* Being first to market with technologically advanced and innovative products can lead to competitive advantage (assuming resources are available to realize the advantage).
- *Branded image* Strong brand names can command premium prices.
- *Matching the company's resources to key success factors in the industry* When a company's strengths match industry key success factors a competitive advantage can be gained.
- *Profit margins relative to competitors* Normally a direct result of successful cost competition.

The weighting and rating of these factors can be applied in the same way as those for industry attractiveness.

11.2.6 Interpreting matrix results

The correspondence of the industry attractiveness and competitive strength positions to the size of the consolidated scores are shown in the following table:

Industry attractiveness	Scores	Competitive strength
High	Greater than 6.7	Strong
Medium	Between 3.3 and 6.7	Average
Low	Below 3.3	Weak

Businesses that are positioned in the three top left cells of the nine cell matrix represent the greatest investment opportunities, with the top left cell (High–Strong) being the most attractive for the allocation of funds. The three cells running diagonally bottom left to top right have the next priority for investment, for they need a steady investment stream to maintain industry position and cash flows. The three cells in the bottom right section of the matrix have a low investment priority and may necessitate that the businesses be divested unless a specific investment opportunity can bring about a turnaround situation.

11.2.7   Life cycle matrix

A life cycle matrix places businesses within a 15 cell matrix with the intention of highlighting the position of each portfolio member within their respective industry life cycle. The horizontal axis rates the company's competitive position (strong, average, or weak) while the vertical axis in Figure 11.4 shows the stages in the industry life cycle from early development at the top of the matrix to stagnation and decline at the bottom.

The numbers against each circle (portfolio company) denotes the industry size by value. Once the companies have been positioned on the matrix the information can be used to support strategic decision-making, especially for investment decisions. The matrix can be used in conjunction with other models and measures, which is important because it does not take into account the profitability of the portfolio companies. This would also support the analysis of strategic fit between portfolio members since the matrix only provides limited information for determining business strategies.

The three matrices that have been outlined should be used to support strategic analysis and not as prescriptive and deterministic models. It is clearly important that the matrices use the most appropriate and up-to-date data. When used carefully, each of the matrices has strategic value, although the greatest benefit is gained when they are used together as this provides a broader picture of the strengths and weaknesses within the corporate portfolio.

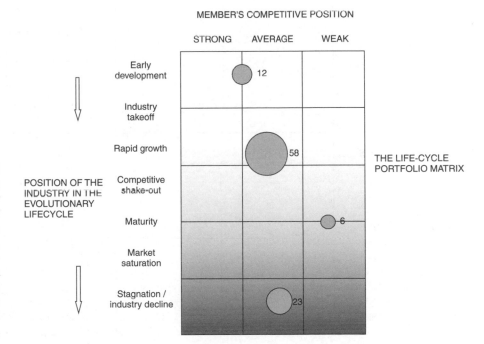

Figure 11.4

Industry life cycle matrix
Source: (From *Strategy Formulation, Analytical Concepts*, 1st Edition by Hofer. © 1978. Reprinted with permission of South-Western, a division of Thomson Learning: www.thomsonrights.com. Fax 800 730 2215).

135

11.3   Strategic Position and ACtion Evaluation (SPACE)

The appropriateness of product development and market development strategies can be analysed using a four dimensional matrix that has the acronym SPACE (Rowe et al., 1994). It is a conceptual device for understanding the strategic posture of a business and the strategic options associated with such a posture.

The usefulness of SPACE lies in its ability to position a business against four strategic dimensions, these being the financial strength of the business, the strength of the industry it operates in, the degree of stability within the general business environment, and the level of competitive advantage the business has compared to its rivals. Examples of how a business can score on the four dimensions are shown in Figure 11.5, and as can be seen, the profile of the business will be determined by its relative position on the four axes. Financial strength is deemed to be important because a business can better withstand adverse environmental conditions, such as high interest rates, if it has access to financial reserves. It also means that a business is in a better position, compared to a financially weak company, if it wants to diversify into more attractive industries or competitively undercut existing industry players. Industry strength focuses upon the attractiveness of the industry in terms of its growth potential and profitability. In an expanding industry, such as that

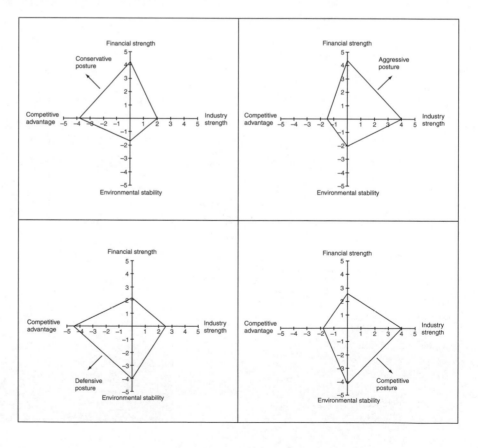

Figure 11.5
Four strategic SPACE postures
Source: (Rowe, A.J., Mason, R.O., Dickel, K.E., Mann, R.B. and Mockler, R.J. (1994). *Strategic Management: A Methodological Approach* 4/E, Addison-Wesley: Reading, Massachusetts. Reprinted by permission of Alan Rowe).

witnessed within the mobile phone market, a business can maintain or increase revenue without necessarily out-performing its rivals. On the other hand, when the market declines, a business will need to protect its position if it is to maintain existing profitability levels. Competitive advantage is therefore important because a business with competitive advantage can maximize the opportunities offered within an expanding market, especially if it is financially strong, and protects its competitive position in a static or declining industry.

When a business is financially strong but does not have any significant competitive advantage over its rivals, and operates in an unstable environment with only a moderate or weak position within the industry, then it is said to have a 'conservative' posture. Alternatively, a business is said to have an 'aggressive' posture when it is financially strong, operates in a strong industry, has a stable external environment and has competitive advantage over its rivals. The most negative posture is the 'defensive posture' because the business has little financial strength and trades within a weak industry. To make matters worse, the wider environment is unstable and it has limited competitive advantage over its rivals. The fourth posture within Figure 11.5 is defined as 'competitive', and as can be seen, it operates within an attractive industry and benign environment, and can compete effectively because it has some form of competitive advantage. Its only weakness is a lack of financial strength which could impede its ability to expand or compete aggressively.

The strategic options associated with the four postures are shown in Figure 11.6. A conservative posture is typical of businesses in mature industries, where the lack of incentive for investment generates large financial surpluses. Yet it is dangerous in the longer term as it reduces competitiveness through lethargy

Figure 11.6
Generic strategies and strategic options within SPACE
Source: (Rowe, A.J., Mason, R.O., Dickel, K.E., Mann, R.B. and Mockler, R.J. (1994). *Strategic Management: A Methodological Approach* 4/E, Addison-Wesley: Reading, Massachusetts. Reprinted by permission of Alan Rowe).

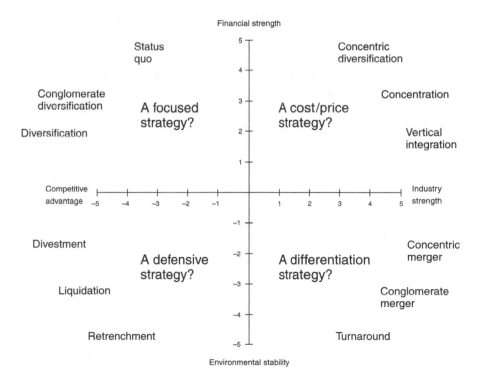

in developing new products and markets. To maintain focus, businesses can sustain the 'status quo' by defending their existing products whilst, if appropriate, 'diversifying' into new markets. This will not be relevant if the business is part of an already successful portfolio.

Aggressive postures imply that the business can compete on price with rivals offering similar products. The ability to out-compete rivals can only be maintained if the business continues to offer and develop products or services with a definite competitive edge. This can be achieved through continued innovation and investment, in what can be described as a strategy of 'concentration' to further market dominance. Concentric diversification (where companies move into new but linked market areas, e.g. dedicated digital services in modern football clubs and branded hotels) and vertical integration can also be used to gain competitive advantage and sustain market dominance. The financial strength of the business is clearly important because it underpins strategic moves of this kind. Indeed, these kind of businesses are key to the development of viable corporate portfolios.

In a competitive posture the critical issue revolves around the availability of finance, as this is needed to maintain the competitive position of the business within its more turbulent environment. The business has competitive advantage and operates within an attractive industry, but this can only be maintained if it can increase its resource efficiency and general competitiveness. Under such circumstances a single business can merge with a more cash-rich business in some form of conglomerate or concentric merger. The business will then be able to 'differentiate' itself by investing in R&D whilst withstanding the pressures of its more turbulent environment through a continued drive to improve resource efficiency. The alternative is to generate sufficient capital internally in what can be described as a 'turnaround' strategy.

The weakest competitive position is the defensive posture. With little financial strength and limited competitive advantage, they are forced to protect their position by greater and greater resource efficiency. This 'defensive' strategy will be difficult to sustain in the longer term, as the lack of financial strength will prevent significant product or service development or entry into new markets. The most logical strategy, in the absence of any corporate merger or take-over, will be survival through retrenchment, divestment, or even liquidation.

One of the dangers of SPACE is that it can appear static, representing a picture at a particular point in time. It is likely that the company will be changing, either by strengthening or weakening its quadrant position, or by slowly moving from one quadrant to another. Indeed, one of the greatest uses of SPACE lies in its ability to focus corporate minds on where they would like to be, and then on how they can get there. For example, it can chart a firm's performance over a specified time period (i.e. 5 years) so that changes are mapped and evaluated. It can also be projected forward (say 5 years) to see the effect that their strategies will, or could, have.

The criteria that underpin each of the four axes are shown in Figure 11.7. A company is then assessed against each criterion using a 5-point scale, with 1 being most negative and 5 most positive. The scores are then added-up and divided by the number of criteria to give the average score for the strategic dimension and its position on the axis. A positive score on financial strength and industry strength would result in a high score (i.e. 4 or 5), whereas a

Factors determining financial strength

	Score				
Return on investment	2	Low	0	5	High
Gearing	3	Imbalanced	0	5	Balanced
Liquidity	2	Imbalanced	0	5	Balanced
Capital req'd/available	1	High	0	5	Low
Cash flow	2	Low	0	5	High
Ease of market exit	2	Difficult	0	5	Easy
Business risk involved	3	High	0	5	Low
Other factors	1		0	5	
Average	2.0			2.0	

Factors determining industry strength

	Score				
Growth potential	4	Low	0	5	High
Profit potential	5	Low	0	5	High
Financial stability	2	Low	0	5	High
Technological know-how	4	Simple	0	5	Complex
Resource utilization	4	Inefficient	0	5	Efficient
Capital intensity	3	Low	0	5	High
Ease of market entry	4	Easy	0	5	Difficult
Productivity capacity utilization	4	Low	0	5	High
Other factors	4		0	5	
Average	3.8			3.8	

Factors determining competitive advantage

	Score				
Market share	5	Small	0	5	Large
Product quality	4	Inferior	0	5	Superior
Product life cycle	4	Late	0	5	Early
Product replacement cycle	5	Variable	0	5	Fixed
Customer loyalty	3	Low	0	5	High
Competitions capacity utilization	4	Low	0	5	High
Technological know-how	5	Low	0	5	High
Vertical integration	2	Low	0	5	High
Other factors	3		0	5	
Average	3.9	−5		−1.1	

(continued)

Factors determining environmental stability

Figure 11.7
SPACE criteria
Source: (Rowe, A.J.,
Mason, R.O., Dickel, K.E.,
Mann, R.B. and Mockler,
R.J. (1994). *Strategic
Management: A
Methodological Approach*
4/E, Addison-Wesley:
Reading, Massachusetts.
Reprinted by permission
of Alan Rowe).

	Score			
Technological changes	1	Many	0	5	Few
Rate of inflation	2	High	0	5	Low
Demand variability	3	Large	0	5	Small
Price range – competing products	2	Wide	0	5	Narrow
Competitive pressure	3	High	0	5	Low
Price elasticity of demand	2	Elastic	0	5	Inelastic
Other factors	1		0	5	
Average	2	−5	−3		

positive score on competitive advantage and environmental stability would result in a low score (i.e. 1 or 2 because the scale is reversed by taking 5 away from the average score).

The appropriateness of the criteria for the dimension it is measuring, and the robustness of the scoring process, are critical to the success of the model. The criteria can be changed if managers feel this is appropriate, as is the number of criteria used. Managers can also use their collective judgement in scoring the criteria if the data is unavailable or too costly to generate.

11.4 Summary

The matrices that have been outlined have one thing in common, they attempt to position a company against a number (usually two) of dimensions. They are used to simplify complex scenarios and as such they can be powerful conceptual devices. Yet they have to be treated with caution because, like all models, they are only as good as the assumptions that underpin them and the reliability of the data that is used within them.

PART THREE

Case Study Analysis and Case Studies

CHAPTER 12

Case study analysis

Our approach to case analysis replicates management behaviour. It involves:

- The intuitive examination of issues that are inter-functional and strategic.
- The salami slicing of a problem in search of significant causes or drivers.
- The creative synthesis and aggregation of the analysis to develop options for the solution of the problem.

Case studies provide deep learning opportunities, especially in the consideration of alternative perspectives and the ability to think outside the box, and with practice, to integrate theory with practice and produce clear arguments.

12.1   Thinking strategically

For business strategy to be effective it is necessary to understand the detail and the big picture. A study by Sasser and Skinner (1978) suggested that successful managers:

- Understood what the critical level of detail was.
- Understood the operation in detail, which was fundamental if they were to understand the key business drivers.
- Instinctively knew when to roll their sleeves up and immerse themselves in detail, and when to delegate.
- Employed a wide armoury of analytical tools and techniques and knew what the appropriate depth of analysis should be.
- Could be unpredictable because they mixed strategic and detailed analysis in apparently random (creative) ways.

This implies that we understand the inputs to the business and the infrastructure (transformation process) that delivers the outputs that current and future customers/markets value. It may also involve moving the organization from 'A' (where it is now) to 'B' (where it wants it to be), which raises a number of issues for the strategic analyst. For example, in getting to 'B' the timing may be crucial – the organization can arrive early and discover there is no competition, because there is no market, or that the competition is there already because they also thought 'B' was a good idea.

12.2 The benefits of case studies to students and practising managers

Deep learning (Revans, 1983) occurs when:

$$L = P + Q$$

Where L is learning, P is programmed knowledge, and Q is questioned insight.

Programmed knowledge is the knowledge we receive through textbooks, research papers and company databases (e.g. market share and company profitability data), etc. In some respects the information contained within case studies is programmed knowledge, and like most programmed knowledge it is usually dated. This does not diminish its utility since it is essential if we wish to benchmark and test new knowledge.

Programmed knowledge requires a learner to remember 'facts' and to be capable of reciting them under examination conditions or using them in their everyday lives. Questioned insight requires the learner to challenge the 'Status Quo' that is embodied within programmed knowledge. For example, to test the applicability of theoretical concepts against case study data and to undertake further secondary or primary research. The outcome of programmed knowledge plus questioned insight is deeper knowledge, even new knowledge. This can be manifested in a number of different ways:

■ evidence of reflection and critical awareness.
■ the ability to produce cogent and convincing arguments.
■ an awareness of alternative perspectives and analyses which are not only theoretically informed, but demonstrate confident integration of theory and practice.

In many ways the characteristics of deep learning are those that we would associate with successfully run organizations.

Case studies can also be used to promote deep learning whilst providing (Johnston et al., 1997, p. 1):

■ Real information about real organizations without having to spend large amounts of time researching organizations.
■ A way of evaluating situations faced by real managers.
■ An opportunity to hold time still so that you can assess a situation without it changing, as it does in real time.
■ A chance to debate and discuss the interpretation and use of data and to undertake meaningful analysis.

■ A mechanism to develop and discuss possible solutions and their implications.

■ A safe environment – you will not be sacked or taken to court if your recommendations turn out to be wrong.

It is also important that we get as close as possible to the contemporary dynamics of the case study companies and the industries that they operate in. This is because all case studies reflect the status quo when they were researched and written, whereas we frequently want to know what the situation is now and how it might change in the future.

The updating of case studies so that contemporary analysis can take place is clearly a valuable $L = P + Q$ process, with the added benefit that it can make case analysis more fun. It also explains why some of the case studies are quite substantive and integrative – they have to be if we want to fully explore the dynamics of their competitive environment as they were then and how they are now. Experience also suggests that students require:

■ Cases to be substantial if they are to convey any meaning.

■ That the knowledge derived from the case is transferable to the students' own organizations.

■ An empathy with the case companies (they recognize them or find them intrinsically interesting).

12.3 Business strategy analysis: A chess metaphor

Business strategy is analogous to chess in so far as the pattern of moves on the board (the nature of the industry structure, its resources and the activity patterns of a business) is more important than the millions of possible moves that can be made by individual pieces. The only problem with the chess metaphor in business strategy and case study analysis is that in a game of chess there are only two competitors whereas in business there are sometimes many competitors. Also, in chess only one move can be made at a time while in business the execution of a strategy involves multiple moves. The chess metaphor does not breakdown completely however because the game is divided into three basic phases, and as Figure 12.1 shows, the three phases can be compared to business strategy and case study analysis.

In chess as in business this classification hides more complex issues. For example, the chess player may appear to have gained a commanding advantage in the middle game – but failure to press home an attack can be disastrous – possibly leading to a draw or even defeat. You must also remember that the Grand Master in chess, although keen to win a tournament, wishes one day to become world champion. The tournaments are a means to an end and not the end in itself: Business organizations do not want to draw or lose, they are in the game to win and keep on winning. Do not overlook this analogy when analysing cases. The game is continuous.

Chess	Business strategy	Case analysis
Opening moves	Understanding the players and defining business objectives.	Understanding the case and the industry players and their business objectives.
Middle game	Analysing the industry and environmental drivers and developing options and determining risk.	Analysing the data and the narrative. Undertaking secondary research and evaluating business performance against business models. Developing options and evaluation risk.
End game	Operationalizing the strategy and monitoring its effectiveness.	Develop conclusions and recommendations based only on what has been discovered in opening moves and middle game
Start over again	Understanding.........	Understanding.........

Figure 12.1
The three phases metaphor.

12.3.1 Opening moves

The real opening moves in chess are not the initial movement of pawns or knights, since the player should have carefully studied the opponent's past performance, their psychology, their favourite opening moves, etc. (i.e. their modus operandi). In case study analysis, it is essential to understand the position of the company in its industry, what its objectives and values are, the type and quality of its competitors, its relationships with buyers and suppliers, its history and so forth.

To understand a case study company and its environment you obviously have to read the case study, and one can read a case study or any set of information and completely misread it, missing the wood for the trees and getting bogged down in detail at too early a stage. We suggest that a case study is read several times and that the first reading should be neither too fast nor too slow. The objective is to familiarize yourself with the case company and its competitive environment. During this first reading you ought to make some notes alongside the text or data (do not just highlight the text as you may forget why you highlighted it!). The second and subsequent readings should be slower, far more deliberate, revisiting your earlier notes and making detailed observations. It is beneficial if more than one person does this, because it enables notes to be compared – you may have missed something which a colleague has 'picked up'.

Case study information can be narrative and data, and both types of information are equally valuable. Many mistakes are made because too much attention is paid to the data without considering the narrative (narrative provides the context), or because too much emphasis is placed on the narrative with scant consideration of the data. The usual outcome from both approaches is that the case study company and the industry are assessed at 'face value'.

Data is a snapshot at a particular period in time (e.g. profit and loss account, balance sheet) and it is important that it is compared with other organizations and industry norms. Historical turnover data, for example, may suggest that the company is increasing its turnover and profits, even when it has liquidity problems (remember that cash is a fact and that profit is a concept) and when it is performing badly relative to its rivals. Market share data can also be presented as 'facts' even though it is an extremely difficult metric to calculate – it is always an approximation and is frequently arrived at from different bases. In the supermarket business there are at least three bases for calculating market share while in the machine tool industry it is very difficult to calculate.

Narrative information can be incredibly rich and valuable, although it should never be accepted at face value. Indeed, it is essential that you distinguish between opinion and facts. The narrative of case studies always contain (to a greater or lesser extent) hyperbole and/or superlatives and opinions which derive from the case narrator, the case company managers, or the case company. What company for example, will not put a positive spin on a bad set of financial results – they are not likely to admit that they are a failing company.

The best (or worst) example of hyperbole in any case study is the 'Mission Statement', which has been described by Eileen Shapiro (1997) as 'a magic talisman hung in public places to ward off evil spirits' or Auberon Waugh's view that it is 'a statement of the obvious'. Mission statements are intended to be broad visions and it is the job of the case analyst to check if the business is moving towards or fulfilling those visions and objectives.

It is therefore important that in the opening moves we try to understand the business's objectives (stated or unstated) and that we test them against business strategy models. Once you are familiar with the broad picture you can move into the more detailed and salami sliced middle game.

12.3.2 Middle game

As in chess the middle game of case study analysis is extremely important (it is where the game is won or lost). The purpose of the middle game is to develop and build on the advantages gained in the opening moves. The middle game is, in case study terms, the detailed analysis of the patterns on the board. Detailed analysis is the salami slicing of the case study information and data and, where necessary, comparing it with conceptual business models. Financial and market/environment data, where it exists, also needs to be subjected to detailed scrutiny. The middle game is also the phase in which you search for contemporary data and information about the case study company and industry and their supply chains. This is an important task in all case study analysis, particularly where there is a lack of financial data.

It is important that your analysis moves beyond broad brush analyses, as the techniques and models used within strategic management should only be frameworks for more detailed analysis. In other words, do not arrive at premature conclusions about the strengths or weaknesses of a business.

The ability to salami slice a case study organization rests on having a good overview of the company from the opening moves stage. If you have completed this stage adequately you will understand the trigger points of the business and industry and reduce the probability of the analysis leading to paralysis (having lots of data that tells you very little).

Hard data is a key feature of middle game analysis, and is likely to include:

- return on capital employed.
- gross, operating, pre-tax and after tax margins.
- changes in market capitalization.
- stock turns or sales/stock ratio.
- time series analysis to evaluate and extrapolate trends in a business (e.g. turnover and profit trends).
- pareto analysis.
- searches for trends in the industry and industry sectors – are growths or declines linear or accelerating.
- correlation investigations between seemingly disparate information, e.g. the links between sales and order volumes, inventory levels and lead times, and comparison of market share with profitability, etc.

It is also a learning opportunity to search for more contemporary data so that we can assess how the company is performing now? For example, what has changed since the case date in terms of industry structure, industry growth and/or industry decline?

12.3.3   End game

The end game is sometimes the phase in chess where players with a commanding lead in the middle game concede a draw or lose the match. Similar outcomes occur in business, which is why it is important that in case study analysis the conclusions and recommendations are robust and operationable. This is why it is important to remember:

1 That even the most poorly run organizations have some strengths or unique resources (do not overlook them).
2 That even the most successful organizations have weaknesses which may make them vulnerable to extended threats.
3 That the end game should be devoted to synthesis and identifying options and risks for the case study company (there are no correct solutions to a business case study, but some are much better than others).
4 That you can consider more than one business model of strategy during synthesis.
5 That conclusions only arise out of your prior analysis and that recommendations are only derived from your conclusions (when you write up a case analysis do not regurgitate whole sections of the case narrative – this does not amount to analysis).

Each of these points is considered in the following sections.

12.3.3.1   Poorly run organizations can have strengths

Students, managers and investors sometimes write off what they perceive to be a failing company without considering all the potential strengths and resources within the company.

12.3.3.2   Successful organizations have weaknesses

The difference between success and failure can therefore be slender, sometimes being determined by the fickleness of the consumer. In addition to the changing competitive milieu, the impact of changing consumer tastes can be significant.

12.3.3.3   Synthesis: Identifying options (no correct solutions)

If analysis is all about salami slicing (dissagregation), then synthesis is concerned with re-aggregation – putting it back together again. Johnston et al. (1997) argue that synthesis is the most creative part of case analysis. Synthesis is concerned with identifying options for the case company. Options should be tested against the criteria of:

- do-ability – in terms of resources and time scales of action.
- political acceptance within the organization.
- possibilities of success or failure.

Synthesis is not about putting the old sausage back into its skin, it is about re-configuring alternative sausages that have new ingredients, and then choosing the tastiest.

Developing options is also a stage at which you should 'phone a friend' to compare and contrast your options with theirs. Also, when developing and comparing options it is useful to think laterally, as most successful businesses and their managers have to think the unthinkable as otherwise they would simply apply the received wisdom of others.

12.3.3.4   Consider more than one business model of strategy

Most students and many managers rely on a single model when they analyse and synthesize a business or a business case study, e.g. the 1985 positioning model of Porter. This limits the range and depth of strategic analysis because there are at least three major approaches to strategy (Eisenhardt and Sull, 2001). These are:

- Positioning strategies.
- Resource-based strategies.
- Rules or criterion-based strategies.

The strategic logic, the sources of advantage and the performance goals for each approach are demonstrated in Figure 12.2.

Eisenhardt and Sull argue that positioning and resource-based approaches are most appropriate in slowly changing/well-structured markets and

	Positioning	Resource-based	Rules- or criterion-based
Strategic logic	Establish position (the more unique the better).	Leverage resources across markets.	Pursue opportunities which may be fleeting.
Strategic question	Where should we be and why?	What should we be and why?	How should we proceed?
Source of advantage	Unique valuable position, with logical, but unique activity systems.	Unique, valuable, inimitable resources.	Key processes and unique but relatively simple criteria.
Duration of advantage	Defensible, but not necessarily 'sustained'.	Defensible, but not necessarily 'sustained'.	Not predictable.
Performance goals	Profitability: profit maximization.	Long term: dominance.	Growth.

moderately changing/well-structured markets (i.e. the old economy). The criterion or simple rules approach, on the other hand, is more suited to rapidly changing and ambiguous markets (i.e. the new economy). We suspect, however, that these issues are less clear cut.

To summarize:

- There is no mystery to business strategy.
- There is not one way to analyse a company and an industry.
- There are no correct solutions, only better ones, and even these are likely to be sub-optimal in 5 years time.

12.3.3.5 *Writing of a case study and arriving at conclusions and recommendations without regurgitating the case narrative*

The seventeenth-century philosopher Bacon asserted that 'writing maketh a man precise', which begs the question of how a case study analysis should be written up so that they are precise. We recommend a report format so that it can be easily digested. This requires them to be:

- Readable.
- Articulate (proofread as you cannot always rely on the spell and/or grammar check).

and for them to:

- Have a beginning, middle and end.

It is also worth avoiding:

- peculiar font styles (except for italics for quotations longer than thirty words).

- fancy clip art to decorate the narrative.
- being vague or too generic.
- the overuse of bullet points – they are only sound bites and they should only be used if you intend to elaborate on them.

12.4   Structuring the report

A report should have the following basic sections:

- A title page with the title of your work (e.g. AB machine tools: combating industrial decline?). It should also contain your name and the month and year you produced the report.
- A synopsis, executive summary or abstract (not all three).
- List of contents with page numbers. You may wish to introduce separate lists for tables, diagrams and appendices.

Note: the page numbers for the synopsis and contents should be in Roman numerals.

- Introduction – this should be where page 1 starts, and where you can use the title of 'Introduction' or an alternative such as 'An Overview of AB Machine Tools and its Problems'.
- Analysis and findings – this could be divided into three or four sections and it does not have to be subtitled 'Analysis'. It could, for example, be called 'Industrial Structure and Supermarkets'.
- Conclusions and recommendations.
- Bibliography and/or References.
- Appendices.

Many of the sections of the report format are self-explanatory, although there are some dos and don'ts for each of the following sections:

- Synopsis/Executive summary/Abstract.
- Introduction.
- Analysis.
- Conclusions and recommendations.

12.4.1   Synopsis/Executive summary/Abstract (not all three)

The Synopsis is usually written after the work is completed. Its purpose is to encourage the reader to study part or the whole of the report. It should be no longer than $1\frac{1}{2}$ pages of A4 and it should be self-contained, unabbreviated and contain no bullet points. It could cover the following areas:

- Brief outline of the problem(s) or your objectives.
- How you addressed the problem(s) or objectives in terms of analysis.

■ Outline of your conclusions.
■ Outline of your recommendations or implications for the case company.

12.4.2 Introduction

The Introduction should provide:

■ An overview of the case company and the industry.
■ The problem(s)/objectives which were the focus of your research.
■ How you researched those problems or addressed those objectives.
■ A brief outline of your conclusions and recommendations.
■ You may wish to add a section on the structure of the report – something similar to an abstract, e.g. 'In chapter 1 the author (do not use the first person) discusses the structure of the machine tool industry . . .'.

12.4.3 Analysis/Findings

This is the major part of the report and it should be broken down into discreet sections that reflect the objectives/problem(s) discussed in the introduction. There are some very specific dos and don'ts which should be committed to memory:

1 Do not regurgitate the case narrative as this does not amount to analysis. In fact, it is normally an indication that the case has not been analysed (but you can directly quote and cite the case to underpin an argument).
2 Case studies are not just confined to theory. Concepts can be integrated with practice so that the analysis is theoretically informed (but do not segregate concept from practice).
3 Do not make bland or generic statement without substantiation. A typical example would be 'it's a well known fact . . .'. To which the response is 'who says so' or 'where's the proof'.
4 Try not to use unexplained superlatives such as 'the supermarkets compete in a dynamic and aggressive environment . . .' unless the constituent parts are outlined and explained (i.e. the components within the environment, the nature of the aggression, and an explanation of the dynamics involved).
5 Do not explore cul de sacs, even when they are interesting, unless they address your objectives and/or move the analysis forwards.
6 Do discuss your finding/analysis as you proceed because you may be able to arrive at interim conclusions.
7 The analysis should be self-sufficient in the sense that managers and students tend to do one or both of the following:
   ■ They incorporate huge amounts of data and information that should be in an appendix.
   ■ They continually refer the reader to the appendix.

(Summarize data or information from an appendix within the narrative of the analysis and refer the reader, if necessary, to the appendix for more complete data).

8   Be consistent in referencing to sources (texts, journals, websites, research papers, etc.) such that you do not alternate between a Harvard referencing system (which is used in this book) and a numerical one, and that you ensure that all sources are full and accurately referenced in the references/bibliography section.

12.4.4   Conclusions/Recommendations

Conclusions can only be drawn on your stated objectives and on the analysis and findings arrived at in meeting those objectives. You cannot speculate on what has not been subject to scrutiny. You may, of course, admit that some of the objectives or problems have not been fully addressed (e.g. through a lack of information) and that your conclusions are speculative in the sense that they are based on the analysis carried out. For example, 'the author is unsure of the impact that the ASDA/Wal-Mart combine may have on the UK supermarket sector, but from the limited evidence available and Wal-Mart's strategy in the USA, one could speculate that ....'

Recommendations can only be based on the conclusions drawn, and they are an outcome of the examination of options in the analysis and conclusions. There also needs to be an underpinning rationale, which again derives from the analysis, for the recommendations put forward. It is also important to be specific when you analyse a company and in the conclusions and recommendations that are made. Degeneration into generalities is both tempting and dangerous, as the following two examples demonstrate:

1   'The company requires us to adopt a synergistic and dynamic Marketing Strategy.' In this statement there is no explanation of what the components of the marketing strategy should be or what the words 'synergistic' and 'dynamic' mean in relation the marketing strategy?

2   'The company requires a more effective and pro-active planning and control system and it is necessary to implement this immediately.' Again, what does 'effective' and 'pro-active' mean in relation to planning and control systems? And is it possible to implement a planning and control system immediately?

12.5   The use of buzzwords

The following are a selection of words and phrases that frequently appear in essays, reports and dissertations. The key message is that they can be meaningless unless you define and contextualize them. They are not listed in any particular order:

Pro-active	Usually undefined.
Reactive	Usually undefined, is it the opposite of pro-active?
Synergy	Unexplained and sometimes accompanied by '$2 + 2 = 5$' (a course in basic arithmetic is obviously required).
Sustained competitive advantage	Frequently used without recognizing that it implies 'continuous' or 'forever'.
Competitive edge	What is the 'edge'? Where is the 'edge'?
Empowerment	In what way and how?
Dynamic	This adjective is meaningless without verbs – it requires definition and contextualization.
Exponential	Usually used in relation to 'growth' when the growth has been linear or flat in places (basic course in mathematics required).
Philosophy	As in New Management Philosophy, Marketing Philosophy and Total Quality Philosophy. The components of the philosophy are rarely detailed or examined in terms of how they can be operationalized.
World class	Another favourite and rarely defined or contextualised.
Best practice	Very similar to 'world class'. Students usually forget that there is no consensus on best practice (O'Shea and Madigan, 1997).
Agile	Rarely defined and frequently confused with 'lean'.
Symbiotic	With what and how?
Short, medium and long term	Time scales are rarely defined.

12.6   An overview of the cases in the book

The cases represent a wide variety of industry in the UK. They are all based on real companies even where the real name of the company has been disguised. Some of them are successful while others are struggling:

The companies are also located in different places along the supply chain relative to consumers:

- *Morrisons* is only one 'remove' from the consumer.
- *AB* is at least eight removes from a consumer.
- *Delamare* is three to four removes from consumers, dependant on products and channels.

The companies are also in different growth sectors of the UK economy:

- *AB* is in a declining sector. The decline started in the late 1950s and has continued ever since.

■ *Delamare* is also in a declining sector with imports now taking at least 38 per cent of the UK tableware market share. Nevertheless there are centres of excellence in the industry which have bucked the trend (e.g. Denby, Steelite and Portmeirion).

■ *Morrisons* is in a moderately growing sector. Overall industry growth in grocery retailing (including small retailers) has grown just above inflation, with the 300 per cent growth over 10 years for Morrisons being mainly at the expense of other competitors.

■ *Alpha* was a supplier to an organization which was the epitome of success in 1990s: Marks & Spencer. In 1990, Marks & Spencer was growing fast at the expense of other retailers in the sector, with Alpha being a slip stream business.

The cases also address a variety of issues in business, marketing and operations strategy:

■ *Morrisons* is an integrative study which encompasses a wide range of issues from HRM to merchandising and marketing strategy to supply chain management. There is also a case study on the UK supermarket sector.

■ *Alpha* appears to be the most single issue case in the sense that it has a clear planning and control problem. However, if you read between the lines you will discover marketing strategy, business strategy and HRM issues.

■ *Delamare* also has a strong operations strategy emphasis and considers important marketing, operational and financial interfacing issues.

■ *AB* is a highly integrative case study. It considers marketing, operations, customer service and design issues against the background of a declining industry.

CHAPTER 13

Wm. Morrison Supermarkets PLC

(Case date: 1996)

The business was founded by William Murdoch Morrison in Bradford in 1899. He started out as a wholesale egg and butter merchant, not dissimilar to J Sainsbury who commenced as a dairy retailer 30 years earlier. The company did not develop spectacularly, but by 1918 it became a private limited company – Wm. Morrison (Provisions) Ltd. By this time the business had changed because it was now a retail organization rather than a wholesaler. In the late 1920s, the business developed into a mixture of stalls within covered markets and lock-up shops.

When the depression came in the early 1930s the business was nearly wiped out, and the business moved back to some of its old roots – market stalls in Bradford and Dewsbury. Almost immediately after the Second World War the company opened Bradford's first self-service store with products individually priced. Whilst the current Chairman and Managing Director, Kenneth Duncan Morrison, was undertaking compulsory National Service from 1950 to 1952, his mother phoned to say his father was ill and would not work again (he died shortly afterwards). She told him she would run the business until he was demobilized and he could take it over if he was interested. Kenneth was very interested.

From 1952 to 1966 Kenneth, along with two brothers-in-law, developed more self-service shops. The most significant breakthrough occurred in 1962 with the opening of Morrison's first supermarket – The Victoria Supermarket. This supermarket was developed from a disused cinema (The Victoria) and it offered free car parking space. It was 2 miles from Bradford city centre, which caused mirth amongst his fellow market traders because they thought he was 'barmy' building a retail outlet out of town. There was a mixture of both luck and judgement in the decision to operate out of town; to begin with Kenneth

Morrison could not afford the rent of a large city centre outlet, but at the same time shopping habits were changing, driven to some extent by increasing car ownership. Morrisons first supermarket was an instant success.

Shortly after the purchase of the Victoria, Kenneth Morrison bought two more supermarket sites including one which pre-empted a Tesco purchase. These two sites were also out of town. In 1966, prior to flotation of the company, the now famous 'M' logo was designed to express the developing corporate image. William Morrison Supermarkets Ltd was floated on the Stock Exchange in 1967, 2 years after Asda. The Morrison share offer of 1.152 million ordinary two-shilling (10p.) shares at 10s.6d. (52½) was very popular – it was 174 times oversubscribed.

During the period from 1967 to 1979 the company developed steadily, not overstretching itself. It was at this time that the company acquired the Whelan Discount Stores, which expanded the Morrison chain into Lancashire, providing a ubiquitous presence along large stretches of the M62 corridor. The Whelan purchase had been the only major acquisition of a retail chain in the company's history, as 95 per cent of growth has been organic. Continued growth led the company to build a new headquarters and new warehousing and food preparation facilities in 1971. In the decade from 1980 to 1990 the development of the company moved into a higher gear. In 1986 the Wm. Morrison Enterprise 5 Trust was established with £250 k of personal money from Kenneth Morrison 'to hone the business skills of budding entrepreneurs'. (The 'Enterprise 5' Trust will be discussed in more detail later in the case study.) By 1987 the warehouse and distribution centre had become too small to effectively service the forty stores in the Morrison business, and a new 600,000 square foot warehousing, packing and distribution centre was opened on a 44-acre site near Wakefield in 1988. It was strategically located near the intersection of the M62 and M1 motorways.

13.1 Contemporary history, development and mission

At the beginning of the 1990s Kenneth Morrison was made a Commander of the British Empire (CBE) for his services to retailing. Then for 2 years in succession (1993 and 1994) Morrisons was judged to be Britain's best performing company by the Institute of Directors. The company was also ranked at 84th place out of 400 European industrial and commercial companies (excluding banking) in 1993, by the Economic Research Team at Germany's Kiel University lead by Professor Reinhart Schmidt (Hassell and Wilsher, 1993). This ranking was above that of Marks & Spencer (85) and Sainsbury (88) but slightly behind Tesco (81). The basis of Schmidt's ranking rests on three weighted measures: profitability (Rendite), financial solidity (Sicherheit) and growth (Wachstum). Details of Schmidt's 'RSW' system can be found in Attachment 14.1 (see Chapter 14 Appendix) of the Supermarket Industry case study.

Kenneth Morrison was described by *The Director* as a 'no-frills supermarketer, who isn't carried away by the group's success'. Apart from their 'price mission' Morrisons have avoided formulating a corporate mission statement. The business was summed up in a speech by Kenneth Morrison to the

Institute of Directors in 1994: 'There are no tricks in our business and no secrets to our success. We don't set profit targets. If you do your job well the profits will follow.'

The process of doing your job well was described by Chris Blundell, the group's Marketing Director, in the following way: 'We have pursued a number of key values which have underpinned our growth and performance. One – everyone from the top to the bottom of the business is trained to be self-critical, almost hypercritical, of our retailing operations. There is no room for complacency and satisfaction with the status quo at Morrisons. Two – the company is extremely cost conscious (again from top to bottom). For example we refuse to pay over the odds for store sites. Three – we regard ourselves as innovative, but not to the point of providing the company and, more importantly, our customers with nasty surprises. Four – we listen very carefully to criticism (and accolades) from our customers in order to provide an almost exciting family atmosphere in our stores plus a wider choice of produce at keener prices than our rivals. Five – we believe in close and businesslike relationships with our suppliers to ensure that they provide us with their best prices and meet our demand and delivery requirements first time, every time. In return our policy is to pay suppliers promptly. Six – we value our employees (not just a cliché) and emphasize craft, retailing and managerial development. We are always looking for potential entrepreneurs and most promotions are from within the business.'

13.1.1 Company independence

Since the mid-1980s there had been a lot of speculation by watchers and analysts of the retail sector on the future ownership of the chain (including hostile takeover bids by rivals such as Tesco). But as one company spokesperson commented, 'it is a company with a Chairman who is involved in the business all the way down to the operational level – he is a hands-on chairman who believes in the continuing independence of the company.'

13.1.2 Growth and performance

Morrisons increased their stores from 45 in 1990 to 81 in 1996, with an accompanying 97 per cent increase in retailing area to 2.9 million square feet. This made the Morrisons store portfolio one of the most modern in the industry. Financial performance had been equally dramatic during the 1990s. For example: turnover (excluding VAT) edged above £2 billion in 1996, which represented a 170 per cent increase on 1990 sales. Operating profit had also increased by 216 per cent over this 7-year period (see Attachment 14.2 in Section 14.3, page 193).

The pressures on superstore growth had intensified since 1996, especially those pressures arising from extreme price competition and their effect on margins that had typified the industry from about 1992. New planning regulations and the negative attitude to superstore development had curtailed new developments, refocusing management action towards the major refurbishment of existing Morrisons stores.

13.1.3 Store location and store design

The company was predominantly a northern company with a large proportion of outlets 20 miles north or south of the M62 corridor in Yorkshire and Lancashire. During the period from 1993 to 1996 a large proportion of the development had been in the Midlands of England (e.g. two in Nottingham, one in Coventry, one in Tamworth and one in Northampton). There were also plans to build new stores in Kent and London. The company had no stores in Scotland.

Many of the stores were in towns that were close to major trunk roads or motorways. The Stoke on Trent store, for example, is only 5 miles from the M6 motorway and 1 mile from the A500 motorway link road. Average store size had grown from 33,900 square feet to 35,800 square feet retailing area in the period from 1992 to 1996 (see Attachments 14.2 and 14.10 in Section 14.3, pages 193 and 200). This had been through major refurbishments to stores in the 25,000 square feet to 40,000 square feet range. Fifteen of the eighty-one stores in 1996 are in the hypermarket category (over 50,000 square feet).

One of the largest stores in the chain was built at Idle, 3 miles from Bradford city centre, in 1988. This store had 72,000 square feet of retailing area. It had thirty-nine checkouts including five for the wine and spirit department. The store was one part of a major retailing development undertaken by the company, and as such it included major non-food retailers such as Great Mills (DIY) and Northern Upholstery. This development was built on the site of the old Jowett car factory – a typical brown field site development. The site was named 'Enterprise 5' and it was strategically situated as an out of town development. Inner city developments had also been pursued, with stores being built close to the town centres of Skipton in 1991 and Huddersfield in 1995.

The company has won prizes for store design, especially with respect to the way they scrutinized the origins of store sites and the town and locality in which the store was built and how they integrated this into the overall structural design of the site. This is complemented within the store with photographs and mementoes of the site's history. In 1994, it paid £13 m per site compared to £22 m to 23 m per site that Sainsbury and Tesco paid. All new developments are controlled by the company's own Project Management Team so that project costs, schedules, specifications and quality criteria are met.

13.1.4 Market street

Morrison stores have grid type layouts that have been supplemented with *Market Streets* that occupy two sides of all new and refurbished stores. The market street concept represents a return to a counter style of service within the supermarkets, being badged and marketed as stores within a store. The market street has Morrison shops selling fresh produce (e.g. fishmonger, butcher, pizzeria, pie shop, provisions, delicatessen and baker) and in some respects they are analogous to the types of stores the company had when it first started trading. Each of the market street stores supports a major shopping route through the larger store, with the layout being carefully designed so that it provides space and visual variety for shoppers.

The market street shops have their own services (e.g. refrigeration units, ovens, specialized preparation areas). These services occupy approximately 12½–20 per cent of store floor area and provide poor efficiency in terms of turnover per square foot. Yet they quickly became a financial success in terms of turnover at the individual market street counters and in the store areas surrounding them. The market street is unique to Morrison stores, although some other chains were attempting to emulate it.

Chris Blundell sums up the philosophy behind Morrisons store design as follows: 'The whole idea, even the arrangement of shelves, is intended to provide visual variety and colour rather than regimentation. The management do not want Morrison stores to look like *another shed*.'

13.1.5 Product offerings

Morrisons did not regard their stores as *one stop shops*, although with over 27,000 lines in every store they were approaching it. They thought of themselves as grocers, even though they stocked a wide range of non-food consumables and durables, from underwear to electrical products. The complete range is stocked in every store, with variations in quantity (dependent on store size) and products to meet local tastes – such as regional beers. The company offered an extensive product range to customers, and their 1986 promotional jingle 'More reasons to shop at Morrisons' and the 1995 follow-up 'There's more, so much more, in a Morrisons store' were meant to reinforce this.

13.1.6 Sources of new product ideas

Product line development and branding strategies were significantly influenced by lower level inputs. New product offerings, for example, were derived from a combination of buyer initiative, suppliers, store staff and customers. Two examples of the type of developments carried out by the company are outlined below:

1 Product ideas which can be launched very quickly and with minimal risk (e.g. new packaging and the presentation of fresh food).
2 New merchandising/products which involve capital expenditure and higher risk (e.g. the *Market Street* concept fell into this category, as did the introduction of self-service *salad bars* – they both required extensive market testing because they were innovative and untried in the industry).

The gestation period for new products varied, with fresh food products taking less than two weeks to introduce to all stores. New additions to the brand range can take many months before they can be launched. A large part of this lead time is taken up with designing the product and the packaging so that it conforms to legislation and does not confuse the customer. It also reflects a deeper desire to not accelerate too fast when it comes to anticipating customer taste. For example, the company were one of the first chains to introduce bottled spring water, and it was poorly received before it became an industry-wide success.

13.1.7 Brands

In 1994, 40–45 per cent of sales were derived from Morrison's own brands. By 1996 this figure had risen to a little over 50 per cent. There are three distinguishable Morrison brands:

1 Bettabuy.
2 Farmer's Boy.

These two brands were confined to volume products such as bread, soft drinks, tinned food and lager, etc.

3 The Morrison logo was used on a very wide range of produce, from flowers, shampoos, washing powder and crisps.

The company policy on branding was not designed to restrict other brand varieties. Customers were increasing their purchases of Morrison brands because of the favourable prices compared with equivalent manufacturers' brands.

13.1.8 Pricing policy

In 1996, the consumer journal, the *Which?* magazine, conducted an extensive research of pricing in a wide range of supermarkets and concluded that Morrisons was the lowest priced of the UK superstores. This supports the stated pricing policy that '... the company is prepared to share some of its profits with the customers' (Chairman and MD report in 1996 accounts).

The pricing of groceries is also identical in every Morrison store irrespective of where it is located. This contrasts with other chains that have regional pricing policies. It was unlikely that Morrisons would introduce regional pricing as it expanded further south because competitive pressures would erode the ability of their competitors to maintain and/or apply differential pricing tactics.

13.1.9 Policies on shelf life

Grocery retailers need to turn their stock over very quickly to meet financial, hygiene and freshness objectives. These objectives were interrelated and interactive.

13.1.9.1 Freshness

All food (fresh food in particular) begins to deteriorate as soon as it is manufactured or, in the case of fresh food, when it is taken out of chill. *Sell by* and *Use by* dates are therefore determined by freshness, hygiene and safety.

Fresh foods such as meat, fish and pre-packed sandwiches have a shelf life of only one day. Milk has a shelf life of 4–6 days (it is usually sold within 2 days). Bread has a shelf life of only 2 days. Even products which have longer shelf lives such as preserves, spirits and tinned food are expected to be turned over every 2–3 weeks.

If forecast demand is over or under consumed the retailer loses turnover and profit because they will have to mark down product that is nearing the sell by date or dispose of it when it goes past the sell by date. Correctional mark downs are less than $1/2$ per cent of sales at Morrisons. If forecast demand is overconsumed turnover and profit are lost because the product is unavailable to purchase.

13.1.9.2 Financial objectives

Supermarkets operate on very tight financial margins, therefore high stock turns provide financial liquidity as well as profitability. Morrisons had a sales/stock ratio (which is almost equivalent to stock turn) of twenty-five times per year, which was amongst the best for the industry (see Attachment 14.2 in Section 14.3, page 194).

13.1.10 Sales-Based Ordering (SBO)

Matching forecasted with actual demand exactly is almost impossible. Morrisons regarded themselves as an industry leader in the application of technology to SBO procedures, particularly in the area of fresh food and perishable products. Perishable products include seasonal products with relatively long shelf lives and little value once the season has passed (e.g. Christmas confectionery, Easter eggs, Mothers Day cards). Products that were not perishable were not on the SBO system. SBO is a process which links the whole supply chain from supplier to consumer demand. It is a computerized system which processes historical demand for each day of the week and each week of the year moderated and updated by actual demand, actual stocks in the pipeline, and promotional and merchandising programmes.

13.1.11 Warehousing and distribution

The Wakefield distribution centre was approaching full capacity by 1993 and the company informed its shareholders (in 1994) that 'in the interests of greater efficiency and to support our further expansion, an additional depot will be established in the North West of England to replicate the Wakefield facilities in the very near future.' By 1995–1996 the Wakefield depot was operating at maximum capacity and additional capacity was being obtained through the use of subcontractors. On the 20 September 1996, when interim results for 1996–1997 were produced, the company announced a £100 million expansion which included four new store openings, nine store refurbishments and a new 700,000 square feet distribution centre at Northwich in

Cheshire, very close to the M6 motorway. A new 100,000 square feet extension to the frozen food facilities at Wakefield was also announced.

The depot at Wakefield had over 400,000 square feet of warehousing for grocery products, approximately 135,000 square feet of refrigeration for fresh foods and 46,000 square feet for bread and confectionery. The depot also contained a small office block where a significant proportion of the Board of Management operated from.

The company owned a fleet of temperature-controlled and refrigerated vehicles. Excess capacity was subcontracted to hauliers. In 1996, the Wakefield depot managed over 600 vehicle movements per day from over 80 loading/unloading bays and handled over 3 million cases of produce each week.

13.1.12 Supplier performance

The distribution depots (including temporarily subcontracted ones) were geared-up for 'right first time' deliveries against the three criteria of timing, quantity and quality of produce. Depot procedures were systemic and any variation from these criteria created a disproportionate work effort at the distribution centre, being immediately addressed by senior management. When produce was received at the depot the transaction time for dealing with it amounted to minutes, with supplier metrics being instantly generated for:

- timeliness
- shortages and short shipments
- damages
- produce quality.

Lateness and short deliveries had a severe impact on product availability within Morrison stores. This situation appears to contradict the views of a number of commentators, who suggest that superstores are protected from shortages by equivalent brand availability. It is argued that shoppers can choose more expensive or cheaper brands. Yet shoppers can also delay their purchase or go to another store for the brand they want. They may even stop shopping at a store if it does not stock what they exactly want. Research (Emmelhainz et al., 1991; Iqbal, 1997) has demonstrated that variable availability has an overall negative effect on customer loyalty and that this has a corresponding negative impact on turnover and profits.

Although Morrisons received few damaged shipments (well below 1 per cent) they had experienced episodes of incorrect product labelling, especially with wines from Eastern Europe.

All the companies' major suppliers were linked to Morrisons by Electronic Data Interchange (EDI), which provided suppliers with firm and forecasted demand requirements on a time-phased basis. It also eliminated paper transactions for ordering and invoicing. The company planned to eliminate 'slow mail' with suppliers before the year 2000.

The company is not overly concerned that their suppliers are accredited with quality assurance systems. They regard these as a means, not an end to assuring quality – Morrisons are more concerned with quality performance, than the number of quality manuals a supplier has. This performance emphasis placed new and existing suppliers under a lot of pressure. Manufacturers were frequently visited and audited to ensure that they had the systems, processes, capacity and quality control to meet Morrisons response time and quality criteria.

13.2 Technology and shopping developments

The company regarded itself as a leader in retail management information systems. All its stores were equipped with Electronic Point of Sales and Electronic Financial Transaction Point of Sales (EPOS/EFTPOS). The company was also monitoring newer developments such as whole shopping trolley scanning and Electronic Retailing Systems (ERS) – a system which uses radio communication connected to a Local Area Network (LAN) to establish two way links so that product prices can be transmitted to shelves whilst simultaneously receiving stock level data and promotional details.

There was a high degree of store management centralization, with new technology reinforcing this centralization. The management believed that buying centralization was an essential ingredient to success at store level. Their philosophy was that managers of stores should not be *order placers* (except for limited line items such as local newspapers) and should concentrate on the effective operation of each store. The centralization was managed through EPOS/EFTPOS so that stores, purchasing and warehouse management were provided with up-to-date demand/sales/margin information. Promotional sales labelling was also centralized through information technology, with promotional 'flyers' being produced through terminals at each store.

Developments in the short and medium term were thought to include new additions to customer service, such as the facility to pay utility bills. Cash points were common to most stores while *cash back* facilities were almost universal for customers with debit cards (cash back is a facility where the debit cardholder can pay for the goods and also ask for a cash sum – usually up to £50 – and the total is debited from the customers bank account). Cash back is an effective way of reducing the retailers cash float as it increases security and reduces banking costs.

The company were also evaluating customer *self-scanning* of products – similar to those introduced into Safeway *Shop and Go* stores. This is a service for customers who have extremely large weekly grocery requirements. Many of the major retailers also have loyalty cards (e.g. Tesco Clubcard, Safeway ABC) where points are credited to the card depending on the size of purchase and cash vouchers provided to the shopper when a specific points total is achieved.

Loyalty cards have many benefits for retailers including the identification of specific groups of shoppers for target promotion of their products. There are also costs associated including database administration costs. Morrisons appeared to be content in monitoring these developments rather than joining it, or as one senior manager pointed out, they emphasize *pounds not points* in their stores.

13.2.1 Store evaluation by management and customers

The company does not use mystery buyers to evaluate stores. Rather, senior management developed a *self-critical philosophy* by frequently benchmarking their competitors and making regular store visits, mostly unannounced. The Chairman makes at least four store visits every week. Senior management visits are designed to evaluate:

- the appearance of both the inside and outside of the store.
- how well produce is displayed.
- the level of customer service being provided.

This was supplemented by talking to shoppers. The purpose was to ensure that there was no gap between service offering and customer expectation. Research of customer perception by store management and senior management covered a wide variety of issues, including pricing, store layout, product range and merchandising.

13.2.1.1 Pricing

Customers thought that Morrison pricing was extremely competitive and that pricing was an important factor in determining where they shopped. The independent research by the *Which?* magazine, that was referred to earlier, supports the price competitiveness of the Morrison chain.

13.2.1.2 Layout

In addition to the positive feedback by shoppers to the fresh food *Market Street* experience, there was also some negative feedback:

- The store was too crowded with shoppers. This criticism was taken seriously by the management. For instance, the Marketing Director commented that 'It's amazing how an indicator of a stores popularity (and business success) could be perceived as negative. Nevertheless, we take the criticism seriously and there are ways, such as longer store opening times and additional checkouts, to reduce crowding.'
- Customers complained when overzealous store managers put up large displays, particularly fresh fruit, vegetables or flowers, at the start of the shopping journey though the store.
- Many customers asked for frozen foods to be moved to the end of the shopping trip. Management have been slow to respond to this issue because it involved major re-organizations to all store layouts.
- Shoppers were critical at the lack of self-selection of fruit and vegetables. Up to October 1996 there was no self-selection – all fruit and vegetables were pre-packed and bar coded. The rationale for this policy was that although self-selection might offer the benefit of higher fruit and vegetable turnover due to increased purchase sizes,

it was outweighed by the disadvantages of stock loss through damage caused by self-selection. This policy has been partially reversed (a reasonable range of produce could be self-selected and weighing facilities had been incorporated at all store checkouts).

13.2.1.3 Shopping trolleys

It has been estimated that over 50,000 supermarket shopping trolleys go astray every year in the UK. Morrisons lose hardly any because they have operated a *deposit* mechanism on their trolleys for over 20 years. The deposit (currently £1) is returned to the customer when the trolley is returned to a collection point – and perhaps surprisingly, there had never been a customer complaint regarding the system.

13.2.1.4 Trading hours and demand

Stores opened for 12–13 hours per day except on Thursdays and Fridays, when they opened for 14–15 hours. Sunday trading commenced in 1995 and was financially successful for all the superstores. Up to 1994–1995 Saturday was the busiest shopping day of the week. The introduction of Sunday opening changed this and sales demand in 1996 was distributed approximately as follows:

Sunday	8%
Monday	9%
Tuesday	9%
Wednesday	16%
Thursday	18%
Friday	22%
Saturday	18%

January and February tend to be low turnover months following the Christmas and New Year rushes. March and April is busy depending on when Easter falls, while July and August are very busy, particularly those located in tourist areas. In September and October there is a relaxation in demand, with the Christmas rush from November to December starting the cycle over again.

13.3 Human resource management and development

There were several programmes for human resource development.

13.3.1 Trainee management programme

This programme recruited in excess of sixty 'A' Level and graduate students annually. Trainees underwent a 2-year programme of *shop floor*-based development reinforced by company-based management skills courses. Many of the trainees also undertook postgraduate programmes such as the MBA. As stated earlier, almost all promotions, even to management board level, are internal.

13.3.2 Craft apprenticeships

The *Market Street* concept required specialist craft competencies in baking, confectionery, fishmongering, etc., with the company creating over 100 craft apprenticeships per year. These apprenticeships were predominantly *on the job* training programmes supplemented by classroom tuition. The success of these programmes can be judged indirectly by the fact that Morrisons were the first company to receive the *Seafish Retail Quality Award* for all fresh fish counters in 1994. In 1996, the chain was recognized as *Fishmonger of the Year* by the *Woman* magazine. They have also won awards for in-store butchery and from the *Pizza and Pasta Association* in recognition of the quality and range of freshly produced in-store pizzas.

13.3.3 Induction, shop floor training and communication

Morrisons believed that people can perform a job more effectively and efficiently if they know what they are doing. This is an obvious statement but part of Morrisons' success has been their ability to operationalize this. Their emphasis on training was necessary because they had a relatively high staff turnover rate (25 per cent of the workforce were casual workers, many of them being students). The induction and training programme for shop floor workers incorporate the use of *buddies* or *sponsors*. Sponsors were employees at the same company level as the new employee and they showed them how to carry out prescribed procedures and routines. The sponsor or buddy did not need to be an employee with long service, but he/she had to be a competent individual who had demonstrated characteristics suitable to mentoring (i.e. be able to communicate well and convey correct information to others). The buddy system also enabled store management to assess the capability of potential supervisors/managers.

Full-time and part-time recruits also undertook a 26-week training programme. The programme begins with a 4-week induction period (incorporating the *buddy* programme) concentrating on company policy and the industry in which the company operates, with the remaining 22 weeks focusing on the particular department that a new employee works in. Throughout the 26 weeks assessments are made so that the company can evaluate the performance of the employee and the performance of the training programme.

Morrisons also placed a high premium on internal communication, with prominent company noticeboards being displayed in the employee areas within every store. This provides a focal point for the diffusion of information from the top downwards. The noticeboard displayed information regarding company and store vacancies, corporate and social events, and store/departmental performance week on week compared with the same period in the previous year. The company also published a quarterly newsletter which included employee achievement and the company's financial performance. At regular intervals each store general manager and personnel manager chaired a meeting during working hours, attended by departmental representatives from the shop floor. The information flow at these meetings is said to be 75/25, i.e. 75 per cent from employees to management and 25 per cent from management to employees.

13.3.4   Enterprise 5 Trust

Human resource development cannot be concluded without some reference to the Enterprise 5 Trust, a charitable trust set up by Kenneth Morrison. The Enterprise 5 concept was initiated in 1986 and its objectives were to provide potential business people with a *head start*. The Trust became a reality when it was incorporated in the Enterprise 5 development in Bradford. Candidates on Enterprise 5 programmes usually undertook a 13-week development programme (three day per week) that covered: marketing skills (including market research), financial skills (including the development of credible business plans); operational skills, awareness of the legal aspects of business (including professional liability), presentation skills; IT skills, etc. An additional and larger centre was opened in Darlington in 1994. It included a purpose built 300-seat conference hall, a restaurant and twenty-one microworkshops. The Darlington centre organized business seminars – one of the speakers had been Eddie George, who was the Governor of the Bank of England.

Income flows for the development of the Trust had came from contracts for IT training for Darlington Borough Council staff and from Training and Enterprise Council (TEC) grants. These were supplemented with sponsorship money from banking and commerce. The Trust was self-supporting, but continually trawled for work in commercial training to support its core objectives. Over fifty successful businesses had been developed. Most of these were retailing businesses or suppliers to the retail sector (e.g. jewellery manufacturing and retailing, food retailing, market gardening, motor cycle accessories, dry cleaners).

13.4   Corporate governance and management structure

The Morrison organization had a very flat structure and a small board of executive directors (six, including the Chairman and Managing Director). There are no non-executive directors on the main board 'as the Board is currently of the opinion that there is no commercial benefit in appointing them'. Although the main Board is small the company has a very strong multi-disciplinary Board of Management (see Attachment 13.1 in Section 13.8, page 176) that acts like a junior board of directors. None of the main Board have worked for the company for less than 22 years, while the general level of continuity within Morrisons can be gauged from the fact that the shortest length of service in the company by any member of the Board of Management was 18 years. The Board of Management had twenty-three directors and its size has grown in line with the growth of the company.

The Morrison approach to corporate governance appears to be pragmatic, as the following extracts from the 1996 Report and Accounts on directors' remuneration demonstrates:

- 'The need to attract, retain and motivate directors of the quality required, but to avoid paying more than is necessary for that purpose.'
- 'What comparable companies are paying but taking account of relative performance.'
- 'The use of performance related elements (e.g. company performance-based share option schemes) to align the interests of directors and shareholders.'

At the store management level there were (in 1996) nine district managers who were responsible, on average, for nine stores each. Each store had approximately four levels of management including the store general manager. Sales, fresh food and personnel managers report to the general manager of the store. The remaining and front line level included department managers and supervisors who were responsible for shop floor staff. Average employment in the newer stores was 450 personnel. The organization of the business, as described one senior executive, was 'designed to add value, not cost'.

13.4.1   Vertical integration

According to the statement of the Chairman in the annual report 'where there is a commercial benefit in doing so, we are fully and uniquely prepared to take on and operate the vital functions which serve our needs. This is illustrated by our commitment to manufacturing and packing many of the fresh food products that we sell.' The policy is operationalized at store level where most of the *Market Street* units have extensive food preparation and manufacturing facilities. The company also has 100 per cent equity holdings in a number of manufacturing and food processing subsidiaries so that they can be fully integrated within the Morrison business.

13.4.1.1   Holsa Ltd

This company manufactures polythene shopping bags and plastic packing materials for all store and packing requirements.

13.4.1.2   Farmers Boy Ltd

'Farmers Boy' was a Morrison brand but the Farmers Boy factory produces pizzas, pies, cooked meats, sausages as well as packing cheese and bacon.

13.4.1.3   Household Potatoes Ltd

This company cleans, grades and packs a whole range of vegetables which arrive in bulk from fields and cold stores. They concentrate primarily on potatoes and carrots and processed approximately 3000 tonnes of produce each week. The operation is also linked to W Todd (Potatoes) Ltd which is another wholly owned subsidiary. In addition Morrisons own and control many activities which other organisations regard as 'non-core', including distribution and transportation and project management.

13.5 Comparison of two Morrison stores

The two stores included in this section (Keighley in West Yorkshire and Skipton in North Yorkshire) are from geographically close but socio/economically different areas, and are illustrative of Morrison store development.

13.5.1 The Keighley store

The store was first opened in 1968. It was the fifth Morrison supermarket to open after the flotation of the company. Since 1968 it has undergone at least six major refurbishments including being totally rebuilt and increased in size. It was also one of the first stores in the chain to have a *Market Street*.

The Keighley store has 34,000 square feet of sales area, which is slightly below the Morrison store average. There are twenty-four checkouts and two surface carparks that can accommodate 600 cars, although it does not have a petrol filling station or a restaurant. The basement level is devoted to non-grocery products and a small range of consumer durables, and is accessed from the main shopping area by a 'travelator' – the shopping trolley wheels at the Keighley store are specially designed to lock into grooves on the travelator.

The store is located less than 300 yards from a large modern shopping centre (the Airedale Centre) and Keighley bus station. It is less than 100 yards from a covered market which was built in the 1970s. The major superstore competitor in the town is a similar-sized Sainsbury store that opened in 1984 and which has been refurbished twice. The Sainsbury development includes four adjoining units that are let to other retailers (e.g. electrical consumer durables and personal computing). The surface car parking capacity of the Sainsbury store is 500 and it had a petrol filling station (acquired in 1996) that was separated from the store by a main road. In addition to the Sainsbury store there were Aldi and Iceland stores close by.

Keighley is 9 miles north-west of Bradford. The Keighley conurbation, which includes the Bronte village of Haworth, has an economically active population of 47,000 in 23,300 households. The predominant industries in the town used to be woollen mills and engineering – almost all the mills in the town have ceased trading and many of the engineering companies have been rationalized. These older industries have been replaced by hi-tech service industries and newer engineering companies (some with foreign ownership). The accessibility of Keighley was improved in 1986 when a new bypass was built, as it had the effect of attracting more shoppers and industry to the town. Although the majority of Morrison customers do live in the Keighley conurbation, there is a large minority who come from other parts of West and North Yorkshire and East Lancashire including Bradford, Halifax and Ilkley.

13.5.2 The Skipton store

Skipton is 9 miles north of Keighley. The town is known as the 'Gateway to the (Yorkshire) Dales' and acts as a local and a national tourist centre. It is a popular market town with an open air market in an exceptionally wide High Street; trading on Monday, Wednesday, Friday and Saturday every week of the year.

The Morrisons store was opened in 1991 on the site of the old livestock market. The design of the store, particularly its entrance, reflects the history of the site. It has a retail area of 40,000 square feet and twenty-six checkouts, with four checkouts dealing solely with wines and spirits. The *Market Street* is more extensive than in the Keighley store and it has a large restaurant and a petrol filling station. There is surface carparking for 480–500 cars, which is important as there is a scarcity of parking space in Skipton during the summer months and in the period leading up to Christmas. In 1996, the company introduced a 'Pay and Display' regime to ensure that genuine Morrison shoppers had parking space (customers are compensated for the parking charge at the checkouts).

There is a Tesco store almost adjacent to the Morrisons store, which has been there since they acquired the site in 1987. The Tesco store is much smaller than Morrisons with a sales area of 16,000 square feet and twelve checkouts. It has a petrol filling station and car parking for 400 vehicles. Both stores are quite close to the town centre – approximately 300 yards. The Tesco store is popular with shoppers, even though a significant minority complete their shopping at the Morrison store because of the greater range of lines provided.

The only other major grocery competitor is the Co-op, which is much smaller than either Morrisons or Tesco. It was essentially a department store until 1995 when the grocery department within the store was doubled in size to 10,000 square feet and the checkouts were increased from five to ten. Checkouts at the Co-op were not EPOS/EFTPOS until 1995. Other competitors include the market traders and specialist retailers. Indeed, the variety of retailing in the town (including Rackhams-House of Fraser) is a major contribution to the town's popularity, and although the Skipton conurbation is less than half the size of Keighley it attracts regular shoppers from within a 40 mile radius.

13.6 Postscript to the Morrison case study

There have been many developments at Wm. Morrison Supermarkets since the case study was researched in 1996. Some of the most significant are listed below:

- Turnover is now over £4 billion and pre-tax margins are still amongst the best in the industry.
- The chain now has approximately 120 stores (an increase of 50 per cent over 1996), with major openings in the Home Counties, the West Country, London, Wales and East Anglia.

- The chain is planning to open three new stores in Scotland in 2003/2004. This may be linked to the bid for Safeway (see below).

- The Keighley store which is featured in the case is currently (2003) undergoing a major refurbishment which will increase the sales area to 40,000 square feet (including an extension to the store's *Market Street*) and provide a restaurant and petrol filling station. The refurbishment is due to be completed in the Autumn of 2003 and is currently 6–7 weeks ahead of schedule.

- In January 2003, the company was ranked No. 10 by *Management Today* from all the companies in the FTSE 100. Inside that ranking the company was placed at No. 1 in terms of 'financial solidity'.

- Perhaps most significantly, in January 2003 the company made a friendly bid for the Safeway group. Safeway shareholders were offered 1.32 Morrison shares for every Safeway share – valuing Safeway at £2.9 billion. At the time of writing (April 2003), this offer (and subsequently offers from Tesco, ASDA/Wal-Mart and Sainsbury) were being considered by the UK Office of Fair Trading (OFT).

13.7 Indicative questions

To answer some of these questions adequately you may need to undertake more contemporary secondary research to supplement the case.

1 Evaluate Morrisons business, marketing and operations strategy and assess its effectiveness relative to the competition.

2 Is Porter's industrial model – and analysis of generic strategies – an appropriate analytical framework for the grocery retail industry generally and the Morrison chain in particular?

3 In August 1999, the ASDA chain was taken over by the giant American retailer Wal-Mart.

- What are the implications for the whole of the UK grocery and why?

- Who, in the industry, are likely to be most vulnerable to this restructuring of the sector and why?

- What threats might it pose for Morrisons in the short term (to 2002); medium term (to 2006) and longer term (say to 2010)?

4 On pages 174–175 in Chapter 14 there is a discussion regarding the nature of competition [or lack of it] in the supermarket industry. Where on the continuum from perfect competition to 'a useful example of a cartel...' do the major chains lie? In your analysis use other arguments than those used on pages 174–175.

5 On page 175 in Chapter 14 there is a statement: '[The Supermarkets] have developed new paradigms for effective supply chain

management, which many organizations in non-food manufacturing are attempting, or would dearly love to emulate

- What aspects of supermarket supply chains would these manufacturers 'dearly love to emulate and why'?
- What are the performance standards, both qualitative and quantitative, which make 'supermarket benchmarking' such an attractive proposition for manufacturers outside the food industry?

13.8 Appendix

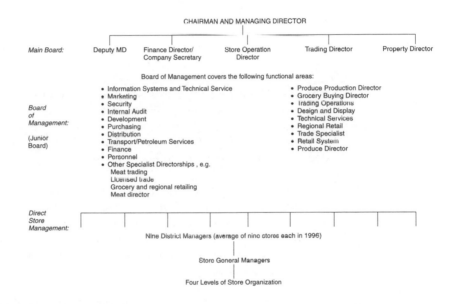

Attachment 13.1
Organization structure at Morrison.

13.9 Acknowledgements

This case study has benefited enormously from the assistance and support of Chris Blundell, the Marketing Director of Wm. Morrison Supermarkets PLC and Bob Sowman, the Director of the Wm. Morrison Enterprise Trust. Valuable information was also provided by Marks & Spencer, Safeway, Sainsbury, Somerfield, KwikSave, Tesco, Waitrose, Budgens, Asda, Co-operative Retail Services and the Co-operative Wholesale Society.

CHAPTER 14

The UK supermarket sector in 1996

The growth of the superstore is a phenomenon of the last half of the twentieth century, and it is generally accepted that they have provided consumers with more and cheaper products. Superstore growth accelerated with the increasing mobility of consumers. Other factors contributing to the attractiveness of superstores include:

- the increasing affluence of consumers.
- changes in consumer lifestyles, particularly since the 1970s.
- the convenience of one-stop shopping for the consumer.
- an increasing range of customer preferences based on their own experiences (e.g. increasing foreign travel and the increased sales of exotic foods and wine).

Superstores have had a significant impact on the retailing sector, with 504,800 retail outlets in 1971 reducing down to 320,000 units by 1995 (the fastest rate of decline occurred from 1980 onwards). As Figure 14.1 demonstrates the market share of the four largest grocers of Tesco, Sainsbury, Asda and Safeway rose from just over 35 per cent in 1990 to almost 42 per cent in 1996. This increases to 58 per cent for the nine largest supermarket chains. They had over 63 million square feet of retail space and almost £50 billion of sales from over 3600 stores (see Attachment 14.2c in Section 14.3, page 195).

The Times made the following comments on price competition in this sector.

Received wisdom has it that the big supermarkets, after years of overcharging us all for our basic needs, have been forced by store-wars to cut back on their greed and hand over some of their loot to the shoppers through lower prices. Received wisdom is wrong on both fronts

(The Times, 18th September 1996, *Pile it high, sell it dear*)

	1990	1991	1992	1993	1994	1995	1996	Est. 1997
Market size £ billion	58.3	63.0	67.3	70.8	74.1	78.2	80.5	85.2
Index of growth 1990–100	100	108	115	121	127	134	138	146
	Market Share %							
Tesco UK	10.0	10.2	10.4	10.7	11.7	13.7	14.2	15.1
*J Sainsbury UK	11.3	11.6	12.3	12.4	12.6	12.5	12.3	12.6
Safeway (Argyll)	7.3	7.4	7.5	7.7	7.8	7.5	7.7	7.8
Asda	7.0	6.7	6.5	6.7	6.9	7.4	7.7	8.0
Somerfield/Gateway	5.2	4.8	4.4	4.4	4.5	4.3	4.2	4.2
KwikSave	2.8	3.3	3.9	4.2	4.1	4.3	4.3	4.1
M&S Food UK	3.5	3.3	3.2	3.2	3.3	3.2	3.3	3.2
Wm. Morrison	1.4	1.7	1.8	2.0	2.3	2.5	2.5	2.7
Waitrose	1.8	1.7	1.7	1.6	1.6	1.8	1.8	1.8
Iceland	1.2	1.3	1.5	1.6	1.7	1.7	1.6	1.6
Total	51.5	52.0	53.2	54.5	56.5	58.9	59.6	61.1
Other large businesses (including Co-op)	22.5	23.4	23.8	23.6	23.1	21.8	22.5	22.4
Total large businesses	74.0	75.4	77.0	78.1	79.6	80.7	82.1	83.5
Small retailer	26.0	24.6	23.0	21.9	20.4	19.3	17.9	16.5
Total	100	100	100	100	100	100	100	100

*Share for J Sainsbury includes Savacentre.

Figure 14.1
Percentage market share of sales in UK.
Sources: The Grocer, MINTEL and extrapolation based on economic growth and planned new store openings and closures during 1996–1997.

It was also suggested that large supermarket chains were 'a useful example of a cartel in operation....*the supermarkets for all the appearance of cut-throat competition are still doing very nicely indeed*'.

Even though differences of opinion exist on competition, the following observations can be made:

- Superstores provided consumers with an increasing variety of produce at much lower prices than before their conception.
- Their buying power is such that manufacturers, particularly in the food sector, are driven to higher standards of efficiency and effectiveness.
- They had developed new paradigms for supply chain management, which many organizations in non-food manufacturing were attempting to emulate.
- They had developed new standards of service that were being copied by smaller retailers.
- Pre-tax margins of 6 per cent by the best performing chains were poor compared to other industries.

14.1 Foodstore classification

Coopers and Lybrand and Malcolm McDonald (1996) provided a broad classification of foodstores together with a range of their strengths, weaknesses and net prospects. The classification comprised:

- Hypermarkets.
- Superstores.
- Discounters.
- Convenience stores.

14.1.1 Hypermarkets

The term hypermarket is reserved for outlets with more than 50,000 square feet of retail area. Their main characteristics are:

- Large food and non-food ranges with product lines that range from 30,000 to 60,000 or more items.
- They have large car parking facilities, usually owned by the store.
- Their size provides them with economies of scale and, therefore, 'value prices'.

McDonald concludes that the major threats to hypermarkets are their anonymous format which provides limited consumer interaction. Planning legislation was also limiting their growth. Their net prospects were poor according to McDonald because they were in 'danger of becoming dinosaurs'.

14.1.2 Superstores

Superstores are sometimes defined as stores with retail areas of 25,000–50,000 square feet. Superstore characteristics were outlined such that:

- They are a 'one-shop' grocery store with product lines that range from 15,000 to 30,000 items.
- They can develop strong brand formats.

More negatively, the superstores of the different chains were deemed to look increasingly similar, and as with hypermarkets, planning restrictions were constraining their growth.

14.1.3 Discounters

These stores usually had less than 10,000 square feet retailing area. They had very focused offers with product ranges sometimes not exceeding 1000 items. KwikSave was a major player in this area, but the discount sector had fragmented with the entrance of players such as Aldi and Netto within the UK market. There was also pressure on this sector from mainstream competition.

14.1.4 Convenience stores

These stores rarely exceed 7000 square feet and they had long opening hours to meet emergency needs. Many of the large players were entering this sector (e.g. Tesco with their Metro stores). There were also a number of competitive pressures, such as:

- ▦ Opening hours of larger stores were being extended to match the convenience stores.
- ▦ The lack of planning regulations to restrict the development of competitor locations.

These classifications were broad and somewhat simplistic, and they did not consider the dynamics of the industry, such as the development of new technologies that facilitate online and virtual shopping.

A different approach to viewing foodstores is shown in Figure 14.2. It is a representation of customer perception based on price (from high to low) and

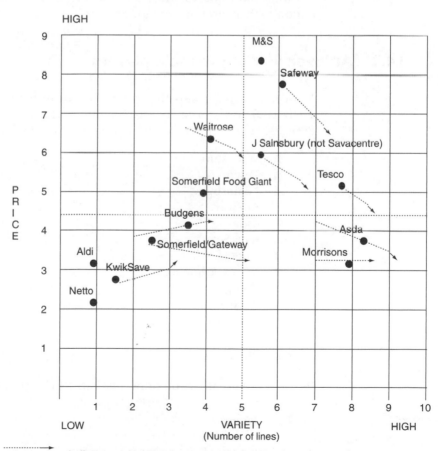

Figure 14.2
All moving to the same end point?
Source: (adapted from Cox and Brittain, 1996).

choice (number of product lines from high to low). This perceptual diagram was first produced in 1995 by Cox and Brittain, but has been updated and demonstrates the direction in which the major chains were moving (or where they would like to be!) in 1996.

14.1.5   History of the food retailers

Although there is insufficient space to provide a detailed history of their development, a 'key dates' overview of food retailers is included in Attachments 14.11–14.15 in Section 14.3, pages 200–204. The following conclusions can be drawn from the historical development of these companies:

- They tend to originate from very humble origins.
- Their histories enabled them to establish cogent and successful business philosophies.
- Business success has not been continuous as most of the chains have experienced episodes of retrenchment.

The suggestion is that one cannot understand these companies without knowing and understanding their historical development – from their foundation to their present configuration.

14.2   An overview of the main players

Brief histories of competing companies from their foundation to the years 1996–1997 are shown in Attachments 14.11–14.15 in Section 14.3, pages 200–204. The competition are reviewed in the following order:

- Morrisons.
- Tesco.
- J Sainsbury.
- Safeway.
- Asda.
- KwikSave.
- Somerfield.
- Marks & Spencer.
- Co-op.
- Waitrose.
- Budgens.

14.2.1   Morrisons

Please see Wm. Morrison Supermarkets PLC case study.

14.2.2   Tesco

Tesco became the UK market leader in food retailing after it had acquired the Wm. Low supermarket chain in Scotland, and by 1996 the chain had 545 outlets all over the UK. The company had also expanded into Europe with 109 stores in France (acquired from the Catteau Group in 1993) and five franchises near the Channel ports. They also had 36 stores in Poland and a 51 per cent stake in Global, a Hungarian chain with forty-five outlets (see Attachment 14.11 in Section 14.3, pages 200–201).

The growth of Tesco had been mainly through successful acquisitions. In 1954, Jack Cohen's (Tesco's founder) winning formula was still 'pile it high, sell it cheap' and it was in that year that Ian Maclaurin (now Lord Maclaurin) became the company's first management trainee. When Ian Maclaurin became Chairman of the company in 1985 he worked hard to find his own equivalent of Jack Cohen's formula. In addition to acquisitions, it involved developing a wider range of stores (not just superstores) and increasing the service programmes within the stores, such as healthy eating initiatives, nursing rooms, pharmacies, etc. By 1991 Tesco had also become the largest independent petrol retailer in the UK. Their leadership in petrol retailing had stimulated fierce competition, particularly after Esso introduced its *Pricewatch* campaign in 1995, reducing fuel turnover at supermarkets by 15 per cent from 1995 to 1996.

The introduction of the customer loyalty card *Clubcard* in 1995 was important in propelling Tesco ahead of its major rival, Sainsbury. *Clubcard* was developed into a *Clubcard* plus *debit card* in 1996 making them the first mover into supermarket banking. In 1996, Tesco claimed to have 8 million *Clubcard* members. It also provided extensive information on the shopping habits of their mainstream shoppers and of minority customer groups such as vegetarians and diabetics. The basic *Clubcard* scheme was expanded in 1996 for frequent shoppers such as students and pensioners whose spending did not always exceed the £10 minimum to qualify for points.

Tesco have four store categories in the UK:

1 *Superstores* Over 25,000 square feet with a large product range and surface car parking: half of the selling space of the Tesco chain was accounted for by superstores. Each superstore, depending on size, stocked about 14,000 lines.

2 *Compact* Smaller superstores below 25,000 square feet. The Skipton store referred to earlier would fall into this category.

3 *Metro* This was a new format – a return to the high street or city centre. They were relatively small stores with selected lines to attract town centre shoppers, e.g. convenience foods, sandwiches, fresh foods, newspapers and wines and spirits. The Metro store was described by one commentator as 'the bijou as opposed to the hypermarket'. There were just over 20 Tesco Metro stores in the UK in 1996.

4 *Express* A combination of convenience store plus petrol station (very similar to Budgens convenience stores) with a relatively narrow product offering. There were only 8 Tesco Express stores in the UK in 1996.

Although the Metro and Express stores were quite successful, preferred new store development was between 40,000 and 65,000 square feet. The average size of stores opened during 1995–1996 was 30,700 square feet (in 1994–1995 it was 28,200 square feet).

The company had four methods of warehousing and distribution:

1 *Regional ambient distribution centre* These were for room temperature products (dry groceries). There were five centres in England and one in Scotland – each centre was about 300,000 square feet.

2 *Bonded warehouses* There were two of these centres, each operating under HM Customs and Excise bonding.

3 *National centres* These were for slower moving and more durable lines such as hardware and textiles. There were also three centres that handled health and beauty lines with a maximum size of 350,000 square feet capacity.

4 *Composite distribution centres* There were eight composite centres in the Tesco warehousing network. They were 'composite' because they handled every type of fresh and frozen food. They are similar to, but not as large as, Morrison distribution centres. Tesco had eight composite centres, each of approximately 250,000 square feet. The introduction of composite centres in conjunction with multi-temperature chambers in vehicles had enabled the group to reduce the total number of distribution centres from thirty-eight to nineteen.

The company operated two systems for SBO – one for fresh foods (fruit, vegetables, milk cheese, etc.) and one for longer life products (cereals, tinned foods, wine, etc.). In 1995, approximately three-quarters of Tesco stores were running the short life SBO system and 95 per cent using the long life system. Tesco also had long experience of EDI. In 1984, the company began sending orders electronically to ten major suppliers. In 1987, Tesco joined Tradanet, the world's largest EDI service and was able to transmit 20 megabytes of data every hour. In 1992, Tesco became the first UK retailer to use EDI with over 1000 suppliers. Tesco could send forecast, as well as actual, orders to suppliers which enabled the supply side to adjust capacity in the short term.

14.2.3   J Sainsbury PLC

J Sainsbury's growth had been through acquisition or joint venture followed by acquisition. For example, the first *Savacentre* hypermarket was opened in 1979 and was a 50/50 joint venture with British Home Stores. There were 12 *Savacentre* stores each with an average retailing area of over 86,000 square feet in 1996. More than 35,000 square feet of these stores got devoted to non-food products including clothes and textiles, and wide ranges of white goods and audio-visual products. A typical *Savacentre* stocked over 62,000 lines.

In 1979, it undertook another joint venture with the Belgian retailer GIB (Sainsbury had a controlling interest of 75 per cent). This was an intentional diversification into the DIY market. The new chain was called *Homebase* and by 1995 there were 83 *Homebase* stores. In 1996, the *Homebase* outlets were considerably increased to 310 with the acquisition of the underperforming

Texas chain. The expectation was that the Texas stores would be fully integrated into the *Homebase* format and systems by 2000 (see Attachment 14.12 in Section 14.3, pages 201–202).

Sainsbury became an international company before Tesco, though its sights were on the North American market rather than on Europe. As long ago as 1977, J Sainsbury had made a strategic decision to invest in the USA and in 1983 they purchased a minority interest in *Shaws*. Sainsbury gained full control of Shaws in 1987. The rationale for the original investment was threefold (Williams, 1994):

1 Sainsbury wished to benchmark the retail technology used by Shaws. (They were a pioneer of bar code scanning and EPOS systems – Shaws had been experimenting with this technology as early as 1974.)

2 The background and culture of the two companies were almost identical (Shaws was founded in 1860).

3 Sainsbury also wished to benchmark American retail trading as opposed to the retail ethos of Europe. Sainsbury regarded the American market as far more dynamic and challenging than that of Europe. Shaws had 96 stores with a total sales area of just over 3.1 million square feet (roughly the same size as Morrisons) in 1996.

In 1994, the group acquired a 16.7 per cent interest (including 50 per cent of the voting shares) in *Giant Food* which has 166 outlets on the American Eastern seaboard. As mentioned earlier, operating margins are less in the USA – Shaws and Giant Food were 3 per cent and 4 per cent compared to the 6 per cent group operating margin (and 7.5 per cent for UK food retailing) at Sainsbury (see Attachment 14.2b in Section 14.3, page 194).

Despite the group's diversification (some commentators describe them as 'diversions') the core of the operation was J Sainsbury Supermarkets which account for 75 per cent of turnover and 87 per cent of operating profit – although the profit in this sector slipped by £40 million in 1996 compared to that in 1995. There were 363 Sainsbury Supermarkets all over the UK in 1996 (Tesco had 545 stores). The average Sainsbury store was slightly larger than a Tesco store (26,900 square feet compared to 25,600 square feet).

Many financial commentators have been critical of Sainsbury's strategy, citing inconsistency and slow response to changing market conditions as major weaknesses. For example, when Tesco introduced their Clubcard in 1995 the Chairman, David Sainsbury, regarded it as just another form of 'trading stamp'. (The Sainsbury family had been instrumental in drafting trading stamp regulations which eventually forced Tesco to discontinue using them in 1977.) Yet 6 months after the introduction of Clubcard, Sainsbury launched their own reward card. Some regarded the policy change as a knee-jerk reaction. Sainsbury were also slow to respond to the price wars that were initiated principally by Tesco in the early 1990s. The *unbeatable value* campaign launched by Tesco in September 1996 featured discounts on 600 popular products and was said to have costed £30 million. At almost the same time Sainsbury launched its *Autumn value* campaign featuring 700 products.

14.2.4   Safeway PLC

Founded in 1977, Safeway stores was acquired by the Argyll Group in 1987. The Argyll Group changed its name to Safeway PLC in July 1996 so that it was more aligned to, and reinforced, its Safeway stores core business. They also owned the much smaller Presto stores. The group had a very mixed store portfolio and variable performance up until 1994–1995. This is when the company drastically reduced the number of stores by divesting the Lo-Cost chain (271 stores) and closing down small and underperforming Safeway and Presto stores. The intention was to change all remaining Presto stores to the Safeway format by 2000. An overview of the group's turnover and operating profit data is provided in Attachments 14.2a, 14.2b and 14.5 in Section 14.3, pages 193, 194 and 197, and it can be seen that turnover growth from 1991 to 1996 was only 35 per cent. Operating profit growth in this period was 48 per cent, which is better than its nearest rivals Asda and Sainsbury.

The company had a loyalty card programme – ABC (Added Bonus Card). This was market tested and rolled out to all its stores in 1995 (Safeway had 4 million ABC cardholders). In 1995, the company also commenced a rolling programme of checkout service improvements, with *improved service* and *value for money* being pivotal to the then innovative national television promotions. Each store had a Customer Service Manager, second in seniority to the Store General Manager. The task of this manager was to 'ensure customer satisfaction' and this involved obtaining customer feedback, sometimes through the use of focus groups. The company also used *mystery shoppers* who provided feedback to the store management and store action teams.

Not all the stores had EPOS – mainly at Presto stores – and the company had been busy developing SBO and EDI with their major suppliers. The company centralized their warehousing and distribution in six major cities supported by specialist centres for products such as frozen food and non-food items. This centralization of distribution had enabled the company to reduce the number of vehicles used by 5 per cent and provide a large saving in vehicle journeys.

One of the most important shopper orientated developments had been the *shop and go* concept. *Shop and go* allowed customers to scan their own shopping and use the ABC card. It was tested in 1995 and because it proved to be successful, it was rolled out to all stores with over 20,000 square feet during 1996. Self-scanning had involved new investments in trolley-based scanning hardware, which had to be user friendly and efficient. It also had to be integrated into the chain's retailing and financial information systems.

14.2.5   ASDA

Asda almost went bankrupt in 1992 due to earlier management decisions to expand by acquisition – they spent £750 million acquiring 60 Gateway stores from Isosceles (who were also in trouble). Long-term debt gearing exceeded 80 per cent in 1991, and this level of debt repayment stalled store development and the integration of Gateway into the Asda format. In 1992 a new Chairman, Patrick Gillam, was appointed, who, in turn, persuaded Archie Norman, the Finance Director of Kingfisher PLC (owner of Woolworths) to become the company's Chief Executive (see Attachments 14.2a and 14.13 in Section 14.3, pages 193 and 202–203). Archie Norman immediately set in train a financial recovery plan that involved a cultural shift in the organization. The first year of his incumbency was preceded by a new Asda mission statement:

> Asda's mission is to become the UK's leading value for money grocer with an exceptional range of fresh foods together with those clothing, home and leisure products that meet the everyday needs of our target customers.

Archie Norman was also ruthless in stopping the cash haemorrhage from the business, duly halving the Head Office headcount, cutting spending on non-essential items (only buying items that were essential to the running of the chain) and stopping all capital expenditure projects. It also involved terminating the employment of underpeforming store managers and reducing wastage and excess stockholding. These actions induced confidence from the City and Asda had a successful rights issue to refinance the Gateway loan and to provide finance for future developments.

The non-financial changes included:

- flattened structures at Head Office and in stores.
- first name terms.
- all employees were now known as *colleagues* (not as staff or managers).
- listening – *tell Archie schemes*.
- management style – mentoring, coaching and dismissal of 40 per cent of managers on non-renewable contracts over a 3-year period.

These cultural changes were a success, although the company still needed to review its antiquated information system and to evaluate the costs and benefits to be derived from new technology. A *blitzkrieg* approach to tackle the deficiency of their information systems was developed, with a budget of £32 million in 1995. It aimed to deliver:

- 'New availability' management systems.
- fully computerized cash handling.
- Online accounting system access by stores (OLAS).
- new fresh ordering system.
- voicemail, etc.

By 1996 sales growth was above industry average and the *blitzkrieg* programme was extended to a second year and focused on:

- Sales-based ordering.
- New labour management systems.

During 1995–1996 Archie Norman developed the *breakout* plan. This included a human resource breakout and concentrated on:

- employee (colleague) development programmes.
- hard targets for personnel managers to reduce labour turnover, absence, premium rate payments and minimum contracts.

Archie Norman became the Chairman of Asda in September 1996 and he was widely regarded as Asda's saviour by competitors in the industry and the City. However, even though sales rose by 45 per cent between 1991 and 1996, and operating profits advanced by 25 per cent (this performance is good but not spectacular for the industry as a whole), the number of stores only increased by two in 1996 (see Attachment 14.2c in Section 14.3, page 195).

Asda store sizes were 50 per cent larger than the average size of the stores of their competitors (Asda average was 41,000 square feet). Its product range was very large and included CDs, videos, and the *George* clothing range. Asda also spearheaded the campaign against the net book agreement and subsequently increased their book sales by 50 per cent in 1996. A cautious *wait and see* approach to loyalty cards appears to have been adopted as only 18 stores were involved in the scheme, and there was no evidence to suggest that it would be rolled out to all the stores.

Asda had eleven distribution centres in the UK (there were none in Scotland even though they had 28 stores). These distribution centres ranged in function from regional combined warehouses to fashion warehouses and slow moving goods warehouses. They also had multi-temperature trailers to supply their stores.

14.2.6   KwikSave

KwikSave was one of the longest established 'discounters' in the grocery sector and up until about 1993 was one of the most successful companies of this genre. It had however faced competition from both ends of the price spectrum: from hard *absolutely no frills* discounters such as Netto and Aldi at the lower end and the price initiatives of the mainstream multiples at the other end (Figure 14.2).

KwikSave announced a new strategy and period of restructuring in 1996 at a cost of approximately £105 million. This entailed the closure of 107 stores and the loss of 1900 jobs from its 26,000 employee base. Most of the store closures were to occur in Scotland (twenty-five closures) closely followed by the South-East of England and the London area. The company Chief Executive Graeme Bowler was confident in November 1996 that the group could relocate 90 per cent of the employees affected because of the '. . . high attrition and staff turnover rate'.

The new strategy was known as 'New Generation KwikSave' and included increasing their own quality label products covering 100 product lines (as alternatives to national manufacturers' brands) and an extension of their own *no frills* economy brands. This meant that there would be a three-tier choice of brand products. Other initiatives included broadening the produce range in chilled and convenience foods and in health and beauty products, and providing more fresh food produce. They also provided additional capital expenditure to refurbish existing stores so that they would be more *user-friendly* whilst simultaneously replacing or upgrading 75 per cent of their business systems. Projected capital expenditure for 1997 was £50 million rising to £100 million in 1998.

Commentators pointed out that KwikSave was attempting, with its extended brand choice and wider fresh produce, to compete with the mainstream stores where the range of choice was already available, and that '... the difficulty will be to distinguish what it is offering from what their rivals offer ... the only way it can be done is on price, which means slimmer margins' (*Times*, 8 November 1996, p. 27). The commentator was also sceptical about the *New Generation* strategy: 'New Generation has a naff ring to it, sounding like a 1970s light entertainment dance troupe, so it is an entirely suitable name for the relaunch of Britain's naffest food retailer.... this is probably the last chance to extricate itself from the corner into which it has been forced.' The launch of *New Generation* was also accompanied by changes to the main board. A Marketing Director was appointed in October 1996 and a new position of Supply Chain and Distribution Director in November 1996.

The average size of a KwikSave store was quite small, being less than 7500 square feet. Income and retail variety was primarily through concessions that were operated by local independent retailers (there were over 1800 of these concessions in 1996). The concession arrangements are managed by Colemans, a KwikSave subsidiary. Most of the concessions provided fresh food and they were encouraged to adopt competitive local pricing positions. They were also encouraged to participate in national promotions organized and co-ordinated by Colemans Ltd. Concession income adds approximately £36 million per year to operating profit.

In addition to upgrading their business systems the group began centralizing their distribution systems – a new multi-temperature distribution centre at Wellingborough was integrated into the group's systems during 1995–1996. The operation of this site is managed by a specialist contractor, but the assets are owned by KwikSave. The opening of the new centre was followed by a phased closure of four smaller distribution centres. In addition to Wellingborough the group had a 225,000 square feet depot at Pitreavie in Scotland. It was converted to a multi-temperature centre in 1995. This particular depot was acquired in 1994–1995 as part of the acquisition of the 117 outlet Shoprite chain in Scotland (20 of the store disposals – mentioned earlier – are from this chain).

14.2.7 Somerfield PLC

Somerfield was successfully refloated as a PLC in August 1996. The earlier core trading format was Gateway, a chain which grew rapidly during the 1980s. In 1989, the chain was acquired for £2.1 billion by the Isosceles group in a highly geared take-over. Isosceles attempted to reduce the debt burden by selling 60 Gateway stores to Asda in 1990 for £700 million. Although reduced, the debt burden remained significant and several strategies were attempted, albeit with little success, to improve their financial performance.

In 1993, a new Chief Executive was recruited to undertake a financial reconstruction of Somerfield Holdings, the parent company. He was able to ring fence all but £500 million of Isosceles debts. He also ensured that funds were available for store and systems refurbishment. The key focus of the new strategy was to be on the Somerfield brand. Sales from 1991 to 1996 advanced by 9 per cent, although the rate of growth was 15 per cent between 1993 and 1996. Operating profits were down 30 per cent in 1991–1996, which was significantly better than the 90 per cent reduction from 1991 to 1993.

In 1996 there were 609 stores, with 343 being badged as Somerfield stores and 238 as Gateway stores. The remaining 28 were 'discounters' and were badged as Food Giant stores. There were no plans to expand the Food Giant chain and the Gateway stores were being disposed of or refurbished into a Somerfield format. The majority of Somerfield/Gateway stores (397) were held on short leaseholds. The average size of Somerfield/Gateway stores was less than 10,000 square feet, although the average size of new store openings was approximately 17,000 square feet. The company also increased their product range by enhancing the choice of fresh food and new Somerfield own brands. Somerfield stocked between 3000 and 12,000 lines depending on store size and geography.

In 1993, the company was poorly served by retailing and management systems since only 30 per cent of stores had EPOS. By 1996 over 70 per cent of stores had EPOS checkouts and SBO was being evaluated. Warehousing comprised fifteen main depots (+2 satellite depots) providing approximately 2 million square feet of warehousing. All of these depots were managed by logistics contractors and all transportation was contracted out to third parties.

Somerfield adopted a similar approach to Asda in the way it reduced organizational and human resource costs. The Somerfield headquarters was substantially reorganized, with poorly performing managers being replaced. The company also closed down over 50 under-performing stores from 1993 to 1996.

14.2.8 Marks & Spencer

Marks & Spencer were a large and cautious international retailer. It had a presence (including franchises) in most continents:

- USA – Brooks Brothers, Kings Supermarkets.
- Canada – Marks & Spencer.
- Hong Kong – Marks & Spencer.
- France – Marks & Spencer.
- Belgium, Spain, Holland, Austria, Greece and Hungary (franchises for St Michael brand).

The opening of the Marks & Spencer store in Cologne's Schildergasse – Cologne's equivalent of London's Oxford Street, was significant because it had a complete Marks & Spencer format. It transformed its UK slogan of 'Quality, Value and Service', into a broader 'Kein Kaufhaus, Weltanschauung' – 'Not a department store, but a world philosophy'.

Not withstanding its international operations, the UK outlets of Marks & Spencer provided the group with 85 per cent of its turnover and 94 per cent of its operating profits. There were 285 Marks & Spencer outlets over the UK with an average store size of 36,100 square feet. Food only accounted for 40 per cent of UK sales, and from 1991 to 1996 the cumulative sales of food only increased by 8 per cent. They avoided becoming involved in super-market price wars by relying on the goodwill of their non-food shoppers in recognizing the high quality of the St Michael brands. Factors negatively affecting food sales included the limited range in some stores and the fact that only 54 stores were opened for Sunday food retailing during 1995–1996.

Marks & Spencer stores were of varying sizes and carried different 'catalogue' ratings depending on location and sales volume. The rating determined the catalogue class of a store, with stores carrying a higher rating stocking a wider range of merchandise.

EPOS terminals were functional in all Marks & Spencer stores – in the 1980s the group invested hundreds of millions in information technology across the supply chain. The company knew (almost) exactly how much of a line item of stock the company had and its exact location, whether it was at the manufacturers as finished stock or work in progress, at a distribution centre, in a store or whether it had just been sold. A live system called MUWS (Multi User Warehouse System) controlled these various aspects of the business. They also developed a system known by the acronym ASR (Assisted Stock Replenishment). This is a non-food SBO system which works in conjunction with MUWS and EPOS. As an item is sold in store it registers via EPOS into the ASR processor which automatically checks if the item sold is in stock. If a minimum stock level is reached an order is automatically generated.

The company had a store-based customer ordering system (SBCO) which was developed in conjunction with ASR. It enabled a customer whose preferred line item was out of stock to order it in store (subject to its continuity) with a promise that it will be available within 3 days. Food produce SBO uses FSAS (food store allocation system). It operates on sales estimates and store trading patterns to ensure sufficient stocks are available for a day's forecast volume. It automatically adjusted itself to register stocks-outs or where high wastage was experienced. The system worked at a high level of immediacy, and the overall sophistication of the system, in conjunction with experience of sales and technical staff, were deemed to be contributory factors to the group's success.

Marks & Spencer claimed that 80 per cent of their food was sourced within the UK (a similar proportion for non-foods). Although they had many suppliers their preference was to single source through Northern Foods, a company that employed 24,000 people and who manufactured more than half of Marks & Spencer's prepared food. In the non-food area I J Dewhirst and Peter Black were their major suppliers.

14.2.9 Co-op

Robert Owen was a pioneer of the Co-operative movement, which together with the Trade Union movement became the foundation of the British Labour Party. The aims and objectives of the early Co-operative movement in the mid-nineteenth century included the banishment unemployment and poverty, the provision of services for sickness and old age, and the education of children 'thus making all people virtuous and happy'. The Co-operative Society began in Lancashire in 1844 when a group of workmen bought and sold goods and any profit made was divided equally among the group (the 'dividend'). The group was designated 'The Rochdale Society of Equitable Pioneers'. The Co-operative Wholesale Society (CWS) was founded nearly 20 years after the establishment of the Rochdale pioneers and by the end of the nineteenth century the CWS manufactured products ranging from biscuits to washing machines and wringers. The Society even bought an 800 acre tea plantation in Ceylon.

The Co-op became the largest grocery retailer (closely followed by J Sainsbury) in the 1950s and still provided a 'dividend' for its members until the 1970s. Perhaps surprisingly, the Co-operative movement was supplier-led and opposed the liberalization of product pricing and the abolition of resale price maintenance (RPM). More recently, it supported the RPM for pharmaceuticals, the net book agreement and the continuance of the recommended retail prices (RRP) system.

The Co-op was a quasi-political organization and consisted of forty different Co-operative Societies in the UK. They were independent of one another but shared similar 'Co-operative values'. There were two principal wholesale arms that served the societies: the CWS and co-operative retail services (CRS) – neither of them serving or controlling all of the sales of the retail outlets. The Co-operative movement had 4600 shops with 2500 of these being retail grocers. The movement had 76 superstores, although Baren (1996) noted that 'some of these operate with turnovers which other retailers would not consider worthwhile'.

Co-operative retail turnover included operations ranging from grocery retailing to funeral services. In the 10-year period from 1985 to 1994 total retail turnover value increased from approximately £5 billion to £7.5 billion. During the same period volume marginally declined. The turnover data for 1993 and 1994 is divided into three categories: food division, non-food division and services. A resume of turnover statistics is shown in Figures 14.3 and 14.4, and it should be noted that the growth in turnover value was less than retail price inflation for the period, which was a continuation of zero or negative real growth over the previous 9/10 years.

Retailing at the Co-op was being reshaped in a number of areas and societies:

- There was a greater investment in new store openings and many of the superstores were being refurbished.
- New and refurbished stores were being equipped with modern EPOS/EFTPOS systems, although few societies had EPOS fully integrated with SBO.
- There was an improved service ethic in the grocery outlets with more stores opening 12–13 hours a day (including Sunday), a wider choice and a higher availability of produce, and the abolition of antiquated practices such as half day openings.

The individual retail outlets still maintained some old habits, such as store managers still being able to return unsold seasonal stock to distribution centres if demand did not meet forecast, which made their stock turnover and store margins look better than they really were.

In late 1995 the Co-op announced that they intended to reintroduce the 'Dividend', although this was overshadowed and pre-empted by Tesco when they introduced their Clubcard.

Division	1994 (£m)	1993 (£m)	Change (%)	1994 Total (%)	1993 Total (%)
Food division Groceries; bread; meat; fresh food; wine and spirits; restaurants and catering					
Total	4954.1	4920.0	+0.7	66	67.3
Non-food division Textiles; fashion; menswear; footwear; furnishing; hardware and electrical; durables; pharmacy					
Total	1059.1	1065.6	−0.6	14.1	14.6
Services Funerals; motor and petrol; travel and others					
Total	1493.8	1325.4	+12.7	19.9	18.1
		7311.1	+2.7	100	100

Figure 14.3
Co-operative turnover data for 1993–1994.

	Largest change (%)	Change classification	Smallest change (%)	Change classification
Food division	+12.4	Fresh food	−2.6	Restaurant and catering
Non-food division	+5.3	Pharmacy and optical	−3.9	Furnishing; hardware; electrical
Services	+15.2	Travel	+2.3	Funerals

Figure 14.4
Largest and smallest per cent changes in each division.
Source: Co-operative Retail Statistics (data does not include results of the successful Co-operative Bank).

14.2.10 Waitrose (John Lewis Partnership – JLP)

The John Lewis Partnership (JLP) is a 'private co-operative' where the employees are the shareholders and operate an inbuilt profit-related/payment-by-results programme. Some of the principles of the partnership are similar to the mainstream Co-operative movement, e.g. labour should hire capital, not vice versa, and labour should keep for itself the profits generated by the business. The governance of the JLP is quite complex and the equity and control of JLP are held in trust by the John Lewis Partnership Trust Limited. There have been two irrevocable trust settlements (1929 and 1950) which determine the organization and control of the Partnership:

- *Chairman* Supported by a central board and principle directors. The latter directing functional operations of the business.

- *Central Council* The Chairman and directors must obtain the confidence of this council. The Central Council is a mixture of a parliament and a shareholders gathering. It is comprised of 130 members, 80 per cent of whom are elected to the council by secret ballot by employees. The other 20 per cent of the council is nominated by the Chairman. There are also standing committees such as the 'Committee for Pay and Allowances' which meets regularly to review, but not settle, pay policy or levels. There are also Branch Councils which usually consists of one Central Council member.
- *Central Board* This is, in effect, the main board. It consists of the Chairman, the deputy chairman and ten directors – five appointed by the Chairman and five elected by the Central Council. Principal directors and other senior management report to this Board.

John Lewis trading consisted of over 23 department stores and 112 Waitrose supermarket outlets plus a number of ancillary manufacturing activities, mainly producing furnishing fabrics. Waitrose accounted for almost 50 per cent of turnover and almost one-third of Partnership profits.

The motto of JLP for over 50 years has been 'Never knowingly undersold'. The Partnership states that this is the basis for providing good value (value for money). However the *Which?* magazine survey of 1995 rated Waitrose as the most expensive supermarket chain in its survey. The price differentials noted in the *Which?* survey could also be ascribed to the location of Waitrose stores: the majority were located in London, the Home Counties, South-East and Southern England. The most northerly store was Evington, Leicestershire. These are regions of higher personal disposable income and less consumer price sensitivity. This area of the country was the basis of Sainsbury's image as the 'middle class grocer', but price sensitivity had been increasing since the 1980s with the entrance of new competition and the dominance of Tesco. In 1995 and 1996, the Partnership opened two new stores described as 'Food and Home Stores'. They are a combination of John Lewis department stores and Waitrose stores with petrol filling stations.

The Waitrose chain was served by two regional composite distribution centres (Milton Keynes and Bracknell). The Milton Keynes depot was managed by a contractor and the one at Bracknell was operated by Waitrose. EPOS was not rolled out to all Waitrose stores until late 1995 and consequently SBO systems were in their infancy.

Like the Co-op, the Partnership management and employees had an aversion to Sunday trading: in early 1995 less than 25 per cent of Waitrose stores were open on Sundays but by June 1995 this had increased to just under 45 per cent.

14.2.11 Budgens PLC

A brief history of the Budgens chain is shown in Attachment 14.15 in Section 14.3, page 204. It was founded in 1872. In 1993, Germany's largest retail chain REWE increased its equity share in the chain to over 29 per cent. Budgens stores were located in the Home Counties, South-East England, East Anglia and the North and South Midlands. The most northerly outlet was in Derbyshire.

During 1995–1996 the company successfully extricated itself from the aggressive discount sector. Although operating margins were relatively low (3.3 per cent in 1996) they were predicted to rise to 3.5 per cent–4 per cent in 1997. Budgens store sizes ranged from 2000 square feet to 15,000 square feet with the average being about 6800 square feet. There were a number of Budgens store formats:

- *Medium-sized supermarkets* Which compete for the 'primary' shopper (10,000–15,000 square feet).
- *Convenience stores* In the High Street and in conjunction with petrol retailers such as Kuwait Petroleum Limited (Q8) and Mobil. There were eleven of these co-branded convenience stores in the group.
- *Village stores* These usually trade under the Budgens' fascia and were located in small communities to serve everyday shopping needs.
- *Fresh Save* These were price competitive supermarkets with lower margins and operating costs. Many Fresh Save stores were being converted to Budgens formats.
- *Metropolitan range* Almost all located in and around London, operating within a Budgens format, but supplying products with an emphasis on ethnic products, convenience foods and food for immediate consumption (e.g. sandwiches). This move is very similar to the Tesco 'Metro' format.

The company had a distribution depot at Wellingborough. It also owned a 46,000 square feet bakery plus a meat processing plant that was integrated with the Wellingborough depot. Excess capacity from these operations provided sales to third party customers.

Budgens were experimenting with free home deliveries in 1995–1996 within a 5 mile radius at one Home Counties store and the success of the operation was being monitored. In 1996, the company became the first UK supermarket chain to launch its own VISA card. This is a credit card which can be used for Budgens or any purchase elsewhere. The VISA cardholder receives a £10 Budgens voucher for every £200 spent in a Budgens store or £500 spent elsewhere.

14.3 Appendix

The Kiel University RSW system ranks company performance on three weighted measures, i.e.: Profitability (Rendite), Financial Solidity (Sicherheit) and Growth (Wachstum). For industrial companies these three measures are each divided into two components. However, the greatest weighting is placed on profitability 'R' (66 per cent). The remaining 33 per cent is divided equally between solidity and growth, e.g.:

Profitability R1 = return on equity before tax

(Rendite) R2   = cash flow as a proportion of sales

Rendite Score = R1 × 44.0 + R2 × 22.0

| Company | Rank 93 (92)* | Sales £billion | Profitability | | Solidity | | Growth | | Total Score |
			R1	R2	S1	S2	W1	W2	
KwikSave	22 (29)	2.32	36.1	6.7	55.5	6.0	13.0	17.7	87.43
Argyll (Safeway)	45 (40)	5.2	30.6	9.0	46.6	16.7	15.1	3.5	70.35
Tesco	81 (116)	7.58	22.3	8.9	59.1	7.1	14.5	5.5	47.74
Wm. Morrison	84 (110)	1.32	22.6	7.2	55.7	5.3	16.3	13.9	47.14
M&S	85 (99)	5.95	21.2	13.0	66.4	10.2	3.5	−2.7	46.77
Sainsbury	88 (91)	9.69	25.1	8.6	53.7	5.6	9.0	7.2	45.52
Asda	318 (84)	4.53	5.0	4.0	47.2	5.0	7.7	6.4	−40.37

Attachment 14.1
1993 RSW score and ranking of British supermarket chains.

*( ) = 1992 ranking.

Financial solidity $S1$ = equity gearing (equity/total capital employed)
(Sicherheit) $S2$ = liquidity ratio (acid test)
Sicherheit Score $= S1 \times 11.1 + S2 \times 5.56$

Growth $W1$ = real average growth of total assets (annualized)
(Wachstein) $W2$ = real average growth of turnover (annualized)
Wachstein Score $= W1 \times 11.1 + W2 \times 5.56$

It should be noted that the weighted scores are not simply added together to obtain the 'total score' in the right-hand column: the six fairly disparate metrics are 'normalized' through the use of a fairly complex statistical process known as z-transformation.

Note:
At least two critical observations could be made of this system of ranking company performance or any other (less complex or more complex):

1 Past performance (this is what the RSW scores are based on) does not guarantee future performance, e.g. KwikSave ranked 22 in 1993. They would not be in Kiel's top 400 at all in 1996 and Sainsbury ranked 88 in 1993 would probably be about 200 in 1996.

2 Even though the calculation of the total RSW score has a quasi-scientific appearance, the rankings from year to year appear to be quite erratic, even though the scores for each company are based on 5-year weighted averages. In addition there is no qualitative analysis (to the author's knowledge) to accompany the scores for each company. For example, Asda under Archie Norman was beginning to implement a recovery strategy for the chain in 1993.

These two observations alone would be sufficient to justify Kenneth Morrison's reticence in ascribing the group's success (recognized by IOD in 1993 and 1994) to some unique Morrison formula. As with Asda and KwikSave earlier successes could easily be turned almost into 'ashes'.

	Wm. Morrison	Waitrose* (J Lewis)	Budgens	Asda	Co-op	M&S	KwikSave	Safeway (Argyll)	J Sainsbury	Somerfield	Tesco
Chairman at year end 1996	K.D. Morrison	S. Hampson	C.T. Clague	P.T. Gilam	G.L. Fyfe	R. Greenbury	S. Keswick	A. Grant	D. Sainsbury	A.G. Thomas	I. Maclauran
CEO/MD at year end 1996	K.D. Morrison	S. Hampson	J.A. Von Spreckelson	A.J. Norman	G.J. Melmoth	K. Oates P. Salsbury A. Stone	G. Bowler	C. Smith	T. Vyner	D. Simons	D. Malpas
Year founded and founder(s)	1899 W.M. Morrison	1904 W. Waite A. Rose D. Taylor	1872 J. & F. Budgen	1965 P.& F. Asquith N. Stockdale	1863 CWS	1884 M. Marks later T. Spencer		1977	1869 J.S. Sainsbury		1919 J. Cohen
Date first became Limited/Public company	1967	1929 – first settlement trust		1965	n/a	1926		acquisition 1973 by Argyll 1987	acquisition 1973	flotation 1996	1932
Turnover 1996 (£m)	2099.4	1384.00	302.8	6042.3	4581.6⁻	7231.6 total 2847.5 food	3511.6	6069.4	13499 total 10909 J Sainsbury	3161	11560 UK 12094 total
Turnover growth (decline) (%)	88 (2 years)	12.6 (2 years)	7 (2 years)	33.4	19	55.9	40.5	28	47	1.6 (3 years)	70
Operating profit 1996 (£m)	126.2	Waitrose 53.2 total 172.8	9.93	316.7	73.3†	940.2 total 885.4 UK	71.5	417.5	829 total 778 UK excl. Homebase	100.5	713 UK 724 total
Operating profit growth (decline) (%)	83 (2 years)		130	76	(25) (3 years)	42 total	(–47) (3 years)	27.6	27 excl. Homebase	132 (3 years)	64 UK
Pre-tax profit 1996 (£m)	127.1	121.2 total	7.58	304.6	26.77†	965.8 total	2.8	125.5	760 total	91.8	675
Pre-tax profit growth (decline) (%)	102	76	196	251	(28.5) (3 years)	64	(–97)	(–7)	20.4	145 (3 years)	34.7

Note 'Growth' is cumulative 5-year growth from year end 1992 to year end 1996 except where stated.
* All Figures refer to Waitrose, unless otherwise stated.
† Based on aggregate of CWS and CRS turnover and surpluses and modified by approximate market share data. Turnover and profit data for 1996 excludes banking; insurance services; funeral services and commercial services which include travel agents.
n/a Not available or not applicable.

Attachment 14.2a Overview of grocery retail multiples in 1996.

	Wm. Morrison	Waitrose* (J Lewis)	Budgens	Asda	Co-op	M&S	KwikSave	Safeway (Argyll)	J Sainsbury	Somerfield	Tesco
Earnings per share(loss) 1996	10.67p		3.2p	7.96p	n/a	23.3p	(14.6)	26.4p	26.8p	23.4p	22.2p
Earnings per share growth (%)	63		129	563	n/a	73	(−130)	(−19)	4	266	23
Net assets 1996 (£m)	545.6	952.0 (J Lewis)	66.34	1657.7	984**	4142.2	435.5	1939.2	3543	722.2	3594
Net assets growth (%)	73.8	10 (2 years)	20 (2 years)	49	34 approx.****	55.9	29.9	34	7 (2 years)	(−40)	48.8
Margin on sales 1996 (%) (Operating margin)	6.01	6.8	3.28	5.24	1.6**	13.1	2.03	6.8	5.99 (group) 7.2 (UK food)	3.18	6.2 UK 2.1 Europe 6.0 total
Margin on sales 1996 (%) (Pre-tax margin)	6.05	3.66	2.5	5.16	0.6**	13.8	0.08	7.07	5.64	2.9	5.84
Sales/Stock ratio (times per year)	25.4	11.6 (J Lewis total)	17.4	23.3	13.9**	17.1	18.17	22.6	17.25	19.3	26.2
Gearing 1996			41.3	16.3	33***			12.8			

Note 'Growth' is cumulative 5-year growth (%) from year end 1992 to year end 1996 except where stated.
* All Figures refer to Waitrose, unless otherwise stated.
** Excluding Co-operative Bank.
*** Aggregate gearing of CWS and CRS for trading activities, excluding Co-operative Bank, i.e. net borrowing ÷ members funds.
**** Net asset growth for Co-op over 3 years for trading activities (excludes Co-op bank).
n/a Not available or not applicable.

Attachment 14.2b Overview of grocery retail multiples in 1996.

	Wm. Morrison	Waitrose* (J Lewis)	Budgens	Asda	Co-op	M&S	KwikSave	Safeway (Argyll)	J Sainsbury	Somerfield	Tesco
Number of stores (UK) 1996	81	112	106	206	4600 total 2500 grocery	285 (UK)	979	479 incl. Presto	375 excl. Homebase	609	545
Growth In UK stores (%) (decline)	52.8	2.7 (2 years)	2.8 (2 years)	0	n/a	8.3 6 years	27.4	(−41.5)	16	(−5.6)	37.6
Total stores including those outside UK 1996	81	112 Waitrose 25 department	106	206	4600 total 2500 grocery	640	979	479 Presto and Safeway	471 excl. Homebase	609	739 incl. five franchises
Total stores retail area 1996 (UK) 000s square feet	2903	n/a	687	8436	n/a	10300	7300	9264	10801 excl. Homebase	6029.1	13397
Retail area growth (%)	61.5		1.5 (2 years)	2.4	n/a	21.2 (6 years)	13.3	9.7	28.1	(−2.6)	38.7
Average store size (square feet) UK	35800		6850	41000	n/a	36140	7442	22700 Safeway 7800 Presto	26906	9900 Average 11000 Somerfield	25600
Weekly Sales per square feet 1996 £ (Note some figures include VAT)	15.23		8.48	13.77	12.1†	13.5	8.4	14.1	18.59 incl. VAT	10.13	18.31
FTE employees UK 1996	17526	18600	3370 approx.	39461	41940**	33170 stores only	18230	47592	70930 approx. supermarket only	23211	80650
Principle source of growth O = organic A = acquisition JV = joint venture	O		O and A	A and JV		O, A, JV	O and A	O and A	O, JV then A	A	A

Note 'Growth' is cumulative 5-year growth (%) from year end 1992 to year end 1996 except where stated.
* All figures refer to Waitrose, unless otherwise stated.
** Excluding Co-operative Bank.
† Based on CRS estimates.
n/a Not available or not applicable.

Attachment 14.2c Overview of grocery retail multiples in 1996.

Tesco PLC	1996	1995	1994	1993	1992
Turnover exluding VAT (£m)					
UK	11560	9655	8347	7581	7097
Rest of Europe	534	446	253	–	–
Total	12094	10101	8600	7581	7097
Operating Profit (£m)					
UK	713	600	513	496	434
Rest of Europe	11	17	8	–	–
Total	724	617	521	496	434
Operating Margin (%)					
UK	6.2	6.2	6.1	6.5	6.1
Rest of Europe	2.1	3.8	3.2	–	–
Total Group	6.0	6.1	6.1	6.5	6.1
Retailing Statistics (UK)					
Number of stores (UK)	545	519	430	412	396
Total sales area (square feet-000s)	13397	12641	11006	10352	9661
Average store size (square feet)	25600	24900	25700	25200	24400
Average sales area of stores opened in year (square feet)	685000	830000	790000	859000	889000
Full-time equivalent employees (UK)	80650	68552	60199	58046	59519

Attachment 14.3
Five-year financial, retailing and employee statistics.
Source: Report and Accounts.

J Sainsbury PLC	1996	1995	1994	1993	1992
Sales (incl. VAT and taxes) (£m)	13499	12065	11224	10270	9202
Operating profit (£m)					
Sainsburys' supermarkets	744	784	697	716	604
Sava Centre	34	41	38	36	28
Homebase	36	31	23	18	15
Texas	(10)				
Shaws (USA)	51	40	31	19	21
Group profit before tax (£m)	764	808	731	735	631
Retail portfolio – number of stores at financial year end					
Sainsbury supermarkets					
Under 15,000 square feet	49	49	49	52	56
15,000–25,000 square feet	87	98	99	99	98
Over 25,000 square feet	227	208	193	177	159
Sainsburys' supermarkets total	363	355	341	328	313
Savacentre	12	10	10	9	9
Homebase/Texas	310	83	76	70	64
Shaws USA	96	87	87	79	73
Total outlets	781	535	514	486	459
Average Sainsbury supermarket size (square feet)	26906	26304	25890	25310	24380

(continued)

Employees – Sainsburys supermarkets

Full-time	36082	33568	n/a
Part-time	79746	67911	n/a
Total	115828	101479	n/a
FTE (approx.)	70930	63245	n/a

1996/1997 Planned Store Openings:

Sainsburys Supermarkets	16 stores	460000 square feet
Planned extensions	25 stores	163000 square feet
Homebase	10 stores	401000 square feet
Shaws USA	11 stores	417000 square feet

Attachment 14.4
Five-year financial, retailing and employee statistics.
Source: Report and Accounts.

Safeway PLC (formerly Argyll Group PLC)	1996	1995	1994	1993	1992
Turnover including VAT (£m)	6500	6217.7	5982.9	5539.0	5039.3
Operating profit (£m)	417.5	382.9	364.8	387.0	327.2
Profit before tax (£m)	429.4	175.6	361.8	417.3	462.6
Fixed assets (£m)	2987.7	2795.5	2654.3	2279.3	1751.7
Net gearing	12.8	17.9	14.8	2.6	–

Retailing statistics – number of stores

	1996	1995	1994	1993	1992
Safeway stores					
Under 10,000 square feet	20	25	27	25	27
10,000–19,999 square feet	116	131	138	144	148
20,000 and over square feet	234	222	200	176	147
Total Safeway stores	370	378	365	345	322
Presto stores	109	169	205	216	212
Lo-Cost stores	–	–	271	274	285
Total stores	479	547	841	835	819

Average store sales area (square feet)

	1996	1995	1994	1993	1992
Safeway	22700	21900	21200	20700	20000
Presto	7800	6100	5500	5700	5300
Number of store with petrol stations	128	105	81	54	31

Attachment 14.5
Five-year financial, retailing and employee statistics.
Source: Report and Accounts.

New stores opening in 1996	17 stores	Average store size 30,600 square feet
New stores opening in 1997	16 stores	Average store size 30,400 square feet

	1996	1995
Total employees	66681	67323
Full-time equivalent	47592	47950

Asda group PLC	1996	1995	1994	1993	1992
Turnover excluding VAT (£m)	6042.3	5285.3	4822.2	4613.8	4529.1
Operating profit (£m)	316.7	251.1	196.7	190.0	180.0
Profit/(Loss) before tax (£m)	311.5	257.2	(125.9)	188.4	(364.8)
Gearing (%)	16.3	NIL	6.0	4.9	61.2
Number of stores	206	203	202	201	206
Total sales area (square feet-000S)	8436	8210	8134	8099	8241
Average store size (square feet)	41000	40400	40300	40300	40000

Average number of 'colleagues' employed by group

	1996	1995	1994	1993	1992
Total	73688	69366	70515	n/a	n/a
FTE	39461	36161	37473	n/a	n/a

Attachment 14.6
Five-year financial, retailing and employee statistics
Source: Report and Accounts.

KwikSave group PLC	1996*	1995	1994	1993	1992*
Sales (including VAT) (£m)	3511.6	3228.3	3020.3	2858.4	2498.2
Profit before tax** (£m)	2.8	125.5	135.6	126.1	110.6
Operating profit (£m)	71.5	134.1	135.5	n/a	n/a
Operating margin (%)	2.03	4.15	4.49	n/a	n/a
Pre-tax margin (%)	0.08	3.89	4.49	4.4	4.4
Number of stores	979	979	861	814	768
Total sales area (square feet-million)	7.3	7.1	6.0	5.4	4.9
Average store size excluding concessions (square feet)	7442	7282	6950	6620	6440
Number of concessions	1849	1864	1665	1560	1507
Concessions and tenant area (square feet-million)	2.3	2.2	2.1	1.9	1.6
Total employees	26081	25108	22502		
Full-time equivalent	18230	17642	15882		

Attachment 14.7
Five-year financial, retailing and employee statistics.
Source: Report and Accounts.

* 53-week years.
** Profit before tax after exceptional items (£87.5m provisions mainly for store closures), i.e. in November 1997 the group announced a closure plan of 107 stores during the 1996–1997 financial year.

Somerfield PLC	1996	1995	1994	1993	1992
Turnover (£m)	3161.0	3156.3	3109.6	n/a	n/a
Operating profit/loss (£m)	100.5	(27.4)	43.4	n/a	n/a
Operating margin (%)	3.18	(−80.8)	1.4	n/a	n/a
Number of stores	609	618	645	n/a	n/a
Average store size (square feet)	9900	9800	9600	n/a	n/a
Full-time equivalent employees	23211	24110	24507	n/a	n/a

Details of retail portfolio (1996 only)

Supermarkets	No. of stores	Retail area, 000 sq. ft	Av. retail space sq.ft		
Somerfield	343	3900	11000	n/a	n/a
Others (e.g. gateway)	238	1300	5000	n/a	n/a

(continued)

Discount Superstores					
Food Giant	28	800	29000	n/a	n/a

Size of supermarket store (square feet)	Number	% of total group retail space			
up–4500	173	10		n/a	n/a
4501–7500	123	14		n/a	n/a
7501–10,000	77	13		n/a	n/a
10,001–15,000	114	27		n/a	n/a
15,001–20,000	59	19		n/a	n/a
20,001–25,000	21	9		n/a	n/a
over 25,000	14	8		n/a	n/a

Attachment 14.8
Five-year financial, retailing and employee statistics.
Source: Prospectus.

NB: Somerfield were listed on the Stock Exchange on 2 August 1996

Marks & Spencer	1996	1995	1994	1993	1992
Turnover excluding taxes (£m)					
General	4090.4	3889.0	3718.6	3380.1	3325.2
Foods total	2847.5	2682.0	2612.6	2387.5	2341.4
Foods UK	2503.7	2374.5	n/a	n/a	n/a
Financial activities	178.9	135.7	122.8	109.9	98.2
Direct export outside Group	114.8	99.8	87.2	73.3	62.7
Total turnover (excluding taxes)	7231.6	6806.5	6541.2	5950.8	5827.5
Operating profit (£m)					
UK	885.4	847.4	790.2	665.0	622.5
Europe (excluding UK)	20.0	20.7	27.9	28.1	25.2
Rest of the world	34.8	28.4	36.4	28.7	15.3
Total operating margin (%)	13.1	13.2	13.1	12.3	11.7
Grocery/food as percentage of UK sales	34.7	34.9			
Total stores (UK)	285	263	n/a	n/a	n/a
Selling area (UK) (square feet-million)	10.3	8.5	n/a	n/a	n/a
Employees					
Total employees UK stores	50638	48994	n/a	n/a	n/a
UK Head Office	3448	3377	n/a	n/a	n/a
Financial Services	860	747	n/a	n/a	n/a
Overseas	10552	10213	n/a	n/a	n/a
Total	65498	63331	n/a	n/a	n/a
Approximate total FTEs	42906	41535			

Attachment 14.9
Five-year financial, retailing and employee statistics.
Source: Report and Accounts.

Wm. Morrison supermarkets PLC	1996	1995	1994	1993	1992
Turnover excluding VAT (total) (£000)	2111633	1811016	1550764	1331561	1124906
Operating profit (£000)	126190	114359	95964	79895	65433
Profit before tax (£000)	127099	116073	97845	83838	62649
Profit after tax (£000)	79199	73114	63184	54626	41809
Tangible fixed assets	815303	711209	603121	508970	435241
Increase on previous year					
Turnover (%)	17.98	15.66	16.84	17.78	22.91
Operating profit (%)	10.35	19.17	20.11	22.10	19.56
Profit before tax (%)	9.50	18.63	16.71	33.82	24.61
Profit after tax (%)	8.32	15.72	15.67	30.66	35.00
Tangible fixed assets (%)	14.63	17.92	18.50	16.94	26.4

Retail portfolio number of stores at financial year end

	1996	1995	1994	1993	1992
0 to 25000 square feet	9	10	10	11	11
25000 to 40000 square feet	57	48	42	37	31
40000+ square feet	15	14	12	11	11
Total stores	81	72	64	59	53
Petrol filling stations	60	52	41	35	27
Average store size (square feet)	35800	35100	34500	34100	33900

Employee statistics

	1996	1995	1994	1993	1992
Full-time	11413	10335	10049	8703	8066
Part-time	8846	7186	6324	5559	5102
Casual	6761	5679	4454	3520	3097
Total	27020	23200	20827	17782	16265
*Full-time equivalents	17526	15348	14325	12363	11391

Attachment 14.10
Five-year financial, retailing and employee statistics.
Source: Company Accounts and Reports.

* FTE calculation = Full-time + (1/2 × part-time) + (1/4 × casual).

1919	Jack (Jacob) Cohen invests Royal Flying Corps gratuity of £30 in NAAFI surplus groceries and sells from stall in the East End of London. 25 per cent gross margin on a £4 turnover on his first day of trading.
1925	First own label product – Tesco tea – derived from T E Stockwell (Tea merchants) and Cohen.
1929	Tesco name first appears above one of Jack Cohen's shops.
1932	Tesco stores limited becomes private limited company. Motto developed: 'Pile it high, sell it cheap'.
1935–1939	Modern food warehouse built and number of stores increased to over 100.
1939–1945	Tesco rationing introduced in advance of government rationing. Purchase land at Cheshunt (now Tesco headquarters) to grow fruit and vegetables.
1947	Tesco store (Holdings) Limited floated.
1950–1957	Number of stores grows to 180 including Williamsons acquisitions of 70 branches. First Tesco supermarket opens in Leicester.

(continued)

1959	First management trainee employed – now Lord (Ian) Maclaurin, current company chairman.
1960	Acquisition of Irwins, a chain of 112 branches in Northern England.
1963	Green Shield trading stamps introduced (abandoned in 1977 after trading stamp legislation).
1964	Resale Price Maintenance abolished after pressure from Tesco and Sainsbury.
1968	First 'superstore' opened in Crawley, Sussex, 40,000 square feet retail area, selling food and non-food lines.
1969	Jack Cohen knighted for services to retailing (Sir John Cohen).
1973–1976	New headquarters at Cheshunt built and opening of first 'hypermarket' near Manchester (73,350 square feet).
1979	Jack Cohen dies. Turnover exceeds £1 billion.
1980	Acquisition of Cartier, Kent-based retailer.
1982	First Tesco store with EPOS.
1983	Becomes Tesco PLC.
1985	Rights issue launched for superstore development programme.
1985 and 1986	Disposal of 48 stores.
1987	£570 million investment in 29 new stores and six new distribution centres.
1987	Acquisition of Hillards, West Yorkshire supermarket chain – 40 stores.
1991	Tesco becomes largest independent petrol retailer in the UK.
1993 and 1994	Acquisition of Catteau (92 stores in France); 51 per cent share in Global, Hungarian chain (45 stores); Wm. Lowe (57 stores in Scotland and the North of England).
1995	Launch of Tesco 'Clubcard' – loyalty card.
1995	Tesco becomes UK market leader in food retailing.
1996	Turnover in UK over £11.5 billion (excluding VAT).

Attachment 14.11
Tesco significant years.

1869	John James Sainsbury with his wife Mary Ann opened their first shop. J J Sainsbury describes himself as a 'Dairyman', selling: butter; eggs and milk. Very similar to Wm. Morrison's business. Their aim was to sell 'the best butter in London' – 'in London' was later replaced by 'the world'.
1918–1939	Chain of counter stores grew from 110 to 250 approximately.
1942	Company nearly goes bankrupt – sales only half of 1939 levels.
1950	First self-service store opened.
1950–1975	Average sales area of stores increased from 2000 square feet to 17,700 square feet. Sainsbury branches reduced from 225 to 201.
1973	J Sainsbury becomes a public company. 85 per cent of company still controlled by Sainsbury family. The share offer was thirty-three times oversubscribed.
1979	First 'Savacentre' stores opened. A 50/50 joint venture with British Home stores (BHS). A typical Savacentre now stocks in excess of 62,000 lines. (In 1996 there were 12 Savacentre stores.)
1979	Joint venture with the Belgian retailer GIB results in the DIY chain 'Homebase'.
1981	First Homebase store opened. (In 1996 there were 310 Homebase stores.)

(continued)

1983	J Sainsbury purchase a minority interest in Shaw, a New England (USA) chain. Purchased because Sainsburys wished to benchmark their EPOS technology and the background and culture of Shaw's was almost identical to Sainsbury's.
1987	Sainsburys gain full control of Shaw (in 1996 there were 96 Shaw supermarkets).
1989	Sainsburys acquire full control of Savacentre group. Sainsburys acquire full control of Homebase.
1994	After 1977 the company decided not to open any more Sainsbury warehouses and subcontract this area of their operations. In 1994 there were seventeen contractor warehouses, each of which is fully integrated with Sainsbury's information systems.
1994	Acquire a minority interest in another USA chain 'Giant Food'. The Sainsbury stake is 17 per cent with 50 per cent of the voting shares. Giant Food has 166 stores and $3.9 billion turnover.
1995	Company acquires 91 Texas DIY stores and commences to reformat them to Homebase standards. This integration is expected to be totally completed in 1999.
1995	Tesco market share overtakes Sainsbury's total food retailing share in the UK. (Heads begin to roll) – 'a number of changes were made to the Executive Board' (Annual Review 1996).
1996	Supermarket operating profits drop to £744 million (1995 – £784 million.).
1996	Introduces Reward loyalty card, 6 months after vowing not to do so, after Tesco introduce theirs. Sainsburys earlier described their loyalty cards as another form of trading stamps which they opposed in the 1960s.

Attachment 14.12
J Sainsbury PLC
significant years.

1965	Asda floated by Peter and Fred Asquith and Noel Stockdale of Associated Dairies. (The company likes to conclude that ASDA is derived from Associated Daries but the AS could come from Asquith. However the money came from both sides – Asquiths and Stockdale – and the idea was Peter Asquith's.)
1965–1968	New store built near Wakefield with free car parking. GEM superstore purchased in Nottingham (80,000 square feet).
1977	Asda moves south – opens superstore in Chelmsford.

More contemporary dates

1989	Asda booming. New store openings push up sales. 60 stores purchased from Gateway at £750 million. New £60m distribution systems opened. Asda third largest retail grocer.
1990	Gateway stores gained Asda identities. Policy to 'chase' Tesco and Sainsbury shoppers.
1991	Slow down in like-for-like Asda sales. Total sales growth slowing and margins slipping. Company attempts to increase prices to maintain margins but drives customers to the competition. Discounters such as Aldi also making some negative impact. Asda moving towards bankruptcy.
1992	'Asda in a mess' (*Financial Times*). Loss before tax of £360 million. City and customers losing confidence in the company. Gearing over 60 per cent (cost of debt for Gateway purchase). Patrick Gillam appointed chairman and brings in Archie Norman (ex-financial director of king-fisher) as chief executive. 'Recovery Programme' started.

(continued)

1993	Archie 'slashes' head office complement. Introduces 'Cheapest On Display' (COD), ruthless drive to reduce operational costs, waste and stockholding costs. New culture engendered in the organization – new mission statement – all employees now known as 'colleagues'.
1994	Economic recovery going well, but still a pre-tax loss of £125 million but gearing down to 6.0 per cent after a successful rights issue for refinancing the short-term Gateway loan.
1995	Third and final year of Recovery Programme. Company now turns its attention to antiquated systems and technology. 'Blitzkrieg concept' born with a first year £32 million budget to upgrade all systems. Company now making almost £260 million. pre-tax profit and zero gearing.
1996	Asda's 'first Year of Breakout'. Acquire the balance of equity in 'George Davies Partnership' (George brand – clothing). 'Blitzkrieg' continued with new investments, logistics, distribution and systems. Turnover above £6 billion. Pre-tax profit £311 million. Asda still third largest retail grocer.

Attachment 14.13
Asda significant years.

1882	A Polish/Russian refugee arrives in England. Starts selling haberdashery from a tray in a village near Leeds.
1884	Isaac Dewhirst, a wholesaler, lends the refugee £5. Michael Marks uses the money to buy stock from Dewhirst's warehouse. Marks trades in Leeds 6 days a week, he has no English and therefore for products which are not individually priced he has a big poster – 'Don't ask the price – it's a penny'. (Note: firm of I J Dewhirst is still a major supplier to Marks & Spencer.)
1894	Michael Marks seeks a partner. Isaac Dewhirst turns Michael down, but suggests Tom Spencer from Skipton, who had worked for Isaac Dewhirst. Tom Spencer invests £300 (representing half the shares of the business) and Marks & Spencer is formed.
1897	Headquarters moved to a warehouse in Manchester.
1903	The Partnership is registered as a private limited company. They now have over forty branches (twenty-four market stalls and the remainder shops, three of which were in London). The new company had a share capital of £30,000.
1904	Tom Spencer dies.
1907	Michael Marks dies at 48.
1911	Simon Marks born in 1888 becomes a company director.
1916	Simon Marks becomes chairman of the company. The company now has over 150 stores.
1917	Israel Sieff joins the board. Israel and Simon shape the Marks & Spencer strategy.
1924	Policy developed to purchase direct from manufacturers.
1926	Marks & Spencer becomes a public company.
1928	'St. Michael' brand used for the first time.
1931	Headquarters moved to Baker Street in the centre of London.
1935	Laboratories established to monitor quality.
1948	Food development department established with strict QA controls. (M&S has been selling ice-cream, confectionery and biscuits since 1920 and in the 1930s a wider range of canned and fresh food.)
1956	New systems and a 'Good housekeeping' campaign introduced to simplify systems.
1964	Israel Sieff appointed chairman on the death of Simon Marks.

(continued)

1975	Stores opened in France and Belgium.
1977	M&S becomes the UK's largest importer of clothing.
1985	St Michael Financial Services launches the M&S chargecard.
1988	M&S acquires: Brooks Brothers (US clothing company); Kings supermarket chain USA (16 stores); St Michael franchise shops are opened in Hungary.
1990	Sales on M&S chargecard exceeds £1 billion.
1989–1996	Franchise operations grow to 50,000 feet retailing space from 81 stores in 19 countries.
1996	M&S moves into 'over the counter' pharmaceuticals with the St Michael brand challenging Boots and Lloyds chemists (market estimated at £1.2 billion).
1996	Opens new store in Cologne, Germany.
1996	M&S announces that it is opening stores in Australia.

Attachment 14.14
Marks & Spencer
significant years.

1872	John and Frederick Budgen establish a chain of grocery stores in Maidenhead, Thames Valley and East Anglia.
1920	Business sold to Alfred Button and Sons Ltd of Uxbridge.
1957	Chain grows to 100 stores; business sold to Cambooker (present day Booker) who financed changes to self-service outlets. Budgen fascia reintroduced after 40 years.
1984	Budgen acquires Bishops grocery chain.
1986	Budgen was acquired by Barker and Dobson group. Large scale upgrading of stores.
1989	Central distribution depot opened in Wellingborough.
1990	Older Budgen stores were sold to Betta and Marks & Spencer. Retained outlets renamed Budgens.
1992	Budgens acquires Gilsons of Slough – craft bankers.
1993	REWE of Germany, acquires 26 per cent share which subsequently increases to 29.4 per cent
1995	Meat processing plant added to Wellingborough depot. Budgens and Kuwait Petroleum Ltd (Q8) establish co-branded petrol forecourts. Also Budgens convenience stores on BP sites.
1996	Budgens launches its own VISA card first in the UK for a supermarket chain. Acquires family-owned grocers (Carters). Budgens most northerly store opened in Derbyshire.
For 1997	'Price Promise' campaign extensively advertised in national press and regional TV to celebrate 125th anniversary.

Footnote:
The company operates four types of stores within the Budgens format:
1   Medium-sized supermarket (primary shoppers);
2   Small village stores (everyday shopping needs);
3   Convenience stores in the High Street with petrol forecourts;
4   Stores, mainly in London, offering a larger range of ethnic and convenience food.
The company also operates 'Freshsave' stores which are discount supermarkets.

Attachment 14.15
Budgens PLC
signifaicant years.

CHAPTER 15

Delamere Pottery Limited

(Case date: 2002)

Delamere Pottery Limited is a small medium enterprise which manufactures earthenware tableware for the mid-price range market. This means that their products were neither fine bone china that demanded premium prices nor economy earthenware with low margins of the type frequently found in discount stores.

The Company is located in Stoke-on-Trent in Staffordshire, the heart of the UK pottery industry. Delamere Pottery commenced trading in May 1997 after the current management successfully purchased the assets of T.G. Delamere & Co Ltd (TGD) from the receiver. TGD had traded for over 110 years before going into receivership in January 1997. The management buy-out of TGD was headed by TGD's Managing Director, Malcolm Lewis, together with a non-executive Chairman and the Production Director. A high-street bank and venture capitalist financed the buy-out and a non-executive director represented the interests of the financial investors on the board of the company.

During the period of receivership (between January 1997 and May 1997) trading was continuous with former directors and employees of T.G. Delamere receiving 'peppercorn' salaries in an effort to make the new company viable and to provide continuity of service to existing customers. Delamere Pottery subsequently retained a significant number of TGD employees who had not been made redundant in January 1997. In May 1997 the headcount was 160, which was less than 50 per cent of the pre-receivership numbers. The company was also successful in retaining the profitable nucleus of TGD's customers.

Delamere Pottery's organization structure (see Exhibit 15.1) consisted of three tiers: senior management, middle/supervisory management and blue collar workers. Malcolm Lewis, as the Managing Director, was responsible for the overall direction of the company, with additional responsibilities for sales and marketing. John Wilshaw, the Production Director, headed up internal operations and had responsibility for new product development and supply chain development. The organization structure of the new company was not dissimilar to that of TGD, even though the management adopted a more

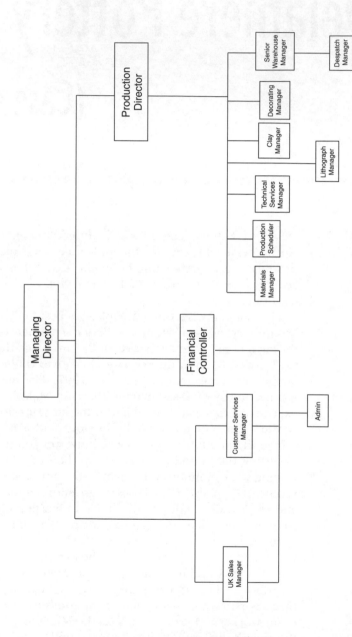

Exhibit 15.1 Delamere organizational structure.

	Year ended	Sales	Net profit before tax
T.G. Delamere & Co. Ltd	31/12/1995	£7586k	£337k loss
T.G. Delamere & Co. Ltd	31/12/1996	£7631k	£239k loss
Delamere Pottery Ltd	30/04/1998	£4400k	£320k profit
Delamere Pottery Ltd	30/04/1999	£4260k	£131k profit
Delamere Pottery Ltd (Business Plan Forecast)	1999/2000	£5125k	£343k profit

Exhibit 15.2
Turnover comparison.

vigorous market philosophy and an approach to business processes that was markedly different than their predecessors.

The level of turnover in the first year following the management buy-out was £4.4 million (see Exhibit 15.2). Previously TGD had chased turnover in low-margin/high-volume markets such as supermarkets and retail discounters, whereas Delamere Pottery had re-focused its marketing efforts on new markets/customers that provided higher margins. Although the 1997 and 1998 turnover levels were less than 60 per cent of the last published accounts for TGD, this still represented 2 per cent of the total domestic and export sales achieved by all UK pottery companies in the earthenware sector. This placed the business in the top ten league of UK pottery manufacturers with the likes of Wedgwood, Churchill, Royal Doulton, Potmeirion and Denby. The ranking ignores foreign competitors from Portugal, Italy and Asia (particularly China, Taiwan, Thailand, Hong Kong and Indonesia). It is worth noting that between 1995 and 2000 ceramic imports as a proportion of total UK market share rose from 27 to 32 per cent. The impact on Delamere Pottery, during their first 2 years of operation, was mixed. Sales in 1998, particularly in the UK and Europe, were healthy. They were assisted by the continuing economic growth of the late 1990s and a favourable exchange rate. Export sales became much more difficult however after 1999, particularly in Europe, when the Euro was introduced it began to depreciate against the Pound.

In light of this increasingly aggressive competition the company pursued a marketing and investment strategy that sought to achieve two primary business objectives:

1 To increase gross margins from 35 to 45 per cent.
2 To improve customer service and responsiveness to demand whilst at the same time minimizing inventory.

15.1 The Market

The UK ceramic industry is one where 'Darwinian' principles dominate in the sense that only the most responsive companies, especially with respect to volatile demand patterns and changing competitive conditions, appear to survive. The UK industry had excess capacity and a number of companies were forced to cease production during the 1990s. For example, Staffordshire Tableware who

	£m rsp current prices	Index	£m rsp at 1996 prices	Index
1996	420	100	420	100
1997	430	102	425	101
1998	440	105	430	102
1999	445	106	432	103
2000	455	108	446	106
2001 (est)	465	111	254	108

Exhibit 15.3

Retail sales of china and earthenware (1996–2001). *Source*: Mintel May 2001.

claimed 5 per cent of the 'casual' and 'mid-range' earthenware market went into receivership in December 2000. During the 1990s Wedgwood also closed two of its major earthenware manufacturing sites.

In the UK most segments of the china and earthenware markets had grown, albeit quite slowly. Total retail sales at 1996 prices, for example, had grown by 6 per cent from 1996 to 2000 (see Exhibit 15.3). More worryingly, UK manufacturer's sales fell by almost 20 per cent in the same period. The general backdrop for the industry was however more benign, with a number of positive market factors operating:

- The UK had a very healthy housing market with a 30 per cent increase in the number of house conveyances between 1994 and 2000. There was also an 11 per cent increase in the total number of households in the decade to 2001. More significantly, the number of single person households had risen by almost 30 per cent during the same period. Factors like these have historically correlated with higher ceramic sales, although demand for tableware products in smaller households tend to be for lower total cost purchases. The decline in the number of marriages – a 25 per cent reduction from 1990 to 2001 – had a more negative impact as the decline tended to affect the fine china market, with marriage gifts being an important proportion of total sales.
- Changing consumer tastes have been influencing general consumption patterns in the tableware market. The de-structuring of formal meal times and the rising popularity of barbecues and other casual dining habits has been reflected in increased demand for 'casual' earthenware and stoneware dinner services. There has also been a growing demand for individual pieces of tableware as opposed to more formal dinner services.
- Fashion and colour co-ordination has had a growing impact on the tableware market. This trend is beneficial to the manufacturers because purchases tend to be more frequent. However, the life cycle for fashion products is extremely short and there is little, or no, opportunity for a producer to obtain copyright for original fashion designs – low cost producers do not entirely copy original designs; they emulate existing designs with small modifications.
- Casual dining accounted for approximately 30 per cent of the retail market for tableware in 2001, and was increasing steadily at the expense of more formal ware. 'Fashion' and 'informality' were

thought to be linked, and Malcolm Lewis argued forcefully that 'changes in lifestyle and tastes, rather than increases in disposable income, fuel demand for fashion and casual ware. The punters are demanding strong colours and adventurous designs. At the moment, hand-painted designs are in vogue and I can see no end to it. The only changes will be those dictated by growing sophistication amongst consumers'.

The UK industry exports a very high proportion of its production, but during the period from 1994 to 1999, exports as a proportion of total sales (at manufacturer's selling price) fell by 7 per cent points to 51 per cent. The principal reason for this has been the relative strength of the Pound, particularly against the Euro. Delamere have been very exposed to the Pound's appreciation in value, as the company exports over 70 per cent of its output, with the majority going into Europe. In response to this the company increased its UK and USA representation and their accompanying marketing efforts.

15.2 Strategy of Delamere Pottery Limited

In mid 1999, the senior management of Delamere Pottery Ltd drafted a revised business strategy and a new Business plan. Three broad statements defined the plan:

1   To continue manufacturing pottery products from the existing site using upgraded plant and equipment giving more efficient and flexible production. The plan to achieve this strategic action covered seven areas:
    - *Planning*   Installation of an integrated Enterprise Resource Planning (ERP) system, with the initial emphasis on Manufacturing, Planning and Control (MPC). The aim was to increase stock turns by 50 per cent, reducing delivery lead times and improving due date performance.
    - *Factory layout*   Re-organize manufacturing with the aim of reducing costs, improving efficiency and reducing process losses.
    - *Sales forecasts*   Examine to determine future departmental loading requirements to optimize manufacturing efficiency.
    - *Efficiency*   To increase employee flexibility and efficiency with the aim of all operatives being capable of standard performance on at least two jobs and improving sales per employee ratio by 5 per cent per annum.
    - *Fuel utilization*   To improve fuel efficiency with the aim of reducing fuel costs as a percentage of turnover.
    - *Quality*   To improve quality assurance and reduce scrap rates from 20 to 15 per cent by 2002–2003 (by achieving at least a 1 per cent reduction year on year).
    - *To enhance communications*   Develop employee motivation and understanding of the business objectives of the company.

2 To enhance the quality and saleability of the Delamere Pottery brand name by continuous improvement of product, service and reliability coupled to a more active marketing programme. As with the first strategic aim, the plan to achieve this strategic action covered a number of areas:

- That the products from the range be sold in-depth into multi-outlets within their major markets.
- That their major buyers were to have complete confidence and satisfaction in the company and its products.
- That the company consistently offered a range of products with designs that met current market needs and trends.
- That the product was perceived as representing value for money to buyers with a record of high stock turnovers.
- That a range of designs and product introductions that manufacturers of associated products would wish to use, thereby maximizing the product offer and exposure of the company name.
- That the company be recognized within the 'Table-Top Industry' as a progressive and innovative organization.
- That the product range has a reputation of saleability so that it is attractive to sales agents/distributors, thereby facilitating selection into the most effective distribution networks.
- That the products attract media coverage to build more consumer awareness of the company name.

The plan to achieve these strategic actions had five parts:

1 *Quality* To ensure that progress was made in improving the required standard of consistency of product, and to ensure that all packaging, marking, palletization or delivery requirements were followed. To reduce the number of credit note requirements caused by quality, breakage or administration errors. The company also planed to obtain ISO 9000 accreditation by 2001.
2 *Design* To ensure that the product range was updated as necessary through planned introductions of new products and to monitor that the latest fashion trends outside the Table-Top field were noted and followed to keep abreast with the latest design trends.
3 *Service* To improve the administrative back up to customers and agents with the following targets:
   - Order confirmations sent within 1 week of receipt of order.
   - Commission statements showing outstanding debtors sent within 21 days of month end.
   - Visits to every major market/territory – at least twice per year.
   - General communication improvement particularly with customers.
4 *Reliability* Ensure that improved delivery performance was maintained, with 90 per cent of orders despatched to schedule and no more than 2 weeks after planned despatch dates.
5 *Brand awareness* Ensure that major buyer within the 'Table-Top' sector of major markets knows the name of Delamere Pottery.

3   Over a 3-year period to improve the level of pre-tax profit to at least 7 per cent of sales turnover (the industry norm). The company thought that this strategic objective would result largely from the achievement of strategic objectives 1 and 2.

Pre-tax profit improvements would come from two directions:

■ Improving gross margin – planned to be two-fold:

(i)   Improved efficiency of manufacturing through improved planning, factory layout and plant upgrade coupled to a programme of more consistent quality of manufacturing and process scrap reduction.
(ii)   Improved margin selling prices through more effective distribution and improving company awareness (a programme of marketing activity and selection of new distribution channels).

■ Additional turnover – this would add to overhead recovery in two ways:

(i)   By offering a short selected range of products to be sold into targeted markets as promotional product under a new brand.
(ii)   By continued in-depth selling of the Delamere brand into major markets, thereby increasing the customer base and the range of products stocked by them.

15.3   Manufacturing and product diversity

The company, like the industry, was engaged in repetitive batch manufacturing with a large number of discontinuities. It produces approximately 65,000 pieces of earthenware a week across four shapes. The number of items within each shape ranges from twenty to sixty. There were eighty-five patterns on the books which resulted in 2750 possible stock keeping units (SKUs), with the number increasing to 5500 if 'selected seconds' were included. Selected seconds, which the company markets, are products that are not of best quality because they have minor faults.

From this product range customers can order any combination of open stock items and/or formal assemblies of SKUs (i.e. tableware sets packaged to their own specifications). The product portfolio is split into four families; Fashion, Everyday, Promotional and Customized. The families display different characteristics in terms of marketing and manufacturing variables.

The *Fashion* family contains a limited number of high-quality specification items which are characterized by short life cycles and a high pattern turnover. The typical order sizes for these products are between £6000 and £24,000 with delivery normally required in less than 7 weeks. To respond to this delivery lead time the management had an inventory policy which stocked semi-finished products and materials for the finished product. The *Fashion* range was experiencing growth but it was difficult to forecast demand because of the fickleness of the fashion industry. It was also difficult to compare prices within such a fragmented area, which equally explains why the company closely monitored *Fashion* sales so that it could run-out potentially redundant stock lines.

The *Everyday* category had a comprehensive range of long life cycle items. Orders for these products were of a similar size to those for *Fashion* products but with a lead time of between 7 and 10 weeks. Such an extensive range required a wide array of flexible manufacturing facilities, especially within the decorating sections. To meet requested deliveries the company stocked moulds, biscuit ware and lithographs for these products (see Exhibits 15.4 and 15.5 for an explanation of processes and terminology used in ceramic manufacturing). Market growth for *Everyday* products was static and highly competitive because price comparisons could be easily made.

The *Promotional* family contains a comprehensive range of Delamere Pottery branded products and a limited range of non-branded products. The markets for these products were highly price sensitive and the main manufacturing concern was to produce at the lowest possible cost. Orders were usually over £20,000 with a delivery lead time of 10 or more weeks. Growth prospects were poor with sales following a negative trend.

Members of the *Customized* family were usually for one-off orders, usually single items. A minimum order size existed for these products because the company had to mix batches of non-standard clay and interrupt decorating section order flows. The delivery lead time for these products was 8–10 weeks with performance against promise date being crucial for future sales.

The company concluded that major buyers attending trade shows would only be interested in new products because decisions on 'known' products would have been made already. This meant that there had to be a major pattern/shape launch each year. Although the company estimated that the direct costs of pattern development would be between £6000 and £25,000, a figure of £8000 was assumed within the business plan. A prerequisite for a pattern going into production was that the minimum annual turnover would be £100,000–£150,000.

The shape of a product is considered to be of secondary importance to its decoration. In a review of its products the company considered removing poor-performing shapes and switching patterns to shapes that show better performance. They were also keen to increase the number of designs for shapes that would appeal to a worldwide market. The underpinning rationale was to create the correct balance within the product portfolio so that the company could respond to changes in world fashion trends. A core element of this marketing strategy was 'new product introductions' and as such the number of SKUs on offer was set to increase. When challenged on the issue of product variety Malcolm Lewis replied 'the particular markets we are entering are fashion conscious and, as you know, fashions are only in vogue for a season'.

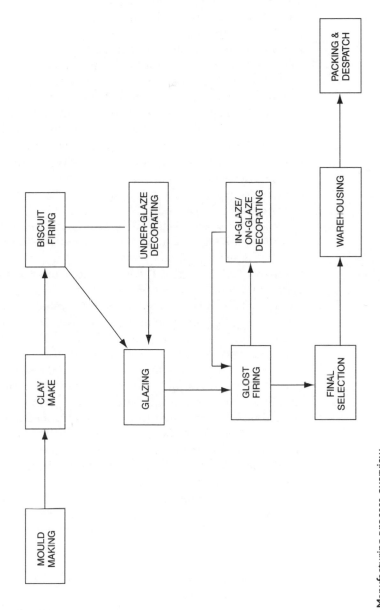

Exhibit 15.4 Manufacturing process overview.

15.4 The first year

During the company's first year of trading a number of policies were implemented. The company had deliberately reduced turnover in order to concentrate on products and markets where they could obtain their target margins whilst simultaneously reducing their cost base (see Exhibits 15.2 and 15.6). To achieve this the company had repositioned their brand and products in the upper to middle range of the earthenware market. They reinforced this brand positioning by winning key accounts with independent retailers and department stores, including Boots, Debenhams, House of Fraser, Fenwicks and the Covent Garden Trading Company.

The brand image of Delamere Pottery was also actively promoted. There had been six full-page features of their products in life style magazines such as Good Housekeeping and Home Beautiful. This had also involved collaboration with major mail order companies who had gained confidence in their product quality, delivery performance and financial stability. Additional continuity was provided by the pricing policy being radically changed so that it supported their brand image and protected their margins – they no longer discounted their prices as the previous company had.

Exports were important for the company and in the first financial year they accounted for 73 per cent of sales turnover with the remaining 27 per cent being for the domestic market. Just over 80 per cent of sales were factored (i.e. a company buys Delamere Pottery invoices and takes responsibility for collecting payments). This assures cash flow, but reduces margin because the factoring company takes a percentage of the sales value. In the medium term, the company was also planning to increase and strengthen its share of the earthenware market to at least 3 per cent by 2002. Indeed, since January 1999 the company has broadened its customer base in the UK and Export markets by nearly 120 per cent (accounts in excess of £12,000 were increased from 30 to 65). The company had achieved this as a result of a planned strengthening of the sales and marketing team: namely the appointment of a UK sales manager backed up by an infrastructure of commissioned sales representatives.

Delamere Pottery's differentiation policy had been the most important factor in obtaining premium prices for their products and in meeting their first-year profit target. Yet John Wilshaw, the Production Director, was insistent that if the company wished to maintain its progress towards target margins and remain competitive for growth in the longer term, major improvements to the supply and cost side of the business were essential. To meet this requirement the company had embarked upon a £250,000 capital investment programme, which was to be fully implemented by the end of December 1999. This programme involved improving process layouts and focusing manufacturing in half of the existing factory floor space. Approximately 50 per cent of this investment was allocated towards the replacement of existing tunnel kilns, which were inflexible and energy inefficient compared with modern intermittent kiln technology (see Exhibit 15.4 for an overview of the manufacturing process). The investment would considerably reduce the cost base because energy and fuel bills represented 11 per cent of production value (PV). In addition to energy costs the company was seeking reductions to all direct costs – they accounted for

Mould	A plaster profile made from a mixture of powdered plaster and water. Made in-house.
Clay making	*Flat making* Manufacture of plates, dishes, saucers, soups, etc. by semi-automatic machinery. The mould forms the face of the article and a profile tool forms the back. Items are made upside down and dried on the mould before removal. *Cup making* manufacture of cups, bowls, etc. by semi-automatic machinery. The mould forms the outside of the article and a profile tool forms the inside. Items are made the correct way up and are dried in the mould before removal. *Casting* The manufacture of articles that cannot be made by either of the previous processes e.g. teapots, coffee pots, sugars, creams, boats, etc. Made by the pouring of liquid clay into moulds, allowing to cast to required thickness and pouring out the excess. The articles are dried to a 'leather' hard state before removal from the mould.
Biscuit firing	Articles in the clay state are placed in a kiln and fired to approx. 1100 °C. Once fired the articles are in the biscuit state and are hard and semi-porous.
Glazing	Articles are dipped or sprayed with glaze. Glazes are mixtures of metallic and non-metallic compounds which give tableware its glossy coating. This physical appearance is produced by the glaze melting during firing and then solidifying as it cools.
Glost firing	Glazed articles are placed in a kiln and fired to approx. 1050 °C. On-glaze decorated articles are fired to approx. 700 °C. At the end of this process articles are in the glost state.
Under-glaze decorating	Colours are applied to biscuit ware prior to glazing. This decorating, up to four colours, may be in the form of machine printing, machine banding and/or hand banding.
On-glaze/ In-glaze decorating	Decoration is applied to glost ware. Application may be by machine printing, machine or hand banding, or lithographing. Lithographing involves the application, by hand, of specially prepared multi-coloured transfers (called lithographs), which are purchased from suppliers who make them to customer specifications.

Exhibit 15.5
Terminology used in ceramic manufacturing.

65 per cent of PV. Other significant cost factors included labour and material costs, as they accounted for 29 per cent and 22 per cent of PV.

The investment programme would, it was hoped, have a major impact on labour and overhead costs. It was equally desirable that it should enhance

Profit and loss details	£000's
Turnover	4402
Profit (Loss) before interest	320
Interest paid	(84)
Profit (Loss) before taxation	236
Taxation (Charge) credit	0
Profit (Loss) after taxation	236
Profit (Loss) for period	236
Dividends	0
Appropriations	0
Retained profit (loss)	236
Balance sheet details	
Fixed Assets	
Tangible	420
Intangible	0
Current Assets	1511
Stock/W.I.P.	797
Debtors	773
Bank and deposits	–
Other	93
Current liabilities	(1402)
Creditors	(466)
Loans/Overdraft	(269)
Other	(667)
Net current assets	109
Net tangible assets	529
Total assets	1931
Total assets less current liabilities	529
Non-current liabilities	(24)
Long-term debt	(24)
Other non-current liabilities	–
Minority interests	–
Total assets less liabilities	505
Shareholders funds	505
Called-up share capital	0.002
Reserves	504.998

Exhibit 15.6
Company accounts for Delamere Pottery Limited at 30th April 1998. *Source*: Company records.

manufacturing flexibility and response times, principally through reduced handling, shorter manufacturing lead times and a reduction of work-in-progress (WIP). These outcomes had to be achieved within existing or improved customer service levels.

The company recognized that the sustained benefits of their marketing strategy and investment programme in the medium to long term was dependent on a coherent manufacturing strategy. This meant that the manufacturing strategy had to be consistent with the marketing strategy. A key component for this objective was the introduction of an enhanced MPC system. This could then be integrated with the other major functions, such as finance, purchasing and sales and marketing. It was also envisaged that planning and control for manufacturing could be placed on an ERP platform, with customer relationship management (CRM) software being gradually incorporated.

In an investigation of customer service it was found that delivery lead times ranged from 22 days to 170 days with a mean value of 76 days. The number of days between promise date and despatch date ranged from 76 days early to 101 days late. It was also discovered that the percentage of orders delivered on or before the promise date was 56 per cent, which represented 63 per cent of the total order value. The research into due date performance revealed that upon receiving a customer order it took on average 42 days for an order confirmation to be sent. When it was discovered that Stock and WIP amounted to £797,000, management realized there was a lack of control within the business.

The board duly approved the appointment of a small consultancy firm that specialized in supply chain management and planning and control systems. After some initial meetings to define business needs the consultancy drafted a detailed proposal for an MPC implementation project. An external project manager was appointed because it was felt that there was a lack of expertise within the company and because it was estimated that it would be a full-time job for 2 years – which would be difficult for a downsized workforce.

15.4.1 Project justification: Performance criteria and benefits

The MPC project proposal was submitted to the Delamere Pottery board in March 1999. It gained approval on the condition that no major capital expenditure on information technology would be required until March/April 2000. The project was justified against a number of broad performance criteria and financial benefits, which are outlined below:

- Improved business liquidity as measured by the acid test ratio from 0.5:1 to 1:1 over the first 2 years.
- Increased stock turns to 8 times per year over the first 1½ years.
- Reduced delivery lead time to 8 weeks (maximum) over 2 years.
- Improved current due date performance to 99 per cent.

The financial benefits attributable to the project were as follows:

1. A £120,000 reduction in working capital, 75 per cent of which would be attributable to the project. This would be achieved through improved management control/reduction of inventory at all stages of the manufacturing process. This would represent a one-off saving, although improvements in subsequent years were not discounted.

2. An increase in pre-tax profits of £150,000, with 25 per cent of this being attributable to the project. This would be achieved through improved systems and procedures that identify loss-making and/or non-contributing products. This would be a 'per annum' benefit for the company.

3 An increase of £2m in turnover, 5 per cent of which could be attributed to the project. This would be achieved through improvements to customer service, mainly by improved delivery performance. This would occur over the life cycle of the project.

Other less tangible benefits included the view that it would be a catalyst for continuous improvement and that it would provide a platform for controlled growth of the business. They also thought that it would assist in the prioritization and construction of detailed action plans for non-manufacturing activities like product development, quality and marketing – because it would interface with most areas of the business.

15.4.2 The project

The consultants emphasized that the project required the full commitment of senior management and that they, like other company personnel, should be actively involved in it. They recommended that all the activities defined in the project, and executed by the project manager, should be continued and refined by senior and middle management and by any other employee involved in the project.

The first set of activities of the project focused on improvements to inventory management because of its financial and operational significance to the company. The project activities that are listed below were designed to establish key files, policies and procedures for the selection and implementation of an integrated business system. As the programme developed, the issues addressed by the project manager would become increasingly multi-functional and strategic and many of the activities would be undertaken in parallel.

15.4.3 The major milestones of the proposed MPC project

Task	Activity	Duration
1	*Initial induction* The project manager would be familiarized with the company, its products, its marketing, its manufacturing systems and methods, its physical and procedural infrastructures and also the corporate and functional objectives of the company. During this period, the new appointment would not make any substantive contribution to business performance.	2 weeks
2	*Inventory management/Inventory transactions* Establish and record inventory levels and conditions for all inventory types. Establish procedures to improve record accuracy, enhance transaction procedures and reduce surplus inventories.	3 months Maintained and developed by the company

3	*Develop item master information*	3 months
	Create the key files for all lines/patterns. The database created must be capable of update and transference to an integrated system at a later date.	Maintained and developed by the company
4	*Non-manufacturing lead times*	In conjunction with Task 3
	Determine current administration lead times, e.g. order entry, sales order processing and other non-manufacturing lead times.	
5	*Product structure/Bill of materials (BOM)*	2 months
	Establish bill of material for A and B class items in current portfolio. Product structure must be comprehensible and useable for marketing, manufacturing, finance and design. Define accountability and responsibility areas for BOM maintenance.	Maintained and developed by the company
6	*Routing and work centre data*	1 month
	Analyse manufacturing logisitics in terms of process capacity, set-up time, standards, etc. Develop prototype routing file and define procedures for maintenance and integrity.	Assisted by company personnel
7	*Purchasing and supplier planning and control*	1 month
	Analyse existing systems in respect of purchase order criteria, links to the financial systems, transaction procedures, vendor selection and performance measures.	Assisted by company personnel
8	*Shop floor control*	$1\frac{1}{2}$ months
	Analyse and develop new shop floor controls including quality reporting, topicality of reporting and possibility of KANBAN signals.	Assisted by company personnel
9	*Demand management*	$1\frac{1}{2}$ months
	Document current procedures relating to forecasting of anticipated demands at aggregate and disaggregate levels. This involves customer order entry, promising mechanisms, and reconciliation procedures between master schedule, inventory and forecasting.	Assisted, developed and maintained by company personnel
10	*Master production schedule (MPS)*	$2\frac{1}{2}$ months
	Develop procedures to link MPS with sales and operations planning and the business planning process.	Established, developed and maintained by company personnel
11	*Communication*	$1\frac{1}{2}$ months
	Recommend and establish improved formal reporting systems within the hierarchy of planning and control.	In conjunction with company
12	*Develop, specify MPC system*	3 months
	Prepare system specification to meet company business needs and prepare cost/benefit analysis for company.	Requires Board decision on completion.

(continued)

Implementation recommendations must provide guidance for generic and user education and the management of the implementation. Must also contain appropriate performance measures (financial and non-financial) at aggregate and disaggregate levels of the business and provide methodology for external benchmarking.

13	*Implement MPC system*	4 months	
	Selection and implementation of MPC system inclusive of education programme for senior managment, project team and user groups. Establish audit procedure.	Major company involvement at all levels	

15.5 Indicative questions

1 Is the developing manufacturing capability and infrastructure (including the MPC project) consistent with the business, marketing and financial strategies of the company?

2 How does a company which is financially highly geared, reconcile short-term demands of bankers and venture capitalists with the longer term 'span of action' necessary for strategic planning and are these demands reconcilable?

3 Undertake some contemporary research of the Tableware Industry: What are the current threats and opportunities for the UK industry and, in particular, how should a company the size of Delamere Pottery respond to them?

4 The MPC project: Is it over-planned? under-planned? ill-planned? well-planned? Or is it merely a diversion which does not underpin the business mission of the company? Whatever conclusion(s) you reach, provide a precise and substantial reason for it (them).

5 Is the business infrastructure at Delamere Pottery appropriate to successfully compete in the 'Fashion Market'?

6 Provide a critical analysis of the 'stated' business strategy: Is it feasible and what changes would you make to it?

(You may wish to use your analyses from Questions 1, 2 and 5 when responding to Question 6).

15.6 Acknowledgements

We would like to thank Woodland Pottery Holdings Ltd for allowing access to, and reproduction of, the material contained within the case.

CHAPTER **16**

Alpha Toiletries Limited

(Case date: 2002)

16.1 Company background

Alpha Toiletries are a subsidiary of a large Midlands-based organization. They develop, market and manufacture a wide range of toiletry products (shampoos, shower gels, aftershave, etc.) for well-known high-street retailers and supermarkets. The company have been trading for approximately 15 years.

The turnover from the operation in 2001 was £9.12 million, with the projected turnover for 2002 being £12 million. The company's key customers were Marks & Spencer and Superdrug, who provided 31 per cent and 37 per cent of turnover respectively. Other significant customers are J Sainsbury (8 per cent of turnover), Romela (2 per cent), Safeway (2 per cent), Medicare (2 per cent) and Proctor and Gamble (2 per cent).

16.2 Products

The products manufactured by the company are nearly all customer/retailer own brand, although they can be broken down into principle groupings:

1 Customer's own brands, which are almost wholly developed by Alpha in conjunction with their customers.
2 Brands which are manufactured from free issue materials on a subcontract basis (e.g. Vidal Sassoon brands worth £177,000 to the company in 2001).

221

16.3 Order winning criteria

The company had long-established relationships with their major customers, and it was felt that the order winning criteria (above and beyond price) for the medium to long term were:

1 Product development capability.
2 Quality.
3 Delivery performance (probably the most important in the short/ medium term).

16.3.1 Product development

Product development was a continuing process and was undertaken in close collaboration with customers. The product range manufactured at Alpha consisted of approximately 450 distinct products. Out of every twelve products developed by the company in a year – with a customer in mind – three or less would be accepted without modification.

Their product ranges also had two basic types of life cycle:

1 The conventional one of introduction, growth, maturity and decline. These products tended to last at least 3 years and were subject to various modifications (not unlike model upgrades in the automotive industry). The modifications could include changes to the product formulation or to changes in labelling, etc. Some were modified so completely that they bore little comparison to the original product, except for a few components contained within the initial formulation.
2 Some products had a shorter life cycle (e.g. 1 year) as the range would be discontinued and replaced by another. These discontinuous life cycles were dictated by customer merchandising policy.

16.3.2 Quality

Conformance quality is crucial in the service of Alpha's markets – all materials have to be traceable to source and large customers such as Marks & Spencer insist on their system of vendor accreditation for Alpha's suppliers.

16.3.3 Delivery performance

Performance against delivery criteria is regarded by the Production and Marketing Directors as 'not good'.

16.4 Product cost structure

The average ex-works product cost structure was approximately:

Materials	55%
Labour	12.5%
Overheads	21%
Profit	12%

Materials were a significant cost driver. Procurement and logistics were therefore extremely important factors in the determination of profit margins and the ability to meet customer service requirements.

16.5 Operations logistics

Alpha manufactured for stock in anticipation of customer orders. Contracts with Marks & Spencer typically covered 6-month periods during which time they were obliged to purchase unsold stock. On many occasions however, unsold stock was purchased by customers at highly discounted prices (sometimes at a 50 per cent discount).

Demand for products were relatively stable throughout the year with the exception of a seasonal increase prior to Christmas as retailers built up stock during the months of October and November.

16.6 Manufacturing logistics

Materials were categorized as 'wet blend' (materials for shampoos, gels, etc.) or as 'alcohol/spirit'-based (materials for aftershaves, etc.). When wet blend materials were received from vendors they were sampled in the company laboratory for microbiological testing of organic materials.

The first stage of the production process was the blending of the wet materials and this was known as 'bulk manufacture'. The capacity of bulk manufacturing was approximately 25 tonnes per day. There were ten blending units, of which two were for alcohol-based products, which were located in an isolated alcohol product manufacturing unit for safety reasons (they were highly inflammable).

After blending, samples are again taken of the blended material to ensure conformance. The remainder of the manufacturing process consists of filling a variety of containers with the blended product, labelling and packing in pack quantities requested by the customer. The finished product was then returned to the warehouse for call off. There were thirteen production lines for filling, labelling and packing, and another five were planned to be added in the latter half of 2002. The process time on these lines was extremely small. Two of the product lines were dedicated to alcohol-based products and were located in an isolated manufacturing unit.

Production volumes were extremely high as would be expected for fast-moving consumer products. The existing eleven wet blend production lines had a total capacity of 100,000 units per day. The two alcohol lines had a capacity of 25,000–30,000 units per day.

16.7 Procurement

Procurement policy was to single source whenever possible except for suppliers of containers. Vendors whose materials are part of Marks & Spencer products require accreditation from Marks & Spencer as quality approved suppliers.

The shortest vendor lead times are 4–6 weeks (for wet materials and packaging materials). Approximate lead times for other components of the products are as follows:

Caps	10–12 weeks
Plastic tubes	16 weeks
Bottles	6–8 weeks

Senior management had no quantitative data on vendor delivery performance against due date, although it was described as 'not good'.

The worst delivery performance for materials was associated with new product launches. Indeed, the logistics for new product introduction were not well-integrated with formal systems.

16.8 Problem evaluation

The Production Director was a recent appointment, and to use her own words, she was 'completely brassed off' with the number of enquiries from customers concerned about overdue deliveries. Her broad analysis of the current situation was that the company had a very short 'time span of action' to resolve fundamental control problems if Alpha was to avoid a permanent loss of competitive edge. She told the Managing Director that they would loose the Marks & Spencer account if drastic remedial action was not carried out. A thorough investigation of the business revealed:

16.8.1 Warehousing

Alpha appeared to hold inventory for their customers and vendors, and the warehouse was struggling to accommodate this level of stock with inventory blocking access and being permanently stored in the receiving dock. It occupied by far the largest proportion of the plant (she estimated 66 per cent of the factory excluding car parks and surrounds). There was also a manual system of inventory recording in the warehouse, and it was struggling to support the number of transactions that were made each day.

16.8.2 Inventory

Total inventory at 20 March 2002 was £2.66 million which gave an average stock turn of 3.4 per year on sales of £9.12 million for 2001 or 4.5 on budgeted sales of £12 million for 2002. The inventory volumes could be classified as follows:

Finished product	40% of total inventory value
Raw materials (chemicals, etc.)	19% of total inventory value
Components (bottles, caps, etc.)	35% of total inventory value
Blended product and other WIP	4% of total inventory value
Packing material	2% of total inventory value

It was evident that stock turns were too low. There was no data available to provide classification of active, slow-moving or dead stock. Inventory and manufacturing information was highly fragmented and it was necessary for the Production Director to speak to at least 4 people, in different functions, to obtain a comprehensive view of inventory records.

16.8.3 Production and requirements planning

The production plan was developed from quarterly or monthly average demand at customer retail outlets. These demand values were aggregated into a spread sheet production plan that had a time horizon of approximately 5 months. There was also a 12-month plan that was based on current orders, i.e. within a 3–4-month time horizon, and also forecast orders which usually occupy the last 8–9 months of the plan. The plan was updated monthly.

16.8.4 Call off of orders

Marks & Spencer products were called twice per week via the EDI network TRADANET. This specified quantities to be delivered and to which depots. Superdrug called off less frequently, about once a week.

16.9 Problem solution

The findings of the Production Director were put into a report addressed to the Managing Director of Alpha and the Chief Executive of the parent company:

I have satisfied myself that there are no effective bridges between business planning, production scheduling and the execution of plans at the operational level. As a consequence the operations of the business are crisis orientated. We are unable to answer basic customer enquiries, such as *where is the job now?* and *when will it be delivered?*. This is not a satisfactory situation for a company where delivery performance is an important order winning criteria and a significant factor in vendor rating by our customers.

Her prescriptions were as follows:

I propose that the company implement an MRP system starting at the earliest possible date. I recommend we use the resources of the parent company to develop Alpha specific software, as an 'off the shelf' approach would not address the fast moving logistics of our business.

The major software development would have three phases:

Phase 1:	Inventory Control (including purchase ordering)	Completion December 2002
Phase 2:	Integration of Purchase Ordering and Works Orders	Completion April 2003
Phase 3:	Bill of Materials (BOM) System	Completion June 2003

I believe these areas are valid in terms of operational priorities.

In addition to this development, when Phase 1 is completed or near completion, we shall require in-company training for the principle users of the system. This training, call it education, should be directed at changing behaviour at Alpha (put bluntly – 'changing mindsets'), particularly in terms of information integrity, the quantification of key business indicators, such as vendor performance and our own delivery performance and the prohibition of informal systems.

She concluded:

'...This needs serious discussion then action approval from the highest level.'

16.10   The counter proposal

The Managing Director received the report with interest although he was a little annoyed that the Production Director had directed a copy to the Chief Executive.

He convened an emergency meeting which included personnel from all the major business functions (i.e. marketing and sales, production, purchasing and finance). He allowed the Production Director to lead the meeting with a presentation of the current state of the operation and her major recommendations.

The presentation was followed by a lively debate chaired by the Managing Director. Marketing and finance were interested in improving 'outcomes'. Marketing and sales complained about current delivery performance and customer service, stating that they were particularly worried about their major accounts. Finance complained about the loss of turnover due to missed deliveries and the amount of working capital tied up in all kinds of inventory.

The Managing Director summed up the meeting as follows:

I agree with the Production Director's analysis and the fact, which is staring us all in the face, that we have to improve things quickly. Whilst I agree with her proposals, they are a long term solution to what, I believe, are day to day problems. That is not to say these are not fundamental problems. I believe we should launch two initiatives simultaneously:

a) We've got to get tough with our suppliers on delivery. They have got to adopt a JIT attitude. This is a job for the Purchasing Manager. But I intend to reinforce this message of JIT supply by writing personally to all our vendors insisting on prompt delivery. And, by the way, I want an additional expediter in the purchasing department to really put the pressure on.

b) Yes, we need a systems solution, but the Production Director's proposals would have little impact until the end of this year. I propose that the company produce production schedules based on actual inventory availability, not on what may be available. This will kill two birds with one stone: it will reduce inventory whilst ensuring that the schedules match customer requirement.

Everyone nodded sagely – except the Production Director.

16.11 Questions

1 Describe and analyse what you think are the major strategic issues within the case study.

2 Fisher et al. (2000) suggest that the 'retail innovators' of the 1st decade of the twenty-first century will be the ones who best combine access to consumer transaction data with the ability to turn that information into action. Explain how and why Alpha will be, or will not be, a retail innovator in the twenty-first century.

3 What do you believe the Production Director means when she says 'I have satisfied myself that there are no effective bridges between business planning, production and the execution of plans at the operational level . . . .'? In what way does her diagnosis impinge upon Business Strategy at Alpha?

4 Imagine you are the Chief Executive of the parent company: Develop a reasoned plan of action for radically changing and improving the Alpha business without jeopardizing the major customer accounts at Alpha.

CHAPTER 17

AB machine tools
(Case date: 1996)

(The company is now A.B. Marwin Ltd. This case is seven years old and products have obviously developed significantly since its writing. Actions taken six years ago should not connect to the new company)

17.1 Company background

Until 1993 Asquith and Butler were distinct and separate machine tool manufacturers that were only one mile apart in Halifax, West Yorkshire.

Asquith was founded by William Asquith in 1865. They initially manufactured all kinds of machine tools, and the development of the company was closely correlated with the woollen and textile industry which experienced rapid growth from the mid-nineteenth century to the early 1950s.

In the early twentieth century, the company began to concentrate on the design and manufacture of radial drilling machines for general purpose manufacturers and horizontal ram type borers for heavy industrial companies. By the mid-1960s the company had become the Asquith Corporation. It had become a machine tool conglomerate with a variety of machine tool manufacturing interests. At this time the Asquith Corporation was not performing particularly well and it was bought out by Staveley Industries, whose primary activity was chemicals.

In the early 1970s Staveley Industries began to re-organize their machine tool portfolio. Poorly performing companies were closed down, new management teams were introduced and new finance became available for research and development of new products. Asquith at Halifax streamlined the production of radial drill products which were moving into the decline phase of their product life cycle, developing a new range of ram type boring machines equipped with the most modern computer numerical control systems (CNC). By 1979 they had developed a new range of vertical and horizontal multipurpose boring, milling, drilling and CNC tapping machines for lighter engineering applications. In 1980, Staveley Industries made a strategic decision to divest its machine tool portfolio – although Asquith had become a profitable operation the industry was extremely cyclical.

The management of Asquith bought the company out in 1981 with the aid of venture capital and the company was registered as Asquith (1981) Ltd. The new company did not buy the facilities for manufacturing the heavy duty ram borers, but concentrated on the development, marketing and manufacturing of an extended but modular range of vertical and horizontal machines. Asquith (1981) had to down-size the workforce from about 400 to approximately 130. The company was then acquired by Marbaix Lapointe Ltd in 1992.

Butler was founded by James Ryder Butler in 1868, 3 years after Asquith. J.R. Butler manufactured most types of machine tool, and like Asquith, from 1918 to 1959 the Butler company became more specialized through the development and marketing of a niche range of planing, shaping, slotting and plano milling machines (a combination of planing machine and milling machine). In the 1970s, the company was acquired by the B Elliott Group and the company name changed to Butler Newall Ltd. During the late 1970s the company briefly diversified into lathe manufacturing, though this was discontinued in 1986 due to the fierce competition from other foreign manufacturers, particularly the Japanese.

In 1991, the company began to suffer with the onset of a new recession and in 1993 the Butler Newall milling division (and its foreign subsidiaries) was acquired by Marbaix Lapointe Ltd.

Following this double acquisition, the senior management of Marbaix Lapointe undertook an in-depth review of the resources at the 2 company sites and in 1994 both companies were consolidated into the Butler site. It was at this point that the two company names were merged becoming Asquith–Butler or AB, a new division of Marbaix Lapointe Ltd.

The new division had a turnover in 1996 of approximately £15 million (not including £2 million in sales for machine tool spare parts) and had a headcount of approximately 120 employees.

17.2 Machine tools

Machine tools come in all shapes and sizes and perform a variety of manufacturing tasks. The UK Machine Tool Technologies Association (MTTA) provides the following generic definition: 'A metalworking machine tool is a power-driven machine, not portable by hand when in operation, which works metal by cutting, forming, physio-chemical (or non-contact) machining or a combination of these techniques.' All the machine tools manufactured by AB employ mechanical cutting techniques (e.g. milling, drilling, tapping) although the company have produced machines which use laser cutting technology. All AB machines also have sophisticated CNC controls.

Machine tools are used by all sectors of manufacturing, including the automotive industry, defence, railway engineering, agricultural equipment, aerospace and consumer durables, etc. These applications are, to some extent, obvious and disguise the ubiquitous nature of machine tools. Indeed, most manufactured and processed products require the use of a machine tool somewhere within their supply chain. Machine tools are also used to manufacture other machine tools.

17.3 The machine tool industry

After the Second World War there were over thirty small machine tool companies in and around Halifax. However, from 1946 to 1996 the UK machine tool industry was decimated through a series of recessions, but perhaps more significantly, from fierce Japanese and German competition. Japan and Germany now dominate the machine tool industry. As the data in Figure 17.1 shows, in 1995 the two countries accounted for almost 46 per cent of world production of machine tools and just over 53 per cent of world exports.

Production $36.5 billion		Exports $21.7 billion	
Country	Share (%)	Country	Share (%)
Japan	25.0	Japan	28.4
Germany	20.8	Germany	24.8
USA	13.5	Switzerland	8.9
Italy	8.2	Italy	7.8
Switzerland	6.0	USA	6.1
Taiwan	4.4	Taiwan	5.0
China	4.4	UK	3.1
South Korea	3.2	France	2.2
UK	2.8	Spain	1.9
France	2.3	Belgium	1.3
Others	9.2	Others	10.6

Figure 17.1
Global share of production and export of machine tools in 1995.

Source: Adapted from Gardner Publications Inc.

17.4 Machine tools and the nature of demand

The industry is highly cyclical with significant changes in demand year on year. This is due to machine tools being capital investments in industries manufacturing capital goods – an area that is highly sensitive to cycles of demand and business confidence. It is aggravated by the time lag that existed between the recovery of aggregate demand in the economy and investment in capacity. This is compounded by the fact that machine tools are hardly ever made for stock, which means that design and manufacturing lead times can be quite extensive (6 months–2½ years), with significant time lags existing between the placement of an order and the shipment of the product to the customer.

These swings/amplifications in demand are a 'Forrester Effect' and they are mainly due to the position of the industry in the supply chain. The effect is partially illustrated in Figure 17.2 and it shows the annual volume index of new machine tool orders from 1987 to 1996. It can be seen that the recession in the machine tool industry commenced 1 year earlier and was much deeper than the general recession in the UK economy as a whole from 1990 to 1995 as measured against the index for employment growth in the economy during the same period.

Year	1987	1988	1989	1990	1991	1992	1993	1994	1995	1996
Index (approx.) new machine tool orders	81	113	115	100	69	83	65	83	101	110*
Employment growth index	94	98	99	100	98	96	95	95	96	97

Figure 17.2
Annual volume index of new machine tool orders and employment growth in UK (1990 = 100).

Sources: Office for National Statistics; MTTA and OECD/Economist Employment.
Index rebased from 1986 to 1990.
* Estimated.

Although the two indexes (sales volume and employment growth) are not totally compatible they do demonstrate the larger amplitude of demand fluctuations compared with macroeconomic movements.

The leading ten export markets and import sources for UK machine tools in 1995 are shown in Figure 17.3. Data in Figure 17.4 also shows export trends as a proportion of the UK machine tool sales and import trends as a percentage of UK consumption. Two significant facts should be noted from these data:

- The UK almost always has a trade deficit in machine tools except during periods of recession (e.g. 1993 and 1994), when exports as a percentage of sales are also high.
- Since 1991 exports from the UK have represented 65–70 per cent of UK sales – which is similar to the AB export proportion.
- The high penetration of Japanese and German imports into the UK – imports from these countries is 41 per cent of UK production and approximately 61 per cent of UK world exports.
- The USA and Germany are the top export markets for the UK, accounting for 28 per cent of UK exports (AB have sales and marketing companies in both of these countries).

Export markets and value		Import sources and value	
Country	Value (£m)	Country	Value (£m)
All countries	441.2	All countries	562.8
European Union	187.5	European Union	220.4
USA	72.6	Japan	142.7
Germany	52.4	Germany	126.5
China	33.6	USA	95.1
France	33.3	Switzerland	38.8
Italy	31.0	Taiwan	32.5
India	16.6	Italy	27.0
Sweden	13.0	Belgium	17.7
Eire	12.8	France	17.7
Spain	11.3	Spain	12.3
Belgium	8.8	South Korea	8.4
Other countries	155.8	Other countries	44.1

Figure 17.3
UK exports and imports of machine tools – leading ten export markets and import sources in 1995.

Source: Adapted from HM Customs and Excise and MTTA data.

Year	Sales of UK machine tools (£m)	Exports (£m)	Exports (%)	Imports (£m)	Imports as percentage of consumption	Apparent consumption in UK (£m)	Trade Balance (£m)
1985	566	266	47	304	50	604	−38
1986	576	269	47	381	55	688	−112
1987	599	306	51	323	52	616	−17
1988	770	386	50	411	52	795	−25
1989	831	399	48	519	55	951	−120
1990	854	489	57	523	59	888	−34
1991	651	411	63	451	65	691	−40
1992	544	329	61	411	66	626	−82
1993	446	339	76	330	76	437	+9
1994	557	361	65	354	64	550	+7
1995	675	441	65	563	71	797	−122

Source: MTTA Office for National Statistics, Taylor Nelson AGB and HM Customs and Excise modified with CECIMO data.

Notes:

- Values are at current prices and do not include spare parts and accessories.
- Apparent UK consumption = Sales − exports + imports.
- Values for imports and exports include new and used machine tools.

Figure 17.4
MTTA trade trends
1985–1995.

17.5 AB product range

Asquith–Butler design, market and manufacture four distinct but associated families of machine tools (see Attachment 17.2 in Section 17.14, page 247):

1 HE: This machine is of Butler origin and has a modular design. There are six major modules on the machine (see Attachments 17.1 and 17.4 in Section 17.14, pages 246 and 249). The average price for an HE machine is approximately £350,000 but this will vary depending upon the specific configuration ordered by the customer. HE machines are usually built as stand-alone CNC machine tools for manufacturing a high variety of components required in relatively low volumes (see Attachment 17.3 in Section 17.14, page 248).

2 TE: The TE machine is also of Butler origin but is a smaller machine than the HE (see Attachment 17.5 in Section 17.14, page 250). Almost all TE machines are purchased as stand-alone CNC machines. There is some similarity of modules between HE and TE models. The same range of CNC systems are also available to customers too. HE and TE ranges compete in relatively high volume, highly competitive markets.

3 LE: Many of the LE machines are configured as machining centres. A typical 'machining cell' is shown in Appendix Attachment 17.6. A configuration of this type was produced for a well-known UK

earth moving machinery manufacturer. LE machines are highly engineered products and the price range is from £650,000 (for a relatively basic version) to £1.25 million (the largest value order for an LE configuration received up to 1996).

HE, TE and LE machines were of Butler origin and were known as the 'Elgamill' range.

4   VN: The VN range is of Asquith origin (The 'V' in VN is interpreted as vertical spindle, although some horizontal machines are produced). Individual machines from the VN range are highly engineered/customized for specific customer requirements and some could be regarded as special purpose machines. A multitude of machine configurations can be derived from modular units. Within the VN range there are three basic sub-classifications: VNCG (see Attachment 17.7 in Section 17.14, page 252), VNCT and VNCR.

17.5.1   Applications of the Asquith–Butler range

General engineering (e.g. subcontract engineers) This sector represents the largest sales value to the company and are mainly supplied by the general purpose HE and TE ranges.

Heavy engineering (e.g. railways, power generation, defence, earth-moving equipment, mining, other machine tool companies such as Cincinnati Milacron) These industries are serviced by HE and TE ranges, but for heavier applications the LE range and verticals are ordered.

Automotive (e.g. machine tools for manufacturing tools, such as body panel press dyes for the auto industry) Again serviced by the HE and TE ranges.

Aerospace (e.g. wing structures, skins and spares) Serviced from the LE, HE and vertical ranges.

17.6   Market share and competitors

The European Machine Tool Directory of CECIMO (European Committee for Co-operation of the Machine Tool Industries) identifies thirty-five major categories of machine tool types. These major categories contain over 400 subclassifications. The company's products predominantly fall into the categories of 'horizontal and vertical milling and boring machining centres'. There were 50–60 competitors worldwide within this category. More importantly, there were just over ten direct competitors in the 'medium to heavy applications' area, with AB having a 15 per cent market share in 1996.

Company	Country	AB products and services in direct or indirect competition
Kolb	Germany	LE and verticals (VNC and VNCT)
Waldrich Coburg	Germany	LE and VN
Ingersoll	Germany	Minor competitor in specialist areas
Rambaudi	Italy	VN, HE, TE
Mecof	Italy	HE, TE
Parpas	Italy	Vert. (VN)
Zayer	Spain	HE, TE
Solaruce	Spain	TE, HE
Korradi	Germany	TE
CME	Spain	TE and VN (partial)
Anayak	Spain	TE and VN
SNK	Japan	TE, HE

Figure 17.5
Major AB competitors and areas of competition.

The HE and TE products faced the most competition, particularly from Spanish Original Equipment Manufacturers (OEM). The Spanish industry was heavily subsidised from the European Union (EU) and had cheaper labour rates than the UK, as did the Italian competition.

There was also competition from the used and reconditioned machine tool sector, particularly for HE and TE products. The buyers of used machine tools are most usually general engineering companies who require a rapid solution to capacity constraints. It was clear that the HE/TE products were very price sensitive and operated in markets where delivery performance was critical.

The major competitors of AB are shown in Figure 17.5, and as can be seen, they were mostly European (Germany, Spain and Italy):

17.7 Product development of Asquith and Butler products

There had been a revolution in machine tool design and capability since Second World War. This had been both user-driven and (perhaps more predominantly) technology-driven.

This revolution really started in the 1950s with the wide availability of tungsten carbide tooling which enabled higher rates of metal removal, which necessitated the development of more powerful and robust machines. In the 1960s hard wired Numerical Control (NC) became available, further increasing the sophistication of machine tools. In the 1970s, NC was superseded by CNC. CNC had advanced to the point where, in the 1990s, they had become almost 'intelligent systems' with complex diagnostic capabilities that could be integrated with computer aided design and computer aided manufacturing systems (CAD/CAM). CNC systems can also be interfaced with management systems such as Manufacturing Resource Planning (MRPII).

There are fewer mechanical and hard wired parts in modern machine tools. For example the introduction of Variable Speed (VS) DC motors and later VS AC motors almost eliminated the requirement for complex gear-boxes and gear change mechanisms. The reduction in mechanical parts has also made machine tools more reliable.

In the 1960s designers were predicting that by the end of the 1970s the factory of the future could be totally unmanned at the shop floor level. Although the timing was optimistic, Computer Integrated Manufacturing (CIM) was installed and running in a number of manufacturing companies. CIM links the major operations and control functions of design, control, handling and internal management. Researchers were also reviewing the possibility of Computer Integrated Enterprise (CIE), where CIM is integrated with systems-based functions of suppliers and customers. The progression from stand-alone CNC machine applications is illustrated in Figure 17.6.

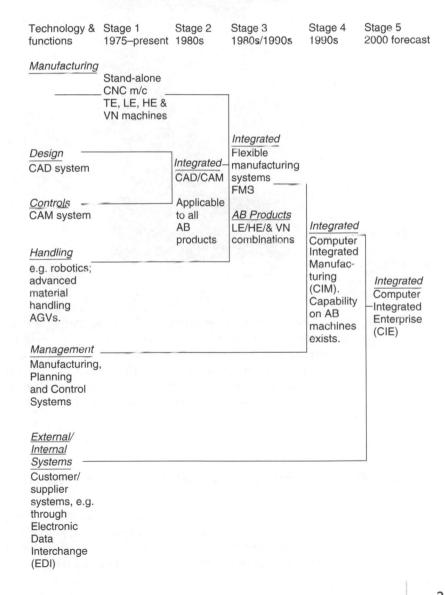

Figure 17.6

Progressive design and technology integration in manufacturing and management systems (incorporating the position of AB products) *Source*: (adapted from Slack et al., 2001, p. 237).

235

Asquith radial drilling machine c. 1900

Butler shaping machine c. 1900

Figure 17.7
Asquith drilling machine
and Butler shaping
machine (c. 1900).

Asquith–Butler designers and senior management closely followed these technological developments and continuously redesigned their products to exploit new technology. The extent of the revolution can be appreciated by comparing the Asquith radial drills and Butler shaping machines being produced in the first decade of the twentieth century in Figure 17.7 with the machine configurations shown in Attachments 17.4–17.7 in Section 17.14, pages 249–252.

17.8 Asquith–Butler business and operations strategy

The AB strategy appears to be based on an holistic definition of their business purpose. They see themselves not just as a designer, manufacturer and marketer of machine tools, but as a provider of 'a total cost effective manufacturing solution that provides capacity, accuracy, speed, versatility and reliability to satisfy specific customer requirements'. According to one company director, it 'defines how the business should be organized'. It included the service provided to customers from initial enquiry all the way through to final commissioning and beyond. Teamwork in a multi-disciplinary environment and effective communication, particularly with customers, were skills that would be required from a wide variety of personnel within the business.

17.9 Asquith–Butler order winning and qualifying criteria

The company had closely scrutinized the factors that contributed to business success, and they can be summarized as given in the following sections.

17.9.1 Price

This was classified as a number one order winning criteria, particularly for the HE/TE range of products which compete in an extremely price sensitive market.

17.9.2 Quality

The intrinsic quality and reliability of the product was regarded as a qualifying criteria (i.e. it allows the company to be considered as a supplier, but it does not guarantee orders). Quality at AB was not confined to the product itself – fast and reliable delivery was also regarded as a quality consideration.

17.9.3 Technology management

Technology was ranked number one – the company needs to be aware of the latest technology at lowest price. This applies particularly to CNC systems. New technology also provides major cost benefits, for example 'multiplexing' where a single control wire replaces complex wiring harnesses.

17.9.4 Innovation

Is only ranked three, particularly for HE/TE products. Imaginative design solutions are however essential for most LE and VN applications. More fundamentally, the industry was reaching a phase in technology where a 'step change' in innovation was imminent. One example of this is 'real' or 'true' five axis machining. The latter was considered a more significant development than the introduction of VS DC drive motors and electronic positioning systems that were widely introduced in the 1970s.

17.9.5 Customization

Demands for customization affect primarily the LE range, and more intensely, the vertical range of products. Customization ranges from the simple provision of additional features, such as special purpose tooling for a standard machine to the design of specially configured machining centres. Effective customization was a highly ranked order winning criteria.

17.9.6 Customer liaison

This was a continuing process that was ranked as a high order-winning and order-qualifying criteria. Liaison did not end at the procurement of a contract, but continued through machine design, manufacturing, final commissioning in the user's plant and beyond. Much of the liaison was conducted through the sales and marketing team, although it also involved service and spares provision, tooling design and manufacturing consultancy. This meant that the AB team had to have the same or a better understanding of the customer's products and manufacturing environment than the customer itself.

Customer liaison was also crucial to the financial solidity of the company. Because the company had extensive design and manufacturing lead times, the company had high working capital requirements. (The total purchasing spend per year was £4.5 million.) Customers therefore had contractual requirements to make progress payments over the period of the contract. Stage payments by customers varied from contract to contract, but the following proportions were not unusual:

- 25 per cent of total cost with customer order.
- 25 per cent of total cost halfway through the contract (e.g. 3–4 months into manufacturing).
- 40 per cent of total cost at final commissioning and customer approval at AB site.
- 10 per cent of total cost at final commissioning and approval at the customer's works.

17.9.7 Brand name

This was a qualifying criteria. The names Asquith and Butler were deliberately combined because they were well-known UK manufacturers with a strong reputation for quality. Brand name does not necessarily win orders, it qualifies the company to compete. Brand reputation in the industry could easily be eroded in one poorly executed contract and was difficult to recover.

17.10 Manufacturing and purchasing strategy

In functional terms the manufacturing at AB can be divided into four basic areas:

1 *Small parts manufacturing*   This included the manufacturing of critical components such as spindles and milling head parts.
2 *Heavy machining*   Confined to strategic (heavy and expensive) parts such as rams, beds and tables.
3 *Sub-assembly*   Ram assembly, control panel assembly, bed assembly, etc.
4 *Final build*   Integration of sub-assemblies, controls, commissioning, etc.

When the new company was formed it was evident that the highest value adding processes were in design, sub-assembly and final assembly. The company therefore decided to purchase, rather than to maintain a comprehensive machining capability. The company did retain the manufacture of strategic components such as beds and rams.

Purchasing could be divided into two categories:

1 Manufacturing of parts where the company would have competence but the investment in manufacturing would not contribute to added value.
2 Components and parts where the company had neither the competence or capacity to design and produce.

It ought to be added that until the late 1970s many machine tool companies had a high level of vertical integration. But with the growing sophistication of such systems and the ability of companies such as Siemens to spend hundreds of millions of pounds on system research and development, it became impractical, and independent CNC design was abandoned in the early 1980s.

17.11 Proposed changes at AB to enhance profitability and meet changing market conditions

The company were considering three major changes to their operation which ranged from the tactical to the strategic. The company were considering these proposals as 'phase changes' which would be implemented over a 2–3-year period depending on market conditions. The three phases were as follows:

1 *Phase 1*   Adopt Assemble To Order (ATO) planning rather than a combination of Engineer To Order (ETO), Make To Order (MTO) or Make To Stock (MTS) particularly for HE, TE and LE ranges. (Adopt over a 1-year period).

2 *Phase 2* Concentrate only on marketing, designing and assembling the products rather than manufacturing the parts for the product – i.e. deintegrating the manufacturing facility. (Adopt over a 2-year period).

3 *Phase 3* Reduce the range offered to LE and VN products only as these are the most profitable product families, even though they only accounted for 20 per cent of the current production volume. The 'First Phase' of Phase 3 would be to gradually remove the TE range, followed by the HE range.

The rationale for each of these phases is outlined below.

Phase 1 Adopt assemble to order
Within the HE, TE and LE ranges alone the company could produce over one million variants from standard options. Even a ram, which is common to HE, LE and TE machines, can be configured into 36 ($4 \times 3 \times 3$) different variants (see Attachment 17.2 in Section 17.14, page 247). Indeed, forecasting exact customer requirements for a completely configured machine was almost impossible. The company could plan manufacturing to meet demand in four distinct ways:

1 *Engineer to order* This was the safest way of ensuring that the specification of a product exactly meets known demand. There was, however, a drawback – the delivery lead time included manufacturing and the design that preceded it. Manufacturing lead time alone for an HE machine could be 8–9 months, and this did not include the detailed specification, contractual negotiations, shipment and commissioning at the customer's plant. Shipment and commissioning could take up to 12 weeks. Engineer to order was also partially suited to the VN range because there was a high level of customization.

2 *Make to order* This is similar to ETO except that design was not sequential with manufacturing in the sense that design can be undertaken in parallel with manufacturing. MTO was more suitable for products where the product modules were fairly standardized (e.g. HE, TE and to a lesser extent the LE families). More customers were specifying lead times that included delivery and commissioning in their works. Engineer to order and make could no longer compete on the basis of short lead times, particularly when competing with the second-hand market.

3 *Make to stock* This is very different to ETO and involves building machines for stock (it was confined to the HE and TE ranges). It has the advantage that a commissioned and working machine can be demonstrated to potential customers. Yet there are obvious problems when the company speculatively builds a machine for an unknown demand. Even if the company built a 'standard' machine featuring the most popular specifications there was less than a 1 per cent chance that it would meet customer requirements fully. This meant that a machine would have to be amended and/or rebuilt and could lead to redundant and excess inventory.

4 *Assemble to order* This required that the company forecast demand and speculate on production at the lowest level of customer requirements, that is, the options that the customer was likely to choose. ATO would also maximise the benefits arising from the modular construction of the machines.

Another rationale cited for the introduction of ATO was that it was used in the aerospace and automobile industries. For example, a typical car can be produced to 50,000 variants, but through the use of master scheduling it could be offered to customers in a much smaller and manageable number of options (e.g. engine size, right- and left-hand drive, saloon or estate, etc.).

Phase 2   De-integrating the manufacturing facility

Phase 2 was a much bolder and controversial proposal than Phase 1. Phase 1 was operational and had few associated risks – it was intended to improve the existing operation in terms of cost and delivery performance, and did not change the structure of the business. Phase 2 contained far more risk, but the management were slowly coming to the conclusion that it offered many opportunities.

De-integration involved sub-contracting all mechanical parts manufacturing and concentrating manufacturing on assembly, machine build and commissioning only. The first and most fundamental argument for de-integration was that the core competencies were in marketing, designing, building and commissioning. A significant issue, however, was that the actual manufacturing of the machines was crucial to the success of the business. They determine the quality of the finished products and the ability to deliver on time, even though their cost impact on the business was no longer as significant as it was previously.

There was also a strong economic argument for de-integration – there was an 'opportunity cost' involved in manufacturing parts for machine tools. Substantial capital expenditure was required for the introduction of improved production capacity and capability. For example, to replace the large machine tools which finish 'strategic' components such as beds would cost an excess of £2 million. The company also believed that the 'opportunity lost' was the ability to invest in more value–adding activities in manufacturing, such as the ability to increase machine tool assembly space and capacity in the context of expected increases in demand.

There was also a strong historical rationale for de-integration. For more than three decades the industry had become less vertically integrated as the technology of the machine tools became more sophisticated. The industry now relied on specialist suppliers who made substantial investments in product and process development. An example was CNC systems: 20 years earlier the company had attempted to design and produce their own CNC systems, only to discover that the pace of development in CNC technology required resources far beyond that available to the company.

It was also argued that the current successful sub-contracting of strategic parts, such as tool changer assemblies and columns, suggested that the whole of mechanical parts manufacturing could be outsourced. Indeed, almost all spares manufacturing had been outsourced successfully, and spares were a critical service element for renewed and new business. Finally, it was argued that the direction of the whole of the engineering industry was towards large-scale de-integration. This was apparent in both the aerospace and automobile industry where over 70 per cent of the product was outsourced. Importantly, it did not include critical parts such as fan and compressor blades.

Rolls-Royce aerospace was cited as an example of a company that sought to reduce engine build time from 150 to 40 days by improving supply chain responsiveness and outsourcing. De-integration at AB was intended to achieve similar objectives.

The company also recognized that there were possible downsides to the proposal, with the most obvious being:

- The company would have less control over manufacturing, including quality control.
- Were there sufficient reliable suppliers with appropriate and sufficient capacity?
- There might be problems with ensuring that small but vital engineering design changes were relayed to suppliers quickly and effectively.
- The possibility that suppliers would pass on confidential design information to AB competitors.
- How would AB ensure that suppliers utilized their capacity to meet AB priorities?

Phase 3   Rationalization

If Phase 2 was regarded as controversial, Phase 3 was even more contentious. The objective of Phase 3 was to gradually reduce the family range to two core product ranges: the VN and LE products. These products were more profitable than the HE and TE ranges because they faced less competition. The data in Figure 17.8 provides insight into the relative profitability of each range in competitive terms.

The TE range, in particular, had been under intense scrutiny for more than 15 years. Even though the cost of the range had been reduced significantly the cheaper competition from lower wage economies always seemed to catch up. The HE range accounted for more than 50 per cent of total output by volume, and even though they were of low margin they could be considered a 'cash cow'. Yet they could also be considered as a future 'problem child' because of the difficulty of improving margin levels in the future, and because management would be reluctant to dispose of a range that had positive revenue flows. Indeed, they could 'hedge their bets' by integrating them into their plans for the development of the LE and VN ranges.

The arguments for disposing of the TE range and for concentrating on LE and VN ranges were as follows:

- The LE and VN ranges provided more scope for customer value-adding activities. That is, they wished to move to markets which required more integrated technology and customization (e.g. Flexible Manufacturing Systems) rather than the 'stand-alone' machine tool sector. The customers in this sector were usually general engineering companies who were very cost sensitive: they usually required a new machine at second hand/reconditioned prices.

Product family	Approximate volume of total output (%)	Family classification	Approximate sales price for each classification (£000s)	Approximate level of competition in each classification
HE	55	ST-HE	250	High
		M-HE	350	Medium
		C-HE	800	Medium to low
TE	25	ST-TE	200	High
		M-TE	250	High
		C-TE	350	High to medium
LE	10	ST-LE	630	Medium
		M-LE	750	Medium to low
		C-LE	1100+	Low
VN	10	ST-VN	300	Medium
		M-VN	700	Low
		C-VN	1200+	Low

Note: The prefixes ST, M and C for each product family refer to the approximate degree of complexity i.e. ST = Standard complexity, M = Medium complexity, C = Complex. These are approximate classifications, but some examples are as follows:

ST-TE: A 'stand-alone' TE machine, without an auto-indexing head, no tool changer and control limited to 3 axes.

M-HE: Usually a 'stand-alone' HE machine with an auto-indexing head, a tool changer and 4- or 5-axes control.

C-LE: Usually part of a flexible manufacturing system or 'machining cell' (see Attachment 17.6 in Section 17.14, page 251, for an example).

Figure 17.8

Sales prices for various complexities of HE, TE, LE and VN products.

- The VN range, in particular, offered a highly differentiated product range (there were many versions of VN) and fewer competitors.
- The LE range was one of the leaders in the 'heavier' section of the market and the range was ideal for providing 'integrated manufacturing solutions'.
- 'Value adding' would reside as much in design and development as it did in manufacturing if the proposal was adopted.
- The TE range, was in supermarket parlance, a 'shelf warmer' in the product catalogue (i.e. it was more for display than for profit).
- A major component of the Phase 3 plan would be to increase the promotional and marketing focus on VN and LE products in order to increase volume demand for these products at the expense of HE and TE.

There were caveats in this plan, and some were more serious than others:

- The company would no longer offer a full range of products in the sector and this might force business customers to shop elsewhere. For example, customers who require LE or VN specifications require HE (even TE products). Sales for VN and LE would be lost because the company could no longer provide a turnkey package to potential big buyers.

- The concentration on VN and LE would require more systems engineers and wider mechanical design skills, particularly if there was a growth in demand for flexible manufacturing systems.
- There would be a demand for a wider variety of technical support at pre- and post-installation.
- The company could become a supplier of 'one offs' – engineer to order. What would be the benefit of Phase 1 then?
- Concentration on the VN and LE range will certainly increase the variety of components to be machined, particularly if customization was increased. This type of production requires exceptionally flexible and agile suppliers, because more variety is invariably accompanied by more frequent design changes to suit the customer. Would the supplier proposals of Phase 2 be capable of handling this?
- Have they got a marketing infrastructure which can cope with this new product mix? – marketing and sales will require much wider technical skills than is presently the case.

It was obvious from the questions raised against Phases 2 and 3 that a detailed business proposal was required which addressed the many variables contained in these two phases of the proposal.

17.12 Questions

1 The company's rationale in respect of key success factors (order winners and qualifiers) are described in the text of the case – given the nature of the industry, the competitive milieu and the 'risk investment' nature of machine tools, what ranking would you assign to key success factors and why? What other factors might you add as being important considerations for the business?

2 Provide an analysis of AB's business, operations, marketing and design strategies and a comprehensive commentary which identifies areas which could be dysfunctional and those which might provide 'competitive advantage'.

3 Provide an economic, supply chain and marketing analysis of the 'Forrester effect' in relation to machine tool demand. How could it be minimized at AB machine tools?

4 In the context of the company's business environment, are the 3 phases of change described in the case ill- or well-conceived?

Are they merely 'fads' and retrenchment or might they enable the company to meet its broad business objectives?

5 Analyse the risks and benefits involved in Phases 2 and 3, including those which are not mentioned in the case. Develop a 'pro-forma

business plan' (including possible timing) for executing these phases. What are the worst possible 'downsides' of these changes?

6   From the limited evidence in the case provide an analysis of the most critical business processes at AB and how they might be improved without implementing Phases 2 and 3 of the company's plan.

17.13   Acknowledgements and Permissions

This case is published with the permission of AB Marwin Ltd. It is intended as a basis for class discussion rather than to illustrate either effective or ineffective handling of management situations. Furthermore AB Marwin Ltd and the authors would like to emphasize that this case was researched in 1996. Since then the products referred to in the case have been superseded by new designs and that actions taken by AB machine tools in 1996 should not be inferred to AB Marwin Ltd. Trade names in the case remain the intellectual property of AB Marwin Ltd.

17.14 Appendix

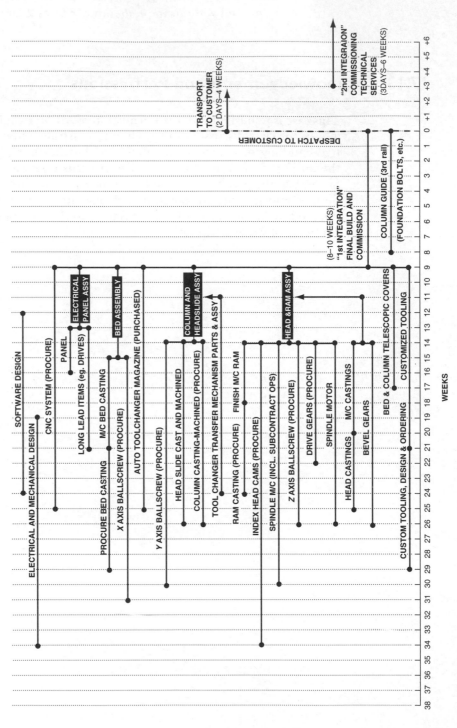

Attachment 17.1 HE MODEL 'SET BACK CHART' For design and procurement of major items and activities.

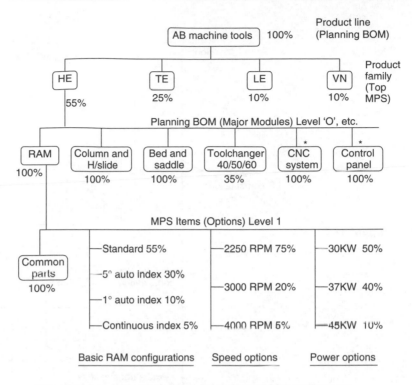

Attachment 17.2
AB product structure.

* Dependent on customer requirements or final machine configuration.

% = Take-off proportions, e.g. every HE machine has a RAM and every RAM has a bill of 'common parts'.

Attachment 17.3
The application of AB products in the volume–variety continuum (adapted from Slack et al., 2001, p. 235).
Source: (Slack, N., Chambers, S. and Johnston, R. (2001) The Application of AB Products in the Volume/Variety Continuum, In *Operations Management*, 3rd edn, © reprinted by permission of Pearson Education Limited).

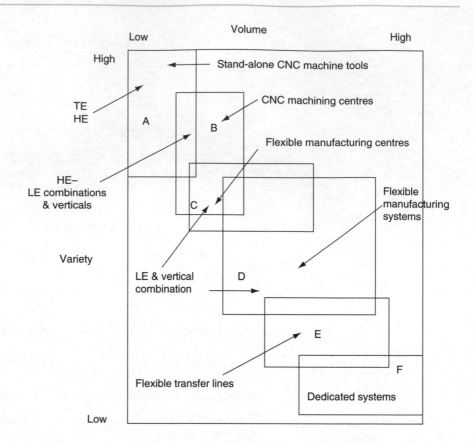

Adapted from Volume–Variety Characteristics of Manufacturing Systems.

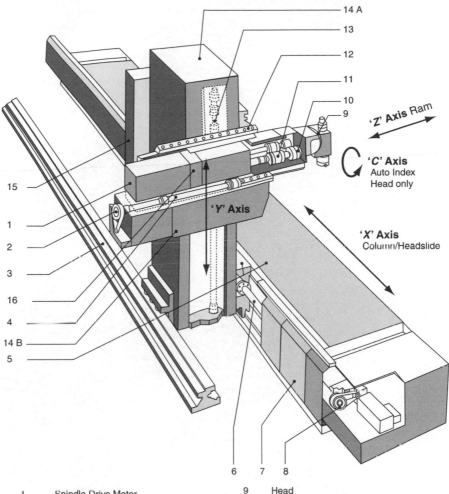

'Z' Axis Ram

'C' Axis
Auto Index
Head only

'Y' Axis

'X' Axis
Column/Headslide

Attachment 17.4
AB Machine Tools
HE Machine horizontal
CNC machining centre.

1	Spindle Drive Motor	9	Head
2	Z Axis Drive	10	Spindle Bearings
3	Column Support Rail	11	Reduction Gears
4	Z Axis Ball Screw	12	Ram Keep Strips
5	Bed and Saddle	13	Y Axis Ball Screw
6	X Axis Ball Screw (up to 8 meters)	(14AB)	Column/Headslide
7	Telescopic Slide Covers	15	Automatic Tool Changer Magazine
8	X Axis Drive (up to 8 meters)	16	Two Speed Gearbox

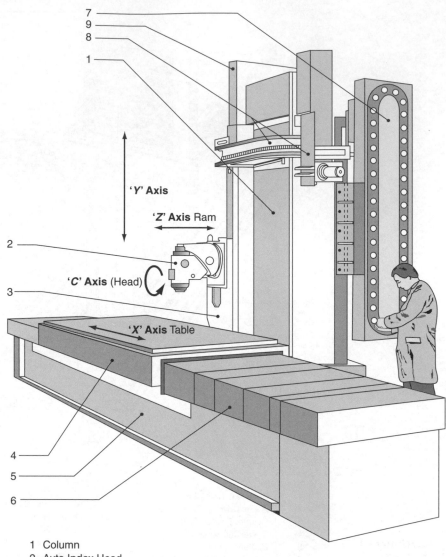

'Y' Axis

'Z' Axis Ram

'C' Axis (Head)

'X' Axis Table

1 Column
2 Auto Index Head
3 Head Slide
4 Table
5 Bed
6 Telescopic Bed Covers
7 Tool Changer Magazine
8 Tool Changer Transfer Mechanism
9 Column Slide Telescopic Covers

Attachment 17.5
AB Machine Tools
TE Machine CNC
machining centre.

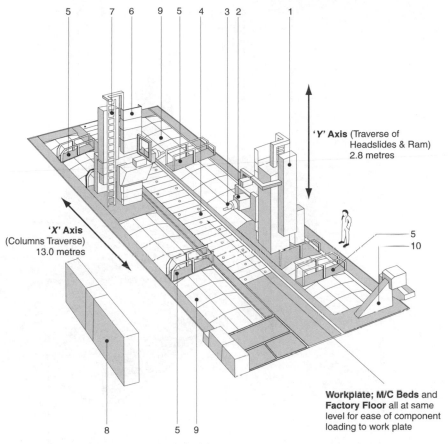

'Y' Axis (Traverse of
Headslides & Ram)
2.8 metres

'X' Axis
(Columns Traverse)
13.0 metres

Workplate; M/C Beds and
Factory Floor all at same
level for ease of component
loading to work plate

Attachment 17.6
Asquith Butler
LE machining cell con-
sisting of twin-opposed
LE machines for
machining heavy earth-
moving machinery
components.

1	60 Station Toolchanger (both machines)	6	Column Slide Telescopic
2	Ram	7	Access Ladders to Columns
3	Auto Index Heads	8	Control Panel
4	Work Plate	9	Telescopic Bed Covers
5	Moveable Access Bridges to Workplate	10	Swarf Management Systems

Note: One advanced CNC system
controls a total of 8 Axes –
X, Y, Z & C on both machines

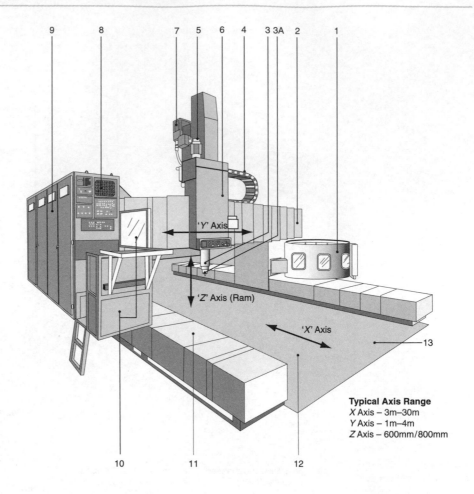

'Y' Axis

'Z' Axis (Ram)

'X' Axis

13

Typical Axis Range
X Axis – 3m–30m
Y Axis – 1m–4m
Z Axis – 600mm/800mm

Attachment 17.7
AB M/C Tools
A VNCG travelling gantry vertical spindle M/C with fixed Bedplate and fixed Headslide.

1	Automatic Tool and Attachment Change Magazine	5	'Z' Axis Servo Motor	11	Traverse Bed Telescopic Covers
2	Gantry Slide Telescopic Covers	6	Ram Carriage/Head	12	Fixed Work/Bed Plate for Component to be machined
3	Ram	7	Spindle Drive Motor		
3A	Spindle	8	CNC System and Console		
4	Cable Drag for Power and Control to Ram Head	9	Eletrical Controls Panel	13	'X' Axis Derived from Travelling Gantry
		10	Operator Platform and Guards		

References

Adair, J. (1988) *Effective Leadership: A Modern Guide to Developing Leadership Skills*, Pan Books, London.

Allison, G.T. (1971) *The Essence of Decision: Explaining the Cuban Missile Crisis*, Little Brown and Co., Boston.

Amit, R. and Schoemaker, P.J.H. (1993) 'Strategic assets and organisational rent', *Strategic Management Journal*, Vol. 14.

Andrews, K.R. (1971) *The Concept of Corporate Strategy*, Dow Jones-Irwin, Homewood, Illinois.

Ansoff, H.I. (1965) *Corporate Strategy: An Analytic Approach to Business Policy for Growth and Expansion*, McGraw-Hill, New York.

Ansoff, H.I. (1987) *Corporate Strategy* (revised edition), Penguin, London.

Baden-Fuller, C. and Stopford, J. (1992) 'The firm matters not the industry', in *Strategy: Process, Content, Context* (2nd edition) (Eds de Wit, B. and Meyer, R.), International Thompson Business Press.

Bailey, A. and Johnson, G. (1992) 'How strategies develop in organisations', in *The Challenge of Strategic Management* (Eds Faulkner, D.A. and Johnson, G.), Kogan Page.

Bailey, A. and Johnson, G. (1995) *The Processes of Strategy Development*, Cranfield School of Management Working Paper SWP 6/95.

Bailey, A. and Johnson, G. (1996) *Patterns of Strategy Development*, Cranfield School of Management Working Paper SWP 1/96.

Balogun, J. and Hailey, V.H. (1999) *Exploring Strategic Change*, Prentice Hall, Europe.

Baren, M. (1996) *How it all began: Up the High Street*, Michael Omara Books Ltd.

Barney, J.B. (1991) 'Firm resources and sustained competitive advantage', *Journal of Management*, Vol. 17, No. 1.

Bowen, D. and Lawler, E. (1992) 'Empowerment', *Sloan Management Review*, Spring.

Bowman, C. (1997) 'Interpreting competitive strategy', in *Competitive and Corporate Strategy* (Eds Bowman, C. and Faulkner, D.), Irwin.

Bowman, C. and Ambrosini, V. (2000) 'Value creation versus value capture: towards a coherent definition of value in strategy', *British Journal of Management*, Vol. 11, No. 1.

Burns, B. (2000) *Managing Change: A Strategic Approach to Organisational Dynamics*, Financial Times Prentice Hall.

Buzzel, R.D. and Gale, B.T. (1987) *The PIMS Principles – Linking Strategy to Performance*, The Free Press, New York.

Campbell-Hunt, C. (2000) 'What have we learned about generic competitive strategy? A meta-analysis', *Strategic Management Journal*, Vol. 21.

Campbell, A. and Goold, M. (1988) 'Adding value from corporate headquarters', in *Strategy: Process, Content, Context* (2nd edition) (Eds de Wit, B. and Meyer, R.), International Thompson Business Press.

Campbell, A., Goold, M. and Alexander, M. (1995) 'The quest for parenting advantage', *Harvard Business Review*, March–April.

Campbell, A., Goold, M. and Alexander, M. (1998) 'The value of the parent company', in *Strategy: Process, Content, Context* (2nd edition) (Eds de Wit, B. and Meyer, R.), International Thompson Business Press.

Chaffee, E.E. (1985) 'Three models of strategy', *Academy of Management Review*, Vol. 110, No. 1.

Chandler, A.D. (1962) *Strategy and Structure*, MIT, Boston, Massachusetts.

Chandler, A.D. (1969) *Strategy and Structure*, Paperback edition, MIT, Boston, Massachusetts.

Cohen, M.D., March, J.G. and Olsen, J.P. (1972) 'A garbage can model of organisational choice', *Administration Science Quarterly*, Vol. 17.

Cox, R. and Brittain, P. (1996) *Retail Management* (3rd edition), Pitman Publishing.

Day, G. (1994) 'The capabilities of market-driven organisations', *Journal of Marketing*, Vol. 58, No. 3.

Dierickx, I. and Cool, K. (1989) 'Asset stock accumulation and the sustainability of competitive advantage', *Management Science*, Vol. 35, No. 12.

DTI (2002) www.dti.gov.uk/quality/people.

Eisenhardt, K.M. and Sull, D.N. (2001) 'Strategy as simple rules', *Harvard Business Review*, January.

Emmelhainz, M.A., Stock, J.R. and Emmelhainz, L.W. (1991) 'Consumers responses to retail stock-outs', *Journal of Retailing*, Vol. 67, No. 2.

Festinger, L. (1957) *Theory of Cognitive Dissonance*, Stanford University Press.

Fisher, M.L., Raman, A. and McClelland, A.E. (2000) 'Rocket science retailing is almost here – are you ready', *Harvard Business Review*, July–August.

Fletcher, K.E. and Huff, A.S. (1990) 'Strategic argument mapping: a study of strategy reformulation at AT and T', in *Mapping Strategic Thought* (Ed. Huff, A.S.), John Wiley, Salisbury.

Frank, R.H. (2000) *Microeconomics and Behavior*, McGraw-Hill Higher Education, International Edition.

Grant, R.M. (1995) *Contemporary Strategy Analysis: Concepts Techniques, Applications* (2nd edition), Blackwell, Oxford.

Greiner, L. (1972) 'Evolution and revolution as organisations grow', *Harvard Business Review*, July–August.

Guth, W.D. and MacMillan, I.C. (1986) 'Strategy implementation versus middle management self-interest', *Strategic Management Journal*, Vol. 7.

Hall, R. and Andriani, P. (1999) 'Developing and managing strategic partnerships', *European Journal of Purchasing and Supply Management*, Vol. 5.

Hamel, G. and Prahalad, C.K. (1994) *Competing for the Future*, Harvard Business School Press, Boston, Massachusetts.

Handy, C. (1993) *Understanding Organisations* (4th edition), Penguin Books.

Hannan, M. and Freeman, J. (1977) 'The population ecology of organisations', *American Journal of Sociology*, Vol. 82.

Hart, S.L. (1992) 'An integrative framework for strategy making processes', *Strategic Management Journal*, Vol. 17, No. 2.

Hart, S. and Banbury, C. (1994) 'How strategy making processes can make a difference', *Strategic Management Journal*, Vol. 15.

Hassell, N. and Wilsher, P. (1993) 'Europe's top 500: dark days at the top' (based on Kiel University ranking of European companies), Management Today, December.

Hedley, B. (1977) 'Strategy and the business portfolio', *Long Range Planning*, February, in Hofer, C.W. and Schendel, D. (1978) *Strategy Formulation: Analytical Concepts*, West Publishing, Minnesota.

Hill, C.W.L. (1988) 'Differentiation versus low cost or differentiation and low cost: A contingency framework', *Academy of Management Review*, Vol. 13.

Hofer, C.W. and Schendel, D. (1978) *Strategy Formulation: Analytical Concepts*, West Publishing, Minnesota.

Hooley, G., Möller, K. and Broderick, A. (1997) 'Competitive positioning and the resource based view of the firm', Aston Business School Research Paper Series RP9726.

Hooley, G.J., Saunders, J.A. and Piercy, N.F. (1998) *Marketing Strategy and Competitive Positioning*, Financial Times Prentice Hall.

Iqbal, T. (1997) 'The implications and effects of stockouts in chain store retailing', Unpublished Dissertation, Staffordshire University.

Johnson, G. (1987) *Strategic Change And The Management Process*, Basil Blackwell, Oxford.

Johnson, G. (1988) 'Rethinking incrementalism', *Strategic Management Journal*, Vol. 9.

Johnson, G. and Scholes, K. (1999) *Exploring Corporate Strategy* (5th edition), Prentice Hall, Europe.

Johnston, R., Chambers, S., Harland, C., Harrison, A. and Slack, N. (1997) *Cases in Operations Management* (2nd edition), Pitman Publishing.

Kaplan, R.S. and Norton, D.P. (1992) 'The balanced scorecard – measures that drive performance', *Harvard Business Review*, January–February.

Kaplan, R.S. and Norton, D.P. (1993) 'Putting the balanced scorecard to work', *Harvard Business Review*, September–October.

Kaplan, R.S. and Norton, D.P. (1996) 'The balanced scorecard: translating strategy into action', *Harvard Business Review*, January–February.

Kerr, S. (1995) 'An Academy classic: on the folly of rewarding A, while hoping for B', *Academy of Management Executive*, February.

Kogut, B. and Zander, U. (1992) 'Knowledge of the firm, combinative capabilities, and the replication of technology', *Organisation Science*, Vol. 3.

Kotter, J.P. (1995) 'Leading change, why transformation efforts fail', *Harvard Business Review*, March April.

Langley, A. (1988) 'The roles of formal strategic planning', *Long Range Planning*, Vol. 21, No. 3.

Lenz, R.T. and Lyles, M. (1985) 'Paralysis by analysis: is your planning system becoming too rational', *Long Range Planning*, Vol. 18, August.

Levitt, T. (1960) 'Marketing myopia', *Harvard Business Review*, Vol. 38, No. 4.

Lindblom, C.E. (1959) 'The science of muddling through', *Public Administration Review*, Vol. 19.

Lipsey, R.G. and Crystal, K.A. (1999) *Principles of Economics*, Oxford University Press.

Maznevski, M.L., Rush, J.C. and White, R.E. (1993) 'Drawing meaning from vision', in *Strategic Thinking, Leadership and the Management of Change* (Eds Hendry, J. and Johnson, G. with Newton, J.), John Wiley.

McDonald, M. (1996) 'The future for the foodstores – challenges and alternatives', Review of a study conducted for Coca Cola Retailing Research Group (Europe) by Coopers and Lybrand in AMBA Management Extra.

McLellan, R. and Kelly, G. (1980) 'Business policy formulation: understanding the process', *Journal of General Management*, Winter.

McWilliams, A. and Smart, D.L. (1993) 'Efficiency v structure-conduct-performance: implications for strategy research and practice', *Journal of Management*, Vol. 19, No. 1.

Mendelow, A. (1991) *Proceedings of the Second International Conference on Information Systems*, Cambridge, Massachusetts, in Johnson, G. and Scholes, K. (1999) *Exploring Corporate Strategy* (5th edition), Prentice Hall.

Miller, D. (1986) 'Configurations of strategy and structure: towards a synthesis', *Strategic Management Journal*, Vol. 7, No. 3.

Miller, D. (1987) 'Strategy making and structure: analysis and implications for performance', *Academy of Management Journal*, Vol. 39, No. 1.

Miller, D. (1992) 'The icarus paradox', *Business Horizons*, January–February.

Miller, A. and Dess, G.G. (1993) 'Assessing Porter's (1980) model in terms of its generalizability, accuracy and simplicity', *Journal of Management Studies*, Vol. 30, No. 4.

Mintzberg, H. (1979) *The Structuring of Organisations*, Prentice Hall.

Mintzberg, H. (1987) 'Five Ps for strategy', *Californian Management Review*, Fall.

Mintzberg, H. (1994) *The Rise and Fall of Strategic Planning*, Prentice-Hall.

Mintzberg, H. (1995) 'The diversified organization', in *The Strategy Process, Concepts, Contexts and Cases* (Eds Mintzberg, H., Quinn, J.B. and Ghoshal, S.), Prentice Hall.

Mintzberg, H. (2002) 'The Structuring of organizations', in *The Strategy Process, Concepts, Contexts and Cases* (4th edition) (Eds Mintzberg, H., Lampel, J. and Quinn, J.), Prentice Hall.

Mintzberg, H. and McHugh, M. (1985) 'Strategy formation in an adhocracy', *Administrative Science Quarterly*, Vol. 30.

Mintzberg, H. and Waters, J.A. (1982) 'Tracking strategy in an entrepreneurial firm', *Academy of Management Journal*, Vol. 25.

Mintzberg, H. and Waters, J.A. (1985) 'Of strategies, deliberate and emergent', *Strategic Management Journal*, Vol. 6.

Mintzberg, H., Pascale, R.T., Goold, M. and Rumelt, R. (1996) 'The honda effect revisited', *California Management Review*, Vol. 38, No. 4.

Narayanan, V.K. and Fahey, L. (1990) 'Evolution of revealed casual maps during decline: a case study of Admiral', in *Mapping Strategic Thought* (Ed. Huff, A.S.), John Wiley, Salisbury.

Nelson, R. (1991) 'Why do firms differ, and how does it matter', *Strategic Management Journal*, Vol. 12.

Nelson, R. and Winter, S. (1982) *An Evolutionary Theory of Economic Change*, Harvard University Press, Cambridge, Massachusetts.

Oakland, J.S. and Porter, L. (1999) *Total Quality Management: Text and Cases*, Butterworth-Heinemann, Oxford.

O'Shea, J. and Madigan, C. (1997) *Dangerous Company: The Consulting Powerhouses and the Business they Save and Risk*, Times Business.

Owen, G. and Harrison, T. (1995) 'Why ICI chose to demerge', *Harvard Business Review*, March–April.

Papadakis, V.M., Lioukas, S. and Chambers, D. (1998) 'Strategic decision making processes: the role of management and context', *Strategic Management Journal*, Vol. 19.

Parker's car guide, April 2002.

Pascale, R.T. (1996) 'The honda effect', *California Management Review*, Vol. 38, No. 4.

Peteraf, M.A. (1993) 'The cornerstones of competitive advantage: A resource-based view', *Strategic Management Journal*, Vol. 14.

Peters, T.J. and Waterman, R.H. (1982) *In Search of Excellence*, Harper and Row.

Pettigrew, A.M. (1973) *The Politics of Organisation Decision Making*, Tavistock, London.

Porter, M.E. (1980) *Competitive Strategy: Techniques for Analysing Industries and Competitors*, The Free Press, New York.

Porter, M.E. (1985) *Competitive Advantage: Creating and Sustaining Superior Performance*, The Free Press, New York.

Porter, M.E. (1987a) 'From competitive advantage to corporate strategy', *Harvard Business Review*, May–June.

Porter, M.E. (1987b) 'The state of strategic thinking', The Economist, May 23.

Porter, M.E. (1990) *The Competitive Advantage of Nations*, The Free Press, New York.

Porter, M.E. (1996) 'What is strategy?', *Harvard Business Review*, November–December.

Prahalad, C.K. and Bettis, R.A. (1986) 'The dominant logic: a new linkage between diversity and performance', *Strategic Management Journal*, Vol. 7.

Prahalad, C.K. and Hamel, G. (1990) 'The core competences of the corporation', *Harvard Business Review*, May–June.

Quinn, J.B. (1978) 'Strategic change: logical incrementalism', *Sloan Management Review*, Fall.

Revans, R. (1983) *The ABC of Action Learning*, Krieger Publishing Company.

Rowe, A.J., Mason, R.D., Dickel, K.E., Mann, R.B. and Mockler, R.J. (1994) *Strategic Management: A Methodological Approach* (4th edition), Addison-Wesley, Reading, Massachusetts.

Sasser, W.E. and Skinner, W. (1978) 'The accomplishing manager', in Skinner, W. (1978) 'Manufacturing in the corporate strategy', John Wiley, New York.

Shapiro, E.C. (1997) *Fad Surfing in the Boardroom: Reclaiming the Courage to Manage in the Age of Instant Answers*, Addison-Wesley, Reading, Massachusetts.

Skinner, W. (1974) 'The focussed factory', *Harvard Business Review*, May–June.

Slack, N., Chambers, S. and Johnston, R. (2001) *Operations Management* (3rd edition), Financial Times/Prentice Hall, Harlow, England.

Slatter, S. (1984) *Corporate Recovery: Successful Turnaround Strategies and their Implementation*, Penguin Books.

Society of Motor Manufacturers and Traders Ltd (2002) www.smmt.co.uk/index.asp.

Spender, J.C. (1989) *Industry Recipe – An Enquiry into the Nature and Sources of Managerial Judgement*, Basil Blackwell, New York.

Srivastava, R.K., Fahey, L. and Christensen, H.K. (2001) 'The resource-based view and marketing: the role of market based assets in gaining competitive advantage', *Journal of Management*, Vol. 27, No. 6.

Tampoe, M. (1998) 'Getting to know your organisation's core competences', in *Exploring Techniques of Analysis and Evaluation in Strategic Management* (Ed. Ambrosini, V.), Hamel Hempstead: Prentice Hall Europe.

The Collins English Dictionary (1991) (3rd edition), Harper Collins.

The Times (1996) 'Pile it high, sell it dear' (18th September).

Walters, D. and Lancaster, G. (1999) 'Value and information – concepts and issues for management', *Management Decision*, Vol. 37, No. 8.

Wernerfelt, B. (1984) 'The resource based view of the firm', *Strategic Management Journal*, Vol. 5.

Williams, B. (1994) 'The best butter in the world: a history of Sainsburys', Ebury Press.

Wilson, I. (1994) 'Strategic planning isn't dead it changed', *Long Range Planning*, Vol. 27, No. 4.

Index